JUSTICE

The Mike Amato Detective Series

A NOVEL BY

LOU CAMPANOZZI

ISBN: 1-4107-3795-0 (e-book)
ISBN: 1-4107-3794-2 (Paperback)

Library of Congress Control Number: 2003092811

This book is printed on acid free paper.

Printed in the United States of America
Bloomington, IN

1stBooks - rev. 05/14/03

DEDICATION

This novel is dedicated to my wife, Nancy, and family—Marc, Nancy and Cassandra, Kim, Derek, Zachary and Mackenzie, Rosemarie, Lorraine, Jill, Cheryl, Mike and Wendy, John, Shannon, Jake and Anthony. When all the chips are on the table and the going gets tough, it is family that sees you through. In all this world there's nothing more important than family, and mine is a very special one indeed!
This novel is for them.

—Lou Campanozzi (May 11, 1943 - October 19, 2002)

From the author's family—

A special thank you to everyone who supported and believed in us that we could bring "Justice" to you. A special thanks to Pat and Steve Walsh who edited and proofread JUSTICE several times. When we thought it was lost, their determination made us believe that it was possible. Thank you to authors, Georgia Durante and Phillip Tomasso, III, who helped us in so many ways. Their encouraging words and guidance helped make what seemed at times as impossible, come true. Thank you to John McNall, Kathy Dunn, and Tony Campione of BowMac Educational Services who helped the "Lou Campanozzi Legacy Project" be so successful. Finally, a special thanks to the people of Rochester, New York, and the officers of the Rochester Police Department. Your continued support was a motivating factor that made us believe that we needed to get JUSTICE into the hands of people who admired, trusted, and respected Lou. Thank you all for believing in us and allowing us the opportunity to keep Detective Mike Amato and Lou Campanozzi's name alive.

Jus-tice, *n.* 1. Being righteous 2. Fairness 3. Rightfulness 4. Reward or penalty as deserved 5. The use of authority to uphold what is just.

Webster's New World Dictionary

"If we do not maintain Justice, Justice will not maintain us."

Francis Bacon

"The more laws, the less justice."

Marcus Tullius Cicero De Officiis

"There is no such thing as justice—in or out of court."

Clarence Darrow

"Courtroom: A place where Jesus Christ and Judas Iscariot would be equals, with the betting odds in favour of Judas."

Henry Louis Mencken

"Justice delayed, is justice denied."

William E. Gladstone

"If you want justice, go to a whore house. If you want a screwing, go to court!"

Source Unknown

ACKNOWLEDGEMENTS

In preparing a novel such as this, it is important to rely on others who have knowledge and expertise in areas not held by the author. Those people add greatly to the story and assist in keeping the story line accurate and real. Based on that, I want to publicly express my gratitude to two people who supplied much of the background information used in the investigation and court scenes. If there are errors in the factuality of the story, it is not because they may have given me faulty information; it is simply that I took certain license with the information they provided.

Dr. Pete DiVasto is a psychiatrist here in Albuquerque, NM. He has made a career-long effort to be there when cops needed someone to listen, someone who helps them sort out their thoughts and reactions to the things that cops see and do. Known simply as "Pete" to cops throughout the state, Dr. DiVasto spent many hours with me discussing the character and background of the fictional killer in this novel.

Mr. Brett Granville, Esq. has been with the Monroe County (N.Y.) District Attorney's Office for about nine years. As an Assistant District Attorney who has worked with cops in the local courts, county courts, and has been the Liaison ADA for the Special Investigations Bureau of the Rochester, NY Police Department, Brett has become a friend to my brother and sister officers. Brett was willing to take my off-hour phone calls and spend time with me as he tried to teach me some of the finer nuances of New York's court system and he was an important source for background regarding the legal scenes in this work.

Thank you, Brett and Pete. I hope I have not done either of you or your chosen professions any disservice.

PROLOGUE

The two cops rode in silence as their prisoner, handcuffed and secured in the back seat of the car, carried on his tirade. From time to time the veteran cop smiled at the rookie, and the rookie grinned in agreement.

"I'll kill you both when I get out! I'll hunt you down like dogs and kill you!" the man shouted for the fourth or fifth time from behind the metal screen.

The defendant had been arrested because he battered his wife. In fact, this most recent spousal beating was the sixth time he had slapped, punched, and kicked the woman in the past four months. He had been busted four times during those passing months, and on each of the prior arrests, the wife had failed to show up in court to testify against the cowardly piece of human crap she had selected to be her husband.

"Take these cuffs off me, you bastard, and I'll kick your ass right now," the passenger demanded. "I'll take that gun of yours and blow your brains out!"

Speaking in short, cryptic words interspersed with police 10-Code jargon, the two cops speculated about the possibility that the wife—who was now being transported to Rochester General Hospital for a fractured cheek bone—would again fail to follow through on her charges and would never testify in court about her husband's violence.

"When I get out of jail, I'll kick your pig ass," the loser shouted madly through the mesh hosiery that added to his natural ugliness.

This time a chuckle accompanied the grins worn by the two cops but it was obvious the older cop was losing his sense of humor.

"You think that's funny? You pig bastard! You're gonna be doing paper work the rest of the night and that dumb bitch I married is gonna drop the charges in the morning. You know she will! She knows what's good for her! I trained the stupid bitch and I know she ain't gonna prosecute nothin'."

The young cop's grin was cut short by Officer Jokovich's big, beefy arm pressed across the rookie's chest as he yelled, "Look out!"

In the same instant, the car screeched to a halt, throwing the foul-mouthed rear-seat passenger forward and slamming his face into the metal cage.

"What the hell?" the rookie questioned.

"Did ya see the dog?" Jokovich asked as he let the car roll forward again. "There was a little black dog that ran right in front of us," the veteran cop explained with a tight, thin smile on his face. The smile grew as he overacted his false concern for the imaginary mutt. "Wow! That was close!" Jokovich dead-panned. "Gee, I sure hope I didn't hurt the little fella." Then, turning his head to look over his right shoulder, the streetwise cop inquired, "How you doin' back there, partner?"

"You broke my nose," the man cried as he tried to stem the flow of blood from his nose with snorts and gagging.

The rest of the trip was made in total silence. Once inside the jail, the prisoner's nose had stopped flowing blood and the jailhouse nurse cleaned his face. The younger cop completed the booking reports as the senior police officer wrote up a report on the near accident, including the specifics of the injury to the prisoner and the phantom black dog.

Back in the car, and on the way to a delayed lunch break, Jokovich broke the silence.

"What are you so quiet about kid?"

"I don't like what you pulled back there."

"Really?"

"Really!" the rookie answered with a tone of anger.

"Why's that?"

"Come on, Trapper. Don't treat me like an idiot. There was no dog, and there was no reason to slam on the brakes. You could have broken the guy's neck pulling a stunt like that."

"He had it coming. Don't lose any sleep over it," the senior man responded.

"What about all that stuff that you've been preaching to me about keeping my cool? You've been telling me not to let someone's mouth make me do something stupid; that I shouldn't let myself get suckered into losing my head. Then you go and pull that dog-running-across-the-street stunt just because the guy was mouthing off."

"What you fail to get is that I *didn't* lose my cool. I *didn't* get suckered in. What I did was intentional and planned."

Again, silence prevailed in the squad car. It was three, maybe four minutes later when the car pulled in behind the Model Lunch. Once the car was shifted into park, Officer Robert Jokovich turned to face the young cop who was in the final weeks of field training under his tutelage.

"Don't get pissed just because I waffled the guy. He needed some justice!"

"What?" the young cop asked with noticeable annoyance. "What the hell do you mean you 'waffled the guy'?"

"When you stop the car fast like I did, you know, because of the, quote, 'little black dog,' the guy's forehead slams into the prisoner screen, and the squares on the screen leave a nice little waffle pattern on his forehead for a few hours."

As the two men exited the car, the rookie cop remained silent and sullen as he filed away the new word of cop parlance.

Once inside the restaurant, Jokovich spoke quietly, almost in a whisper. "Okay, kid, now I'm gonna teach you another lesson."

The young cop stared out the window.

"You're pissed about what I did because you think I did it for revenge, to get even with that scumbag for what he was saying. Right? Well, kid, you're wrong. What I did back there was for the sake of justice. It was street justice, but sometimes that's the only kind of justice there is."

"Come on, Trapper. The guy was drunk and he was just running off at the mouth, just shucking with you. You tell me that I have to grow a thick skin in order to do this job, and then you do something like that because some drunk is mouthing off."

"You're wrong, kid. I didn't waffle him simply because he was mouthing off. I did it because he has no respect for his wife, for the law, for us." The big man wiped off his fork before he continued the lecture. "Once a guy, a guy like that shitbird we just booked, gets the idea he can avoid what he's got coming...well that's when you have to rattle his head and let him know there is some justice in the world. That's when he gets a taste of swift, sure, and *effective* justice."

"Justice? You say 'justice'? I thought justice was for the courts."

"Kid, wake up! If you think you're gonna find justice in court, you're gonna have a very short and very miserable career. I'm here to tell ya that getting punched, getting shot at, getting spit on, well maybe that's all part of the job. But, when some shithead like that guy gets to thinking he can pull his sort of crap without some form of punishment following, that's when he's gotta learn there's some pain in it for *him!* If he thinks he can kick the guts out of his old lady and then just walk away from it, he'll eventually think he can kick the shit out of you or some other cop and walk away from that too!"

"So, what are you telling me, Trapper? Are you saying that waffling a guy is okay if *you* feel it's the best way to serve justice?"

"I don't know if what I'm saying is all that fancy, rookie. All I'm telling you is sometimes if you don't give them a little street justice, there ain't gonna be any justice at all. Then, pretty soon we're the ones who are afraid of *them.*"

When their post-midnight breakfast arrived, Jokovich took a sip of coffee, and spoke without malice, without emotion. "I want to ask you a question, Mike."

The rookie took note that it was one of the very few times his training officer had used his first name instead of the usual reference to him as, "Kid." Looking up, Officer Amato said, "Ask."

"How many times in the past ten weeks that you've been riding with me have we gotten out of the car at some corner along Joseph Avenue or Clinton Avenue and rousted some of our more notable citizens?"

"Four, probably five nights a week."

"So, about 40 or 50 times, right?" Without waiting for a response, the older man continued. "So when we get out of the car and they know we're gonna bust up their crap game, their drug dealing, or whatever the hell it is they're doing, why is it that they don't jump us? Half of them are armed with guns, knives, pool sticks, brass knuckles, or some other damn thing. They outnumber us and outgun us, so why don't they fuck with us?"

"Because they know if they jump us, there'll be 10 more cops arriving. If the 10 additional cops can't handle it, then there'll be 25 cops, or 50, or whatever it takes to get control of the situation. And," the kid-cop added with a grin, "they know we'll make the rest of their summer a living hell."

"So then, do you get my point, kid?" Trapper Jokovich asked without interrupting his chewing. "They know that if they go over the line, if they put their hands on us, if they get too froggy, then there's gonna be hell to pay. They know there's gonna be justice...*instant* justice, *street* justice."

The young cop swallowed and then asked, "Yeah, right, but do they toe the line because they respect us or because they fear us?"

"Fear, respect, honor, hate, love...I don't care what the hell it is. All *I know* is *they know* there'll be justice, the kind of justice they understand. I don't care what emotion they feel! All that matters is that we go home at the end of the shift. That's all that counts. Remember what I already taught you...It's better to be judged by twelve than be carried by six!"

The kid stayed silent, so Jokovich continued his dissertation on the ways of the world. "Is it justice that this mope we had tonight kicked his pregnant wife and busted her jawbone, and all he'll get is a month, maybe three months—if anything at all—in the county jail? Is it justice that a drunk driver kills a fifteen-year-old kid and a smart lawyer gets him off with driver's school? I don't know, Mike. You tell me. What the hell is justice?"

After the meal break, the beat-up cop car moved silently through the neighborhood. Jokovich again broke the silence.

"This ain't no boxing ring, kid. There are no rules out here on the streets. Your job is to go home at the end of the night, to go home to your family. Our job isn't about fighting fair. It's all about fighting to win. If he hits you once, you hit him twice. If the bad guy throws a punch, you crack him with your stick, and crack him hard! If he comes up with a club or a knife, you cap the son-of-a-bitch!"

The young cop let the subject drop and it was never again discussed between the two men. That night, while taking off his uniform, the rookie had to admit he had lost some of the respect and admiration he had held for the man who had tutored him over the past two-and-a-half months.

Then, as the weeks passed into months, and months became years, the rookie turned into a veteran and he did, ever so rarely, deal his own versions of street justice to the unlawful who crossed the thin line that separated acceptable criminal behavior and pure viciousness.

He found he could never totally justify the actions to himself, but down deep in the recesses of his id, where the secrets of conscience are kept, he understood and accepted the concept of...and the need for...street justice.

PART ONE:

JUSTICE SOUGHT

LOU CAMPANOZZI

CHAPTER ONE

THE SQUAD

While I hoped to draw a jack and fill in a possible queen-high straight, Rebecca Chilsom silently prayed she would live to see her mom. My prospect of filling the straight died when Romano dealt me a six of clubs. Rebecca Chilsom's hopes faded as the madman's hands formed a circle around her neck and slowly squeezed the life out of her. As those two mismatched events played their course, the homicide squad—unknowing and almost uncaring—was pushed into a case that would impact almost every subsequent event for the remainder of each detective's life. For most of us, it would be the case that defined who and what we are.

On that cool September evening a couple of years ago, I sat cloaked in blissful ignorance as the squad kibitzed their way through the ritual of our Almost Monthly Poker Game. The bliss came from watching and listening to the group exchange sarcastic barbs, high-fives and bursts of laughter that came from deep in the belly. The ignorance was based on allowing myself the luxury of being smugly content...and foolishly expecting things to always remain as they were then.

My name is Mike Amato. After more than 25 years in the cop business, the last seven of which have been as the Lieutenant in charge of the Violent Crimes Unit, I can say I've seen it all. I can say that, but I know it never was—and never will be—true.

Unfortunately—or fortunately—as we shuffled and dealt cards, I had no way of knowing that in a year's time the card players around the table would be at each other's throats. In a matter of months the good-natured sarcastic remarks would lack any true spirit of fun. Instead, the remarks would become caustic and take on an angry antagonism that would stab at the friendships and kill the equanimity that then lived so passionately in the present, private, violent work-world we shared. In the months and years that would pass, the straight citizens would lose all faith in the squad and our credibility would be questioned. Parents would fear to allow their children out of their sight. Panic would overtake each mother when her child was two minutes overdue and the city would find itself under the manipulation of a psycho serial killer.

All this would come to pass because of one man...one man who coveted the city's children...one man who found joy in choking the life out of our children...one man who pleasured himself in killing cruelly and delighted himself by tormenting the mothers and fathers of his victims.

We liked to get together for a good card game at least once every month, however, for one reason or another - most often a fresh homicide - the games were often delayed for a few weeks or a month, and so we ended up having them sporadically. Somewhere along the line, Bobby St. John changed the name of the event from the "Monthly Poker Game" and hung it with the present tag, "The Almost Monthly Poker Game."

Taking a break from the game, I made myself a sandwich and grabbed a fresh beer. After finishing the meal-like snack, I leaned back on the couch, put my feet up on the coffee table in front of me, took a long pull on the beer, and surveyed the members of my team. Smiling, I was struck with the thought that nothing could break up the squad—and just as suddenly, I admonished myself for the thought. Making predictions like that, my cynical id warned me, was like giving the squad the kiss of death. Whenever one predicted a sure thing, the sure thing became not so sure...and such was the case in this instance. Strangely enough, as it turned out, what would end up destroying the squad would be the one thing that held us together—the endless parade of homicides that drove us...and seemed to consume our lives.

Frankie Donovan is the senior member of the group with about 53 years of life behind him, 28 years of police experience under his 46-inch belt, and approximately 20 years of detective work to his credit. He's an Irishman through and through, who is quick with a smile, has a booming voice, and works like a mule. Whenever we receive a new kid in the squad, he always spends at least six months with Donovan. I don't give a damn about how good a detective the new guy was supposed to have been back wherever he came from, he could still learn a lot more from Detective Francis Xavier Donovan.

Sitting across from Donovan (who was studying his cards as carefully as he studied every aspect of an investigation) was Robert "Bobby" St. John, a guy with an uncanny memory for details. Like Donovan and me, St. John is divorced. He's a quiet, conservative kind of guy who is not one to take part in the crass jokes and verbal sarcasm offered by most of the squad members. Because of his Master's Degree in English Literature and his almost aloof approach to life, some folks looked at him as being too "uptown"…especially for a black guy. He also has a certain live-and-let-live philosophy about life, leaving the detective unruffled by the beliefs of others.

Even when he takes a ribbing from the others in the squad, which usually is done on a daily basis and most often due to him correcting their sloppy grammar or offering a quote from the classics, he gives that little smile of his and returns to work. It would be incorrect to say that Bobby St. John is arrogant or conceited. It isn't that at all. He's simply a man who has very high personal standards, expects a lot out of himself and, more often than not, he delivers.

The reason he's called "Bobby" is not simply a reference to his first name. The nickname had been hung on him because of his love for England, the classic English authors, and his impeccable style. The story is that some old-time sergeant had said, "The new black kid should have been a tight-assed Bobby in England, rather than a street cop over here!" As is the case with most nicknames, the off-hand remark stuck with Robert St. John and he became, forever after, Bobby St. John.

"This frigging provolone cheese smells like dirty socks," Jimmy Paskell announced as he scooped some chips and pretzels into a dish. "How do you guys eat this shit?"

"It's supposed to smell like that," Tommy Romano responded. "It keeps riff-raff like you away from it."

"Damn! I'll bet you some juvie basketball freak in the ghetto has old, rotten sneakers that smell better than this crap."

I smiled at James Harold Paskell's assessment of the cheese I dearly love. He had been in the squad for over three years and I never ceased to be entertained by his observations on life, politics, and any other thing that came to his attention. Paskell likes to seem tough on the outside, but he's also subject to a slight tinge of paranoia that's constantly fed and nurtured by other members of the squad. His nickname, Rooster, comes from the fact that his hair, unless recently combed and sprayed, tends to stand up as if someone is holding a static-charged balloon over his head. A casual inquiry about his choice of tie, or an observation that he doesn't appear to look well, is enough to send Paskell asking everyone he encounters for the remainder of the day what they think about his tie or questioning if they think he looks sick.

Tommy Romano, Paskell's constant critic, is the newest member of the squad. The kid is as sharp in his investigations as he is in his stylish suits. Besides showing an uncanny instinct when it comes to investigations, he has a very large family of aunts, uncles and cousins who seem to have the very connections we often come to need in assorted investigations. If you ever need to build a patio, clean out your chimney, get a carburetor for a '58 Cadillac, or find a midget barber, Tommy will have an aunt, uncle, cousin, or close friend who can help you. He has a natural ability to pick up the smallest details, commit them to an infallible memory, and bring them into play days or weeks later. I like his style and I admire his dedication to the job.

What I don't like about Romano is that he cheats on his wife. He doesn't let it interfere with the job, but it's generally well known he has a girlfriend—maybe two, or it could be three—on the side. Between the long hours he works and then also having an affair going on the side, it's surprising that the kid stays married.

And finally, there's Gail Walz. Gail is as attractive as a woman may be without being beautiful. Besides her casual elegance, the detective's five-foot, seven-inch frame is well-toned by continuous workouts. Added to that is a full head of blond hair that's usually pulled back into some type of braid or roll while on duty, but off-duty, at a squad gathering such as this, she usually lets it fall loose and sexy around her face.

Going by her personnel file, Gail is 32 years of age, but looks slightly younger. Although she's only been a cop for about 11 years, and has a mere five years of experience as an investigator, she has an outstanding reputation for doing her job. In Vice, she had worked some of the toughest undercover cases and developed a reputation for having nerves of steel. Later, when she went to work in Clinton Section, probably the roughest patrol section in the city, Gail Walz efficiently handled—and solved—a heavy load of robberies, assaults, rapes, and other major felonies. To her credit, she cleared almost twice as many of her cases as did the other detectives working the same area.

The woman has just the right balance of being one of the guys, while still maintaining her integrity as a lady. Walz could get "down and dirty" with any suspect, or any cop for that matter, and still every man on the job knows she won't stand still for any abuse because she's "just a woman." On the few occasions when some male cop who over rated his potential to be suave, came on a little too strongly to Gail, she would let him down gently...or leave him a quivering mass of neutered jelly. It was all up to the guy...and how much he wanted to push the issue.

She hadn't been my first choice to fill the vacancy left by Al Verno when he transferred out of the squad. I know a man of the new millennium isn't supposed to think about such things, but the reason I held back on wanting Walz in the squad is that she's the single parent of an eight-year-old daughter. Yeah, okay, so I get labeled as being a sexist pig for my old-way thinking, but I know what demands this job makes on cops, and when I need a team to be called in, I can't wait for the damn babysitter to show up.

All that aside, in the time she had been on the squad, Walz never disappointed me. She did her job, and she did it very well. Maybe she works so hard because she's trying to prove herself to me and the other men; maybe she's just dedicated. Whatever it is that winds her clock, she is one hell of a good detective as far as I'm concerned.

Going out on the balcony of the apartment, I lit a cigarette and blew the smoke into the cool, almost cold, early autumn night air. My continuing thoughts about the squad put a smile on my face. It would be a gross understatement to say I was pleased to be a part of it all…and the work we churned out day after day, week after week.

Returning to the warmth inside the apartment, I got back into the game and smiled at the squad's fresh round of traded insults. To an outsider it would sound as if they hated each other's guts. But to us it was the music of friendship at its best. Paskell had just bluffed Bobby out of a nice pot, so it was time for the Rooster to take his punishment.

"Nice job, Jimmy," St. John said as he leaned back in the chair. "Maybe you'll use the money to buy a new pair of pants."

"What's wrong with my pants?"

"Nothing, nothing at all. Forget I mentioned it," Bobby. "Hang on to them…they'll probably come back in style someday."

As Paskell sought counseling from Donovan about his pants, Gail had just gotten herself a beer and was returning to the table. "Hey, Tommy, can you slide your chair in a little so I can get by?" she asked more in a command than a question.

"Sure thing," Romano said politely and everyone waited for the follow-up slam that was sure to come. "But maybe if you'd lose 20 pounds, your ass would fit through there."

The insult was greeted with a couple of loud exaggerated coughs, groans, and grins.

"You, know, Tommy, maybe you're right," Walz said as she slid behind the man. "I hate to say this, but maybe I should lose a few pounds. You know, if I was to lose 20 pounds or so, I would be quite trim." We all knew there was more to come as Gail paused to look at the first two cards that had been dealt to her. "But you, well, if you lost 20 pounds you would still be a Neanderthal asshole!"

The comeback was greeted with more hoots and hollers as Donovan and Walz high-fived each other.

I swore when the pager on my belt began to emit the annoying beeping.

"Who's the on-call team for tonight?" Romano innocently asked his partner in an exaggerated whine as I made my way to the phone.

"I'm sorry, Thomas, but I really don't recall," St. John answered with a proper British accent and a broad smile.

"Well, gee-golly, if it isn't you and me, well, then, it must be…it sure as hell is…blubber butt and the Rooster!"

Walz gave Romano a slap to the back of his head as she said, "And it's a good thing me and Jimmy are on call or else you and the English professor would leave the squad with *another* open case at the end of the year."

By that time I was on the phone, talking to one of the dispatchers. The information she provided was kind of sketchy, but the woman was only relaying the information she had gotten from the cops on the scene.

Hanging up the phone, I announced, "They want the on-call team over on the 100 block of Scrantom Street. All the dispatcher has is some officer called out with a dead child and asked for a sergeant. The sergeant then asked for us."

The two detectives already had their coats on and were at the door when I advised them, "Give me a call and let me know what the hell's going on."

"Probably just a SIDS death," Walz offered. "You stay and try to win some of my money back, Lieutenant."

"These crib deaths are the worst damn things. I hate taking these calls." Paskell complained to his partner.

"Me too, Jimmy. But it isn't going to get any better with us standing here."

Twenty-five minutes later the phone rang. Donovan picked up the receiver, listened for about five seconds, and extended the receiver to me.

"Yeah?" I asked.

"You better get down here, Boss. We have a seven year-old female, deceased, in a vacant lot. She was reported missing earlier today by her mother. Some neighbors who were just coming home found the body. It's a homicide. No doubt about it."

I made a quick call to my boss, Major Art Winston, to inform him of the latest homicide to hit the city. I then left the card game…and had no realization at the time that I would also be leaving behind an old set of values, standards, and beliefs that had carried me this far in life but would no longer sustain me in months to come.

CHAPTER TWO

DEATH OF AN ANGEL

Becky Chilsom died as she lived—in sparse innocence. The killer had her body dumped without mercy or kindness in a vacant lot on Scrantom Street. The neighborhood had once been home for the upper-middle class, then the middle class, and then the lower-middle class. These days it's a neighborhood for those who make up the lower income strata of Rochester. The big houses have been modified to become apartments and duplexes to provide a home for hard working people who are struggling to get by. Where total failure had landed, and the house was no longer necessary or profitable, there stood an empty lot, becoming another piece of property gone off the tax rolls. Such was the place that surrounded the still, lifeless, grayish body of a young girl who would forever remain years from puberty.

I crossed the city in near-record time and headed north on Clinton Avenue, another street that had seen better times. When the Citgo gas station loomed up ahead, I slowed and made the left turn onto Scrantom Street. The cars belonging to residents formed a solid line on the north side of the street, the only side that permitted legal parking. The six marked police cars and two detective vehicles formed a similar solid line on the south side, in front of No Parking signs and the vacant lot that had become the child's near final resting place.

Yellow crime scene tape had been strung from a fence post on the west side of the lot, around a light pole marked with the silver-colored, metal number 27, to a tree at the other end of the lot. Light pole #27 was obviously the gathering spot for the cops and investigators who had converged upon the scene. By the time I arrived, the crime scene technicians had lit the dark area with portable lights and were in the process of completing a spiral search of the dismal place. I got out of my car, took a second or two to absorb the scene, and then moved to where Detective Gail Walz was talking with an uniformed lieutenant and a police officer.

"What have we got, folks?" I asked as I nodded a silent greeting to Lt. John Sensabaugh and the young copper next to him, but the question was directed solely to my detective.

Walz went into the briefing. "About 10:15 tonight, a Virginia Washington came home after visiting her mother. The Washingtons live there, in the house just to the west of the vacant property. As she was putting her daughter to bed, Mrs. Washington looked out the girl's bedroom window and saw what she thought was a body over there where our victim is. Washington called a friend across the street, one…"

"One Randy Tyrell," Sensabaugh filled in.

"Right," continued Walz offering a smile of thanks to the muscular Lieutenant. "Anyway, Tyrell goes out with a flashlight and after a minute or two, he finds our victim. The police are called; they confirm Tyrell's findings, and then we got called. Jimmy is doing a door-to-door check with two uniform cops and I have the scene. Tyrell lives over there, in the two-story house with the long front porches on both floors," Walz advised as she pointed with her ballpoint pen to a house across the street and slightly west of our position.

"Do we have an identity on the victim?" I asked as I looked over Gail's shoulder toward the spot where the body rested.

"It's not confirmed as of yet, but based on the physical description, the clothing, and the school bag, Lt. Sensabaugh is 99 percent sure it's the body of one Rebecca Chilsom, age eight, who was reported missing late this…well I guess by now it would be late *yesterday* afternoon."

When my eyes shifted to Sensabaugh, he smiled at me, took a couple of short puffs on his ever-present pipe, and went into his soliloquy.

"The child was reported missing early last evening, around six o'clock last night, Friday night that is," he said to clarify the time span now that it was very early Saturday morning. "Maple Section officers took the report, and put out a citywide broadcast. Later, maybe about eight o'clock, they requested assistance in doing a neighborhood door-to-door check for the victim. The evening shift lieutenant sent one of our troops over there to help out."

"Maple Section?" I asked. "Maple Section is way the hell on the other side of town."

"Yeah, right, Mike," Sensabaugh confirmed. "The victim's home address is over on Child Street, right near the corner of Jay Street. It's about four, four-and-a-half miles from here, but with these damn cutbacks the city keeps making, district lines don't mean anything anymore. We have to send out troops all over the damn city in order to cover things." He paused to see if I had any other brilliant interruptions to lend to the briefing, and then continued. "Anyway, one of our guys was sent to help out with the neighborhood check. As far as I know, they didn't come up with anything other than a red car had been seen cruising the neighborhood some time late in the afternoon, right around the time the girl came up missing."

John Sensabaugh is a through-and-through street cop who has become a legend within the ranks of Rochester's 700 cops. At the age of 45, he still had a powerful, trim, muscular body that was evidence of his workouts and long recreational runs through the city's streets and parks. He's a command officer who loves his cops - and they adore him. His troops especially enjoy adding to John's legend status by circulating the most recent, "Wait-'til-you-hear-what-the-Lieutenant-did" story. Besides being a highly active and productive cop, he's an able administrator who has made a career out of short-cutting red tape and getting things done within, around, or without the Rochester Police Department's alleged administration. Consequently, while the man is loved by real cops, he is not well liked, trusted, or embraced by the Department's silk-tie executives.

"According to the information our copper picked up when he was helping out over on the other side, this body here is the Chilsom kid. The coat, book bag, slacks, blouse, even the sneakers, fit the description exactly. And besides, Mike, take a look at this."

I looked down at the picture Lt. Sensabaugh held in front of his chest as he focused a flashlight on it. On the two-inch by three-inch piece of paper was a photo of a smiling little girl with one front tooth missing. Her brown hair was pulled back, but a couple of ringlets fell down the sides of her face. The lighting used by the photographer had created a white light behind her head, as if imitating a halo.

After covering some of the basics with John, Gail and I walked over to the body. The crime scene technicians had created a safe path to and from the body, so that nothing got trampled in the area as cops, detectives, bosses, medical examiners, and technicians did their job of finding out what and who had taken the life out of Becky Chilsom.

I looked down at the small body that had accumulated only eight years of life on this screwed up planet that created angels like her…and the monsters who kill them. The child's body was on her back, looking up at the stars of a clear, cool autumn night. The right arm was down, along the side of the body, and the left one was bent at the elbow, with the palm up, next to her head, as if she were waving goodbye to the beleaguered world she had known. The right leg was straight. The left one was bent at the knee.

"That's exactly the way Wendy sleeps," Gail Walz commented to no one in particular.

My eyes scanned the body, going over her forehead, eyebrows, cheeks, ears, nose, lips, chin, and neck. Days from now I would not remember what the victim's face looked like, but would be able to describe every feature of the face and the presence or absence of wounds. It was a defense mechanism I had built over the years, so that all the elements of the face were committed to memory, but yet my mind was not encumbered with the burden of seeing the victim's face in total, of knowing the victim personally.

Searching for wounds, marks, any evidence at all, my flashlight worked down the body, over the arms, hands, torso, legs, and feet. The light moved back to the crotch of the victim's light blue slacks, to the moist, dark spot.

"Make sure the Medical Examiner's people are aware of that," I said to one of the technicians who was finishing photographing the area.

"Semen?" Gail asked.

"That would be my guess," I responded, and then asked, "So what do you think was the cause of death?"

Detective Walz knew I was going to ask the question. It was one I asked every detective on the squad at every death scene. I wanted them to be able to think and form opinions without hearing my opinion first.

"Right now, from here, my guess is strangulation, manual strangulation. Going by the two marks there on the left side of the neck," she said clinically as she pointed the beam of light from her small flashlight at the spot. "Then, going by the one clear mark with a second lighter mark on the right side of the neck, I would say she was choked from the rear and that the killer had at least two fingers around the front of her neck when he was doing it. Probably, when they get her to the morgue, they'll find the thumb marks on the back of the neck." When there was no response, she asked, "So, Lieutenant, do I pass the test?"

"I would have to give you an A, Detective. That's just the way I would have called it."

"Of course, that's all subject to an autopsy."

"Of course," I replied.

About 15 minutes later, Gail Walz, Jimmy Paskell, and I huddled for a briefing about ten feet from the body. The sum total of everything we had done at the scene amounted to very few facts. We had the body of an eight-year-old girl dumped in a vacant lot; she was most definitely the victim of a homicide; and, it was going to take a lot of effort to solve the case.

"Is the neighborhood check complete, Jimmy?" I asked.

"We covered every house on both sides of the street, and any other house on the side streets that may have had any line of view to the scene. Fien Street is over there and Princeton intersects at the other corner. There are three houses I have to go back to because either we didn't get an answer the first time around or because someone in the family was gone. The bottom line is that no one saw anything, except one woman who saw a red Mustang, possibly an older model, stopped in front of the vacant lot about 10 o'clock tonight. She can't say what he was doing, how long he was here, or even if 'he' was a he."

"Some witness saw a red car over by where the kid lives," Lt. Sensabaugh volunteered.

"A Mustang?" Paskell asked.

"I don't know for sure. The witness was sketchy," Sensabaugh answered with a shrug and couple of quick pulls on his pipe.

"We'll need to get to that witness," Walz said to her partner as he continued to stare down at the victim.

"Okay, here's what we do," I spoke up. "Walz will come with me to notify the parents. Jimmy, you finish up here at the scene. Make sure the neighborhood is done 100 percent. I don't care if we wake up every soul around here, just make sure it gets done. See what the Medical Examiner comes up with when he moves the body, and see if you can get them to commit to a time for the autopsy tomorrow. When you get done here, hook up with me and Walz and we'll take a look at where we are at that time."

"Do you want anyone else called in?" Paskell asked after he jotted a note in his spiral pad.

"Not yet. We'll need them all in tomorrow, bright and early." After a second thought, I added, "Call Donovan's place and make sure the game is over. It's almost two in the morning now. If they haven't called it a night already, tell them they better get some shut-eye because their asses will be hustling tomorrow…and tell them tomorrow is going to start early and be a very long day for one and all."

On the way back to the car, Walz used her portable radio to arrange a meeting for us with one of the sergeants over in Maple Section, the patrol district that had taken the initial missing person report.

Once in the car, I started to say, "You mentioned Wendy before…"

"She's taken care of," she said as if reading my thought. "Her father has her for the weekend. He takes her once a month, and this was his weekend."

"That's good," I commented. Then added, "I mean it's good the two of you have a working agreement."

"Well, as long as we don't live together, we seem to get along fairly well…and it makes it easier for Wendy," the woman replied as she looked out the passenger window.

Gail Walz and I drove in silence as the car crossed the Bausch Street Bridge. At Smith Street and Child Street, we met up with Sgt. Isaac Perez.

It was a brief meeting that lasted long enough for me to inhale my way through a cigarette. Perez is one of those up-and-comers who has steadily demonstrated he's got the knack for being a pretty good street boss. His briefing was complete and concise.

"The kid gets home from school about 2:45 in the afternoon. She normally lets herself in the apartment and then stays there until the mother gets home from work." He paused long enough to take a bite out of an apple that was evidently part of his midnight shift meal, and then continued. "Last night, the mother, one Betty Chilsom, comes home from work at about 5:00 p.m., as she usually does, and she sees her daughter isn't home. She begins to call around to a couple of the kid's friends, and also calls her married brother who lives a few blocks away, but no one had seen the kid. Finally, at 6:18 p.m., the mother calls us. Officer Eric Tyler took the report, notified Lieutenant Williams, the on-duty C.O., and then they got together with a couple of cops from around the city, did a neighborhood search, and put out a countywide broadcast on the kid. The bottom line is that all they come up with is that the victim was last seen at Garcia's Corner Grocery, on Child Street, about a block-and-a-half from the kid's home. The best estimate is that it was somewhere around 3:15 to 3:30 p.m. when she was at the store. At the time, the witness, Roberto Garcia, the owner of the store, noticed the victim talking to a guy in a small, red car. The car, according to the witness, is not too old, but then again, not too new. Garcia says he thinks the car is a foreign model."

"Did he think it might be a Mustang?" Walz asked.

"Not that I'm aware of," Perez said as he shook his head back and forth. "All I was told by the evening shift was that he thought it was foreign, possibly a Honda."

Perez stopped to take a second bite of the apple. "And, that's about it, Boss. The only other thing is that the technicians made a bunch of duplicates of the victim's picture, and we have them out to every patrol district in the city." Almost apologetically, the young sergeant added, "We had to borrow cops from Genesee Section, Lake Section, and Clinton Section, just to do the neighborhood check. We're just too short on personnel. I don't know, Lieutenant. It's like the politicians just don't give a shit about things anymore."

"They will next year," Walz stated flatly.

Perez wrinkled his eyebrows as he bit into his apple.

"It's an election year," Gail responded to his silent question. "Cops and crime will be back in vogue then."

"Amen," was all I could say.

We got back into the unmarked car and turned left on Child Street, stopping in front of a two-story residence marked with the number, 401.

The blood and guts don't bother me. Seeing death has little impact on my psyche. I can handle the cuttings, shootings, and other assorted and creative evil that man does to his fellow man. However, if the truth be known, I would much rather walk into a down-and-dirty bar brawl rather than go to someone's home and tell them a loved one had become the latest homicide statistic. And, when it comes to kids, the task is ten times more arduous.

One minute later, Detective Walz and I were knocking on the upstairs apartment door of Betty Chilsom. The house had originally been a large one-family home, but somewhere along the line it had been converted into a duplex. Because we were still dressed in the casual clothing of the card game, Sgt. Perez accompanied us, so as to verify our police badges and identification cards with his uniform.

"I'm Detective Walz, and this is Lt. Mike Amato," Gail said in a charming way with an incongruent sympathetic smile.

"You found my baby?" Mrs. Chilsom said as she looked over our shoulders, searching the top of the flight of stairs for signs of her daughter.

"Well, we, we do have some, some unfortunate circumstance, some unfortunate news," Walz stumbled.

Time has taught me there's no easy way to say what needed to be said. Stumbling and mumbling only makes the family more anxious and hurts them more as they try to guess the sorrowful news that is being dribbled out to them.

"We found your daughter's body," I said directly but softly, as if the tone could possibly soften the impact of the words. "She was murdered, Mrs. Chilsom."

With that out in the open, we moved into the neat, cramped apartment, and with an arm around the gasping woman, Gail guided her to the couch. Her brother and sister-in-law, who had obviously been in the kitchen when Betty Chilsom opened the door, came into the living room, and Sgt. Perez repeated the news for them. We three cops then stood silently and let the family deal with the news. After allowing them enough time to absorb the information and get past the worst of the sobbing, I moved in to conduct the interview that needed to be done now, now while the mother was the weakest and most vulnerable.

After thirty minutes of questions, crying and answers, my concerns were satisfied. The mother was not, in all probability, the murderer of little Becky Chilsom. She answered all of our questions and verified what she had told the cops earlier in the night when she reported her daughter missing. The only new piece of information we received was that the victim's father was long gone and had been out of Betty Chilsom's life even before Becky had made her way into the world.

Rebecca Chilsom had been the product of a brief, albeit torrid relationship between Betty and her cocaine supplier. From the day she learned she was pregnant, her lover had nothing more to do with Betty and she had nothing more to do with him or the drugs he supplied. After a stint in a rehab center, Chilsom had gone into job training. When the baby was born, she made ends meet by cleaning offices at night and caring for her daughter during the day. When Becky was old enough to start school, the mother had taken a job at a local factory where she soldered contact points on small motors. As the Chilsom woman made her way into supervision at the factory, her child demonstrated a higher than normal intelligence and was moved into one of the newer city schools for gifted children.

When we had what we came for, we excused ourselves and made promises to stay in touch whenever there was a new development in the case. Sgt. Perez made arrangements to have the three family members transported to the Medical Examiner's Office to make a positive identification of the body. With that out of the way, Detective Walz and I made our way back to the PSB - the Public Safety Building.

"It's so damn hard to get the words out," Gail said as I made a U-turn on Child Street and pointed the car towards downtown.

"There's no nice way to say the words, so you just say them. It's like taking off a bandage," I commented. "You have to rip it off in one, quick motion, rather than peeling it back inch by inch."

There was a full minute of silence before Walz spoke. "May I say something, Lieutenant? You know, make an observation?"

"Sure."

"You were kind of rough on her for awhile. The brother was getting a little pissed."

"So? What's your point?"

"Look, I know the, 'You work for the victim' speech and all, but you were kind of rough. That's all…just an observation."

"Walz, you're a good detective. You love snooping, and asking, and interrogating. However, you're weak in one area and that's in the area of being pushy. The fact of the matter is that parents are involved in a high percentage of kids' killings. The time to go after them is right after the body is found. That's when they're vulnerable, and when they're vulnerable is when you need to attack." I took a sneak peek at her to see how she was reacting to the information. She seemed to be okay with it, so I continued. "We *do* work for the victim. That's it, plain and simple. We can't concern ourselves with whether or not the minister likes it or what the press thinks. We owe it to the victim to pull out all the stops and go for the jugular. Now then, if you're tired of the 'We do it for the victim' speech, try this one on. You're a cop, not a social worker. You can't worry about treatment, post traumatic syndrome, how they will handle the baggage, and all that crap. You're a cop. You're doing God's work! So, screw them all, and just do your job."

"You smooth-talking devil," Gail Walz said as she gave me a stiff punch in the right bicep.

Once in the squad room, I smelled the comforting aroma of fresh coffee brewing. Jimmy Paskell was already at the computer, feeding in his report of the night's activities. His coffee cup was full, so I poured one for me and motioned the offer of one to Walz as she briefed her partner on the interview with the victim's mother. Gail waved off the coffee. Allowing her time to catch Jimmy up on our part of the investigation, I poured a stiff shot of *Sambuca* into my coffee cup from the bottle I still keep in my lower left desk drawer.

"Did you make contact with Donovan and the others?" I asked over the four-foot high wall that framed my cubicle to the Paskell-Walz cubicle twenty feet away.

"Yeah," Paskell answered, but he seemed distant, as if answering automatically.

I walked down the narrow passageway and found myself amused by the city's new PSB décor that looked more like an insurance office than a real detective bureau. Approaching the detective I asked, "What's wrong, Jimmy?"

The detective reached for the three-sectioned, hinged picture frame on his desk and handed it to me. "Did you see the victim, Lute?" he asked. Without waiting for a response, he said, "She looks just like Tamara."

I looked at the desk picture of the blond girl seated on James Pakell's lap and nodded. "Yeah, there is a resemblance."

"It kind of blew me away, I guess. You know what I mean? It was like looking down at my own daughter."

There were a few seconds of silence before Gail broke in and said, "There was a red car seen over where the kid was last seen alive, Jimmy. The witness, who, by the way, we need to get back to this morning, says it was a Honda or something foreign."

"Yeah, yeah," Paskell said as he nodded. "I heard you say that."

"How sure is your witness that the car she saw on Scrantom Street was really a Mustang?"

"She was, I guess, pretty firm on it."

"Was she positive?" Walz pressed.

"From what the cop who talked to her said, she was positive. She said it was a hatchback, like one of the older 1970's Mustangs."

"'From what the cop said'?" I asked. "What the hell do you mean by that?"

"The cop that made contact with her said she was positive it was a Mustang," he answered, sounding somewhat offended by my question.

"What the hell, Jimmy? Didn't you interview her?"

"Well, the kid that talked to her said she was pretty firm on it, and, well, he seemed to know what he was doing." Paskell was defensive because he knew I was going to rip him a new ass.

"Jimmy, this is *our* case. *We* do the interviews. If someone else turns up a lead, we're the ones who follow up on it. What the hell's the matter with you? You know better than that! Why the hell are you letting a uniform cop do your job?"

"What the hell's the big deal, Lieutenant?" Paskell asked angrily as he stood up. "Okay, so we'll go back tomorrow and talk to her!"

I slid off the desk and took one step toward Paskell's workstation. With my right index finger extended and pointed directly toward the center of his face, I said, "You bet your ass *you'll* go back and talk to her tomorrow. What you did was sloppy, short-cutting, and you know it!"

"Okay," he said somewhat sharply.

"Okay," I repeated less sharply, believing I had made my point.

It was four in the morning when I finally thought about heading for the apartment I call home. Being that it would take me a half-hour to get there, and then I would have to get up in less than three hours to be back in the office, I decided to pull a sleep-on-the-desk gig for the next few, short hours.

As I drifted off to a light sleep, my mind replayed the scene I had had with Jimmy Paskell. I bawled myself out for being so...so assertive with him. My brain told me maybe I should learn to lighten up a little. "If I lighten up, then they lighten up, and when they lighten up, we stop solving homicides," my lips told my brain.

CHAPTER THREE

THE FULL-COURT PRESS

Saturday morning's sunrise found me sleeping on top of a couple of desks. Something, maybe the kink in my neck, brought me around to semi-consciousness, and a yawn sucked some much needed air into my lethargic body. After rolling off the desk, I yawned my way across the hall to the men's room. The metal locker with an ace of spades drawn on it by one of my crew (probably Tommy Romano) was kind of a home away from home. In it I found the toiletries I needed in order to make myself somewhat presentable after a three-and-a-half hour nap.

After taking what cops call a "Whore's Bath"—washing under the armpits and splashing on some cologne—I brushed my teeth, shaved, and slipped into fresh underwear and a clean, pressed, white shirt, along with a conservative, striped tie. My clothes from the night before were rolled up into a ball and tossed into the bottom of the metal locker. By the time the teams started to drift in at 7:45 a.m., the coffee was brewed, and I was sipping my second cup of the day. With no one of importance in the building on the weekend, I lit my third cigarette of the morning.

Bobby St. John was first through the door, followed closely by Donovan. As the clock rolled around to 8:00 a.m., Tommy Romano entered the squad room, carrying a box of donuts. After everyone poured coffee, picked through the donut box to find the one that suited their taste for the morning, and a second pot of caffeine was churning, the briefing began.

"Jimmy and Gail will be in around nine-thirty this morning, so I'll give you the highlights." With that introduction, I went through the missing person report, the neighborhood checks around Child Street, the finding of the body, what we picked up from the area where the victim was found, and the interview with the victim's mother. "The red car is the main issue. It's the only lead we have for now, so we need to tie it down and see if the two red cars are, in fact, the same red car."

"Who's doing the background, Boss?" Tommy Romano asked.

"Well, Paskell and Walz have the case. They'll work the red car lead when they get in. I want you and Bobby working on the victim's bio. We have a lot of loose ends, and we need to tie them up. Who are her friends, and who are the friends' parents? How does she get along in school? Is the mother as righteous as she appeared to be last night? What about the father? Is he gone, or does he still have an interest? I want to know everything there is to know about her."

"We're on it," Bobby St. John said as he assembled a fresh notebook, copies of reports, and the victim's picture into his briefcase.

"In the meantime," I said as I drained the last of my third cup of coffee, "Donovan and I will work on tracing the victim's last few hours and see if we can nail down the area from which she was abducted." With that said, I went around the room and asked for input.

When it came to Donovan's turn, he summed it up neatly. "Right now, we have to go with the assumption the kid was abducted somewhere in or very near her neighborhood. She was obviously taken somewhere after the abduction, probably sexually abused, and then dumped. He had, roughly speaking, about four hours to do the entire deed. That means our bad guy has wheels." Then he cautioned, "Don't lock in on this red car, but keep it up front in your head."

"Should we get in a huddle and say a prayer?" Romano asked with a smirk in his eyes.

"Lieutenant," St. John moaned. "When are you going to get me a real partner instead of this jester?"

"Screw both of you," I said and flipped them off.

Child Street runs north and south on the city's west side. From its origin at Lyell Avenue, to its end at Danforth Street, the two-lane roadway is lined with homes and small businesses. Some of the houses are large, and some are small cottages, but all provide adequate shelter for the working-class families who live in them. As is the case with most of Rochester's neighborhoods, the length of Child Street is a nurturing spot for the next emerging ethnic group. Over the course of the last hundred years, the mailboxes of the Chilsom home had born the family names of Schmidt, then O'Rielly, and then Fazio, followed by the Washingtons and Jeffersons, and more recently, Rodriguez. The street had now become comfortable with its multi-national role, and no longer was one ethnic group obligated to move out when the next group began to arrive.

Frank Donovan parked the car close to the red brick automotive store that's near the Chilsom residence. It was still too early for the kids to venture out from their warm beds on this cool autumn weekend day. Consequently, Donovan and I attracted the attention of only two wandering dogs as we made our way up the steps to the victim's apartment that was now the gathering point for her limited family.

Frank began to work his way north, as I went door-to-door to the south. When we reached the end of the line, we crossed the street and began to work our way back toward each other. This is the not-so-glamorous part of a detective's life, but it's usually the thing that breaks cases more often than forensics and computers. We began our trek at 8:45, and met up again shortly after 11 o'clock.

"So, what have you got, Frank?" I asked as I lit my tenth or fifteenth cigarette of the day.

"I have one neighbor who saw the victim...actually talked to the victim...just before three yesterday afternoon. Becky Chilsom had just gotten off the school bus, and the witness, whose daughter goes to the same school as our victim, said hello to the victim, and saw her go toward the Chilsom home. She can't really say she saw the kid go inside, but she saw her within 20, maybe 30 feet of the front of the house." He paused long enough to see if I was going to toss in a question. I didn't, so the big man continued. "A second person, a guy right across the street from the victim's house, saw Chilsom kind of skipping or what he calls, 'hop-scotching' south from the house, toward Jay Street. He's not sure on the time, but says it was before 3:30 in the afternoon, because that's the time he goes to work."

"Anything else?"

"Well, I also talked to the first witness' child. That kid, one Veronica Supota, says that she's two grades ahead of the victim, and she knows her from the neighborhood more so than from school. She says the Chilsom kid was normal, usually happy, and very smart in school. Neither she nor the mother has any idea who may have hurt the kid. Neither one has ever seen a man around the house and they don't know anything about the father. On my second witness, I just made a note that we'll need to check out his place of employment to see if he showed up on time for work Friday. Personally, I didn't get any vibes from him, but what the hell, who knows."

I flipped my cigarette into the street and began my summary. "The people who live downstairs, below the Chilsoms, are Hermino and Bernadetta Cruz. They're both in their 70's and the old man has cancer pretty bad. The wife says the Chilsoms are good neighbors, very polite and quiet. She did hear the victim come home from school yesterday at what she calls, 'the normal time,' but can't pin it down. She says she heard the kid coming back down the stairs about 20, maybe 30 minutes later. The significant thing is that the Chilsom kid told Mrs. Cruz that she was going to the store to get milk, and asked if the Cruzes needed anything."

"Well, that kind of ties in with my guy across the street, but I'm still gonna check him out at work on Monday." Donovan noted with a nod. "Anything else jump up?"

"Nothing. Not a damn thing."

"Have you heard anything from Paskell and Walz?"

"Yeah. They called in about nine-thirty and said they were going to hit the witness over on Scrantom and then come over here. They said they'll hook up with us before they go see the Garcia guy at the corner store."

"Well," Donovan said as he looked at his watch, "that's almost an hour-and-a-half ago. What the hell are they doing?"

"I had to chew into Paskell's ass last night. He bought some information that a uniform cop came up with, and he never went back to personally confirm the information with the witness. I guess he's trying to cover his butt real good now."

Frank Donovan was not one to criticize other cops, especially if they weren't around to defend themselves. However, I could see he had something on his mind. "What are you thinking?" I asked.

Donovan squinted his eyes as if he were trying to see something in the air that wasn't there. Then he spoke. "I'm wondering what the hell's up with that kid. I mean, I like Jimmy, like him a lot, and he's a damn good investigator, but lately he's had his head up his ass."

"I think he's got some problems at home. I don't really have anything to base that on, but, I don't know, just a couple of things he's said lead me to believe he's getting pressure from his old lady."

"The old, 'You're-never-home-anymore' routine?" my partner asked without sarcasm.

"I don't know," I answered quite honestly. "I guess so."

As we headed back to the car with the intention of calling the errant team on the radio, Paskell and Walz pulled up. When they were out of the car, Paskell came up to me and asked to speak privately. We moved over toward one of the large oak trees that lined the street and I lit a fresh smoke.

"I'm sorry about last night, Boss," he said with his head down. "I was out of line, and, ah, I guess I was, you know, I was kind of defensive."

"It happens, Jimmy," I said and then blew a thick stream of blue-gray smoke in the air. "Just don't let it happen too often."

He let my warning go without commenting, but knew we had reached an agreement...and more importantly, he knew he better comply with the agreement.

With nothing more to discuss in private, Paskell and I walked back to where his partner and mine were standing. "Gail and I went back to the Gardner woman, the lady who saw the red car. As it turns out, she doesn't know a Mustang from a trailer truck. What happened was she told the cop who was interviewing her, that she saw a smallish red car, and as she was trying to describe it, she said it had a hatchback. The cop asked her if it had a hatchback like a Mustang, and she said something to the effect of, 'Yeah, I guess so'. Based on that, the cop tells me she said she saw a Mustang." The embarrassed detective looked from me to Donovan to see if he was going to hear a great big, 'I told you so!' but when we remained silent, he went on with his story. "Anyway, just to see if we could get a little more out of her, me and Gail took her around to a couple of shopping areas, and had her look at cars. The best she came up with was she's pretty sure it was just like or very similar to a car we saw parked over on Clinton Avenue and Avenue A, and that car turned out to be a 1989 Honda Civic."

"She's sure of the make?" Donovan asked.

"Not sure," Paskell answered. "She says it's similar in size and shape, but can't be for sure about it being the *exact* same make and model." He hesitated for a second or two, and added, "But, there's more."

"Are you going to tell us?" Donovan questioned, with an edge of annoyance in his tone. "Or, do you think it would be more exciting if we asked?"

"Chill out, Frankie," Paskell said as he feigned a punch to the bigger and older man's midsection. The comment and punch were meant to show us he was not intimidated by Donovan's remark, but Paskell's quick nervous glances to me and then Walz showed he knew he had been chastised by the man he admired most. "While we're talking to the Gardner woman, her 10-year-old son, Damion, comes into the room. We're talking to his mom about the car, and he drops it into the conversation, kind of nonchalantly, that two kids from Hawkins Street, right around the corner from Gardner's place on Scrantom Street, were playing in the empty lot up until about nine o'clock last night. Now then, if that's the case, and the Washington woman saw the body there at 10:15 p.m., then the killer only had about an hour, or an hour-and-a-quarter to dump the kid's body." Paskell paused once again, and quickly added, before Donovan could bust his chops again, "We tried to run down the two kids on Hawkins, but they're not home. We need to go back and hit the place again."

I popped in with my burning question. "What time does Gardner put the red car at the scene, and what's the car doing?"

Walz took over from that point. "Martha Gardner is very sure it was just before 10:00 p.m. when she went to pull down her shades in the living room of her house. She fixes the time by some TV evangelist she always watches. Anyway, her house is across the street, just north and slightly west of the vacant lot. She said she was pulling down the shades when she saw this red car right under the street light and notices that it's parked with the driver's side to the curb, like on the wrong side of the street. At the time she didn't think too much of it and sort of passed it off as being someone who was dropping off Mrs. Washington, the woman who first saw the body. However, what made her take notice was that the dome light in the car was on, and it didn't look like anyone was in the car. At the time she remembers saying to herself, something to the effect, 'That fella's going to get his car stolen if he leaves it all alone like that'."

"If that was our killer, the son-of-a-bitch probably pulled up to the curb, dragged the body out, and then got back in the car and boogied the hell out of there," Donovan mused and received a round of affirmative nods from our small group.

The four of us kicked around a couple of questions and a few ideas. Eventually, we decided that it would be best for Jimmy and Gail to return to the Scrantom-Hawkins Streets area and find the two kids, and that Frank and I would cover the interviews at the Garcia store. When Tommy Romano called us on the radio and announced he and St. John were running into little success and a lot of brick walls, we made arrangements for the entire squad to meet for lunch in about an hour or so. At that time we would catch up on our various bits of information.

"We're going to get this sick bastard" Jimmy Paskell said eagerly. "You watch, Lieutenant. We're going to nail this guy."

"What makes you so sure, Jimmy?" I asked.

In a less enthusiastic voice he said, "Because we have to, Boss. We have to!"

Garcia's Corner Grocery, formerly the Jay and Child Pizzeria, is not really on a corner, but actually sits about two doors away from the intersection of Child Street and Jay Street. The place, like many of the other stores, mingled with several vacant small shops and a neighborhood bar that managed to survive in spite of the neighborhood's many changes over the years. Garcia's is the type of small neighborhood Mom-and-Pop stores that dot our entire city and probably every other urban area in the country. The shelves and the odors inside the place reflect the ethnic makeup of the area. Puerto Rican foods sit next to jars of Italian spaghetti sauces and directly under the sign that announces customers are welcome to place an order for chitterlings. For security purposes, the check out area is close to the large door that causes a tiny bell above it to ring every time a customer enters or leaves. Stepping into the place brought instant memories of the corner store we had in our neighborhood, on Prospect Street, when I was a kid a hell of a long time ago.

From the two concrete steps leading to the store, I looked back over my shoulder and could see Becky Chilsom's house. It was diagonally across the intersection to the northwest. In my younger days, I probably could have hit it with a well-thrown baseball.

Donovan asked the woman behind the cash register if we could speak to Mr. Garcia, and when her eyes asked him what business he had with her husband, Frank displayed his badge and said quietly, "It's about the little girl." The woman, made an abbreviated Sign of the Cross, and disappeared into a back room.

Roberto Garcia is a short, bulky, somewhat muscular man in his 40's. His friendly ways made us feel welcome, but it was obvious caution was not far below the surface of the smile. Guiding us to a back room of the store—it's actually the Garcia family kitchen—he invited Frank and me to sit at the table with him.

He started the conversation with, "I have children of my own, you know."

"Then you know how important it is that we speak to you," Donovan said with a polite smile and an affirmative nod.

"I know that, but I also fear for them." Not waiting for us to ask who or why, the grocer continued, "A man who does something like this to an innocent child would also think nothing of attacking the children of a man who is a witness. I'm not going to hide it...I'm afraid to talk to you about this thing."

Donovan went into a little patter he had shared with thousands of witnesses over the years. He told the man his name was not going to be made public and that he was doing the right thing by sharing whatever information he had with the police. It did little to placate the man, but Garcia drew a deep breath and said simply, "Ask what you need to ask."

Donovan said he understood and respected the man's concerns and thanked him for his honesty. Then he went directly into the interview. "The officers who took the report last night told us you may have seen the Chilsom girl in front of your store yesterday and that she was with a man in a car. Can you tell us exactly what you saw?"

"I was at the cash register, checking out a customer, when I looked outside. I don't know why, but I just looked outside and I saw Rebecca. She was not really in front of the store, but maybe five feet past it. I looked to see if her mother was with her, because the two are very close and the girl isn't usually around without the mother. I figured she was okay because she was talking to a guy she knew. So I just thought something like it must be her uncle or somebody like that, taking her to the store. When the customer I was waiting on left, I got busy putting some things up on the shelves and it wasn't until later that I realized little Rebecca never came in the store." When neither Donovan nor I said anything, Garcia raised he hands, palms up toward the metal ceiling, and shrugged. "That's it, officers. That's all I know."

Donovan had the man's attention and his trust, so there was no point in me joining the interview. My role was to watch our witness and look for hints of lies or hesitation. Besides, I already knew what Frank's next questions were going to be.

"You say you had the impression she knew the guy she was talking to, right? What makes you say that?"

"Rebecca was on the curb, kind of leaning in the car. Kind of like this," Garcia said as he laid one forearm over the other in front of his face and rested his chin on the top arm. "It looked like she was talking to the guy, I guess kind of friendly."

"Why do you think it was friendly?" Donovan asked. "Help me understand."

"I don't know why," the storekeeper said a little defensively.

Frank Donovan calmed him with, "You know, Mr. Garcia, the mind is a strange thing. It picks up little clues, like little signals, and it makes sense out of them. There's a lot of research that says people's impressions are usually pretty accurate." The polished detective cited some bogus study that was supposedly done by the University of Rochester on the subject and then waited a second to set up his next question. "My job is to help you remember why you got that impression, you know, the impression that they were friendly. Now, in order for me to do that, I have to ask you a hundred little questions in order to jog your memory and see why you got that impression." He patted the man on the knee, and then he added, "I don't doubt you for a second. You appear to be a hard working, very honest man. I just want to help you remember. You see?" As soon as he received a nod from Garcia, Donovan asked, "So what makes you think they were friendly?"

"She was close to the car, leaning into it. You see what I mean? If she was afraid, she would have been back, back away from the car. That's all I can say, officer."

"Oh, okay, I understand," Donovan said with another pat on the man's knee. "Now let me ask you this, what can you tell us about the car?"

"It was red and, I don't know why, but I told the cops, the officers who talked to me last night, that it was maybe a foreign car. I don't know why I said that. It's just the impression I got."

"The way I got it from those cops is that you thought the car was a Honda or a Toyota. What made you think it might be a Honda or a Toyota?"

"I just said that as a…a for instance. You understand? I said it was probably foreign, like a Honda, a Toyota, one of those cars. And, before you ask me why I thought that, I just saw it as kind of a small car and, at least to me, small cars are usually foreign cars."

Shifting gears, Donovan hit the question I was waiting to hear. "Who was the customer you were waiting on when you saw Rebecca outside your store?"

"Mrs. Rosario. She lives on Colvin Street. But, please, if you talk to her, don't tell her I gave you her name. She's a good customer. I wouldn't want her to think I involved her."

"Don't you worry about it, Mr. Garcia. She'll never know you whispered her name." Donovan made a note or two in his pad, and then looked up, appeared to be deep in thought, and then asked, "You

31

say you thought the girl was talking to her uncle or someone like that. Did you see it was a man she was talking to?"

"No, there's no way I could see inside the car. I don't know why I said an uncle. I don't know if it was a guy or a woman or what in the car." Garcia rubbed his left cheek and then added, "For all I know, the car could have been empty and maybe she was just looking inside it."

The interview lasted a few more minutes before we thanked the man and shook his hand. On the way out of the store, Donovan asked innocently as he stepped behind the counter, near the cash register, "Is this where you were?"

"Yes. Exactly. I was there, and when the customer I was helping asked for some vigil candles, to place in front of her statues of the saints, I reached back, right there over your head, to the right, and got a box of four candles for her."

Again we thanked the man for his time and before leaving him, asked him to take a ride with us to look for similar cars. He attempted to beg off, but Frankie Donovan made a quiet plea for Mr. Garcia to do that what he would expect someone to do if such a tragedy should befall his own family. The plea worked and in less than 15 minutes Roberto Garcia pointed out two Hondas as examples of the car he had seen parked in front of his store the day before.

"Well?" I asked Donovan after we dropped off the man and began to move toward our car. When my partner gave me a quizzed look, I elaborated. "I know you went behind the counter to see if he could have actually seen what he said he saw. Could he have seen it?"

"Absolutely," Donovan said. "When you turn around toward the candles he said he got for the Rosario woman, you can see down the street at least fifty feet in either direction. Plus, with the store being above street level like it is, he would have been looking smack down at the top of the car and been able to see the kid at the passenger side but nothing inside the car."

Colvin Street is only a couple of short blocks from the Garcia store, so it took about five minutes for us to find Carmella Rosario. The street is lined on both sides with two-story, wood-clapboard houses, fronted by spacious porches and well-kept front yards, many of which are enclosed with chain-link fences. Once we located the elderly woman, it took less than five minutes to determine she had seen nothing. She had not seen the little girl, had no recollection of a child talking to someone in a car and had not yet even heard about the death of Becky Chilsom. The woman was helpful and I got the impression she would have loved to seen something that would put some zest in her drab life, but she had no recollection of seeing anything or anybody. She had gone to Garcia's to buy bread, milk, and some oatmeal—it was getting to be oatmeal weather she noted. The small vigil candles had been a last minute thought when she recalled that she was down to her last two candles to adorn the Lady of Fatima shrine she had established in the corner of her small living room.

As we were about to leave, Mrs. Rosario asked one favor. "I know you two men are detectives, but could you maybe ask the policeman who patrols here to watch out for us older people?"

"Of course," Donovan and I said almost together. Then Frank asked, "Is there a special problem, something in particular you're concerned about?"

"We have a lot of ruffians around here. There are drugs and some troublemakers that need to be watched. It's getting so that you're afraid to leave the house anymore. Even when I was going to Mr. Garcia's store yesterday, I was being followed. It was probably someone who wanted to grab my purse. I was scared, but I didn't show it," Carmella said with a wink. "I stopped and let him pass. He drove by very slowly, but he knew I was on to him."

"We'll mention it to the lieutenant who works over here. He's a good man," I said as I nodded. "He'll get his officers on it."

We again turned to leave, but Frank, perhaps motivated by some instinct, stopped. From the bottom of the steps leading to the woman's enclosed front porch, he asked, "He was in a car? What kind of car?"

"Oh, I don't know cars anymore." She stopped to chuckle at herself and then added, "Not that I ever did know cars. It was just a little red car."

Donovan and I shared a look and we both cocked our eyebrows.

"Is the car from around here?" I asked.

"Oh I don't know. I don't think I ever saw it before, but then again, like I said, I don't really pay attention to cars."

"Could you tell us what it looked like, how it was shaped? Was it newer? Older? Big? Small?" I pushed for something, some little clue. That was when Saint Jude, the Patron Saint of Lost Causes, kicked in.

"Oh, that's easy. It was just like my grandson Kenny's car. In fact, when I first turned around, I thought it was Kenny, but his back bumper is missing—from being careless and backing into a fire hydrant. When this car went by, I could see it wasn't Kenny's. It had a back bumper."

"Was it kind of like Kenny's car, or was it just like Kenny's car," Donovan quizzed.

"Exactly like Kenny's. Exactly," Mrs. Rosario answered, her gray head bobbing up and down in affirmation.

Using the Rosario phone, it took two minutes to call Kenny Rosario and learn his car was a 1992 Honda Civic…a hatchback model.

The team assembled for lunch at a pizza place on Lyell Avenue. After placing the order, we sat around two small tables we had pushed together and began our briefings. Paskell and Walz went first, followed by the St. John-Romano duet, with Donovan and me bringing up the rear.

"We nailed down the kids who were playing in the vacant lot," Gail Walz said as she pulled her hair back and pinned it in some mysterious fashion. "There were actually four of them—two brothers and two other neighborhood kids. They were trying to set a fire in the lot, so they were very hesitant to admit it was them, but with my undeniable charismatic ways, I was able to win them over," she said and then reached her right hand over her shoulder to pat herself on the back.

"Do you see the over-inflated ego that a great detective like me has to put up with, Lute?" Jimmy Paskell asked. "She was nothing until she teamed up with me. Now she takes all the credit."

"Both of you, cut the crap!" I demanded with a chuckle. "What did they say?"

"Well, as I was saying before I was most rudely interrupted," Walz said with an exaggerated and very dramatic huff. "The four of them had been playing in the alleys and in the lot from about seven in the evening until a little after nine o'clock. And, before you ask," she said as she held up both of her hands to silence the question she knew was forthcoming. "They fix the time by the fact that the two brothers got their bottoms paddled by their mother for coming home after nine o'clock."

"In other words," Romano chimed in, "they saw nothing!"

As the pizza was placed in front of us, Walz and Paskell added some other odds and ends to finish the details of their day's work. Jimmy then grabbed a slice of pizza that trailed mozzarella cheese from the pan to his end of the table. "So what do the Bobbsey Twins have to add?" he asked as he looked from Romano to St. John.

"Our victim was eight years old," Tommy Romano said dryly as he extended a center finger in front of Paskell's smiling face. "She was in the third grade at Number 16 School on Orange Street. She was considered to be very bright, a 'teacher's delight' as her teacher put it, close to her mother, and interested in science and space. There's no one in her class—and we talked to about nine or ten of them—who had anything bad to say about her. She was a little shy with boys, but was well liked."

As Romano took a bite of pizza, he signaled his partner to continue. Bobby St. John jumped right in. "The victim's father, one Charles Delgato, has a rap sheet for burglary, larceny, assault, possession of drugs, possession with intent to distribute, sale of drugs, and a couple of other lesser charges. The somewhat interesting thing is that he was driving an orange or rust-colored Volvo when he got busted the last time. The bad news is the last bust he had was nine days ago, for a burglary in Ontario County. He's still cooling his heels in their county jail and therefore couldn't be directly involved in the victim's death."

"And, who's got the car now?" I had to ask.

"It was impounded as evidence in the burglary," St. John said with a shrug. "We called the jail and talked to the detective who had the case. It's confirmed. He's still in jail and the car is still in the impound yard."

As Bobby reached for his soft drink, Romano summed up. "The whole day was a bust, Lieutenant. The only other piece of information we have is that the teacher, the principal, and the kids we talked to don't know anything about a red car. They don't know anyone at the school who has a red car except for a reddish or maroon van driven by one of the office staff."

Now it was our turn. I gave the rundown on the neighborhood check. Donovan reviewed our interview with Roberto Garcia. After he handled the round of questions thrown at him from around the table, I went into the information obtained from Carmella Rosario. The confirmation on the type of car brought some smiles. However, the smiles faded with questions about how we could be sure it was the same car the Gardner woman had seen on Scrantom Street, and if we could even be sure it was the same car seen by Garcia.

With mixed emotions, I was taken by the pessimistic approach the investigators took regarding the lead. It was true, the day had accomplished a lot but the lot equaled very little in the way of firm leads. The fact of the matter was we were no closer to solving the case than we were 14 hours earlier, as three of us looked down on the lifeless body of Rebecca "Becky" Chilsom.

The lunch ended with Donovan and me compiling one list of things that needed to be done by the end of the day; a second slate included the leads and questions that would have to wait until Monday. Under the former was the need to photograph Kenny Rosario's car, to have Roberto Garcia and Martha Gardner look at the photo of the car, and to get the results of the autopsy that should already be in progress. Monday's list included getting the Department of Motor Vehicles to punch out a list of every 1987 through 1994 red Honda cars registered in Monroe County and canvass the other teachers and kids at Becky Chilsom's school. Sunday would be the day to go through every departmental file, computer listing and criminal record, looking for child molesters and red cars.

As we stood up to leave the corner restaurant, Jimmy Paskell asked who was going to eat the last piece of pizza. Naturally, the entire squad said he could have it. And, just as naturally, the second he reached for it, every one of them said they really wanted it.

Paskell hesitated, and then, realizing he was being put on, snatched up the cold, limp wedge and shoved it into his mouth.

The detective's chewing was interrupted by the Dispatcher notifying the Paskell-Walz team to call the Medical Examiner's Office. Using the cell phone, Gail made the call, nodded a few times, offered a pair of "Uh-huh's" and asked "Are you sure?" three times.

At the end of the two-minute call, she advised the table, "Cause of death is manual strangulation. Toxicology still needs to be done, but the ghouls don't expect anything unusual. But, get this…the stain on he kid's slacks is not semen…it appears to be jelly, like jelly from a donut."

"What the…?" two of us at the table asked.

"The ME says there's an undigested donut in the victim's stomach. He says she probably had it in her stomach less than an hour before she was killed."

The news added more things to the lists the team had compiled, however, as we left the restaurant we all suspected—in fact we knew—the lists would grow. But at the time we had no way of knowing that Becky Chilsom would be only the first victim of this frustrating case.

And we had no way of knowing the killer was watching us…watching and smiling.

CHAPTER FOUR

DOING WHAT IT TAKES

Sunday morning's stream of autumn sunshine found me where I had dropped Saturday night—sprawled on my sofa. I lifted my head off the sofa arm and moved my feet carefully, so as to avoid disturbing Max who had his butt planted on the cushion and his chin resting on the other arm of the beaten piece of furniture. Regardless of my care, the mutt picked up his head as soon as he felt my movement. Once we exchanged good morning acknowledgements - me stroking his head and him wagging his tail hard enough to wiggle his rear end - I made my way to the bathroom.

I then led the way down the stairs from the apartment to the front door of the building. As my closest friend found a suitable bush against which to raise his leg and relieve himself, I managed - with some notable strain and audible moans - to bend over, pick up the morning newspaper and stand erect again. Once we were back in the apartment Max, begged for his treats. The two of us were very proud of the West Highland Terrier's ability to walk the full length of the tiny kitchen on his hind legs and still manage to catch the treats in mid-air.

After the coffeepot got up a full steam of gurgling, I opened the paper and was brought back into the reality of the day. The murder of our young victim had come in too late to be part of Saturday's morning paper, so there on the front page of the Sunday morning *Democrat and Chronicle,* was the story about the murder of Rebecca Chilsom. Even though Rochester, New York, is a city of almost a quarter million people that experiences 40 to 50 murders a year, the killing of one of its youth is still outrageous enough to take on the importance of front page news.

Having finished pouring over the story and snorting at some of the misinformation, I tried to scan the rest of the paper, but to little avail. My mind was geared into thinking about what was being done, and more importantly, what needed to be done. The weekend had thrown a crimp into the investigation and many leads would have to go unchecked until Monday morning when the rest of the town came to life. Betty Chilsom's alibi of being at work couldn't be checked until the company where she worked opened up for business tomorrow. For the very same reason, confirming the neighbor—the one who saw our victim skipping down the street—had actually gone to work at 3:30 p.m. would also have to wait for normal business hours. The Department of Motor Vehicles wouldn't even begin to run the massive printout we had requested until their computer people came in tomorrow. Finding the rest of the Chilsom kid's school friends and teachers would also have to wait for another day.

It seemed like the whole damn case was on hold until Monday morning!

While the coffeepot did its thing, I lit a cigarette and slipped some mellow Joni James CD's in the player. Once the female crooner's tones filled the empty spaces of the apartment, my mind began to work. I jotted down every aspect of the case I could think of on the pad that remained, with some permanence, on the kitchen table. The list was in two somewhat neat columns. The first column noted things that had been done or were now in progress; the second column contained everything that needed to be done. As far as I could see, there were no loose ends…but still, I felt I should be at work, doing something about a killer running lose in my city.

The apartment seemed small and confining as my feet paced the rooms looking for some activity. Max, my little white shadow, paced with me as if wanting to be near whenever I found whatever it was I seemed to be seeking. Then, strictly out of impulse, I called Diane.

"Did I wake you?"

"Michael?" she asked with sleep in her voice.

"Yeah, it's me," I responded with a slight grin. "Don't you recognize the love of your life's voice?"

"I recognize the *ex*-love of my life's voice," she answered with what I imagined was a smile "It's just that I didn't expect to hear from you this morning...I mean based on what I just read in the paper, I thought you would be at work."

"Yeah, well," I stumbled. "Paskell and Walz are working that case and the new kid, Romano, is helping out. It's going to be a busy week for all of us, so I'm kind of holding Donovan, St. John, and me in reserve. Besides, everything that can be done is being done."

"But you would rather be in there with them than sitting at home doing nothing, right?"

My ex-wife knew me too well, and as usual, she had no hesitation in demonstrating to me how well she knew my mind.

"No, not really," I lied to her accurate assumption. "There's a lot of things on hold until Monday morning and then it's going to be a rat-race week." There was a lapse of conversation before I got to the point. "So, do you want to join me for some Sunday breakfast?"

"Are you serious?" she asked, as I pictured her holding the phone out arm's length and looking at it in disbelief.

"Diane, you asked me to stop swearing, and I stopped swearing. You want me to slow down a little, so I slowed down. You don't want me to drink, so I pretty much stopped drinking. You want me to take time out from the job now and then, so I'm trying to take a time out." There was a pause to allow her rebuttal time. When she didn't take it, I gave a little laugh and continued. "So do you want to go out for breakfast or don't you?"

"I would be pleased to have breakfast with you, Michael," Diane said in a most pleasant voice. "You name it."

A half-hour later I was in my Corvette, traveling through the city on my way to meet Diane...and wondering why I was doing this instead of going to work where I belonged.

Even in a casual sweat suit, with her hair pulled back in a quickly assembled roll of some type, Diane was radiant. We exchanged platonic cheek kisses when she came through the door of the restaurant and joined me in line, waiting for a table. After being seated, we began a benign conversation about her trials and tribulations in the hallowed halls of Kodak. I smiled, nodded, and grimaced in all the right places, thoroughly bored by the topic...but happy to be close by her. As was her habit, Diane ordered eggs Benedict, and just as predictable, I ordered *Frattata*, a skillet of eggs, sausage, potatoes, green peppers, cheese and onions—sort of an Italian version of the Mexican breakfast *burrito*.

As plates were set in front of us, my pager transmitted an annoying beeping that caused both of us to stop in mid-motion. Offering my date a shrug, I pulled the antagonistic instrument off my belt and looked at it. Detective Paskell's cell phone number was illuminated in the digital glass at the top of the pager. Following the telephone number were the added digits of 9-1-1, indicating the call needed immediate attention. The message both pleased and angered me.

Excusing myself, I said to Diane, "This better be important."

When Gail Walz answered the cell phone, I repeated the same four words to her.

"It is, Boss," she said solemnly. "The killer just called our victim's mother."

"He did what?"

"The killer called Mrs. Chilsom and told her how he killed her daughter...and how much he enjoyed doing it."

"The son of a bitch," I said through clenched teeth into the mouthpiece.

"That's not all, Lieutenant. He said there's going to be more!"

Diane was gracious as she excused me from our meal, but still could not resist saying how it was just like old times. All I could do was apologize as I slid a twenty-dollar bill on the table and told her we would get together again very soon. She said something, but I was already on my way to the door of the restaurant.

In fifteen minutes I made my way from Park Avenue, on the city's south side, to the home of Betty Chilsom on the far west side. Jimmy Paskell answered the door, but instead of letting me into the apartment, he maneuvered me back outside.

"Gail's doing an in-depth interview with Mrs. Chilsom right now, so I figured it would be better if we left them alone," he said almost apologetically. Once he got my nod, he continued. "This morning, at about 9:15, the Chilsom woman got a call. The caller asked if she was the mother of the victim and she confirmed that she was. The caller then told her he had some important information for her and she needed to write the information down and get to the police right away. Thinking she was talking to a witness, or at least to someone who was going to help us find her daughter's killer, she told the guy to go ahead. He then told her that he had choked her daughter to death and how she kicked and gagged all the while he was choking her."

"What kind of sick mother fu…?" I started to ask.

"That's not all. Mrs. Chilsom began to cry and asked him why he did it to Rebecca and why he was doing this to her. He told her there were going to be more kids killed…that his intention was to make a lot of people suffer."

"What about voice, accent, age, possible race or nationality?"

"Gail's going for all that now, plus any background noises, his exact words, all that stuff. And, Lute, there's more."

"Like what?"

"The caller asked Chilsom if she had large breasts because he said her daughter was already developing 'nice little nubs', as he put it. He told her he enjoyed playing with them."

"This sick bastard is going down!" I said with venom.

"He is, Lute. That he is!" Paskell confirmed for me…and perhaps for himself. "We're going to get this one. And, when we do, I want some private time with him."

Shifting my anger to constructive thought, I told the detective, "And we're going to need a trap on Chilsom's phone. If he's got the balls to call once, he might call again."

"I'll handle it when we get done here," Jimmy confirmed.

Paskell and I stood on the porch in silence for another ten or fifteen minutes. I wanted to go into the apartment and hear what the woman was being asked…and what she was saying, but knew Walz and the woman needed uninterrupted privacy if Gail were to pull every tiny fact out of Betty Chilsom's tormented mind. Finally, impatience got the best of me and I told Paskell I would meet him and his partner in the office when they were done with the victim's mother.

As I entered the Public Safety Building, Tommy Romano was walking out the front door. After giving him a quick briefing of what had gone down at the victim's home, he gave me an update on the backgrounds of the main players in the case.

"Betty Chilsom has a few busts for possession of drugs, but nothing in the past seven years. Garcia, the guy at the grocery store has been busted for a chicken-shit gambling charge. The Gardner woman is clean, so is Washington, the lady who found the body. However, the Rosario woman took a hit for shoplifting, would you believe, back about ten years ago. Other than that, no runs, no hits, and no errors."

"Where are you going now?" I asked.

"That's the good part," Romano smiled. "Randy Tyrell, the guy who lives across the street from Virginia Washington, has two arrests for Endangering the Welfare of a Child. I'm going down and talk to him, but first I want to meet with the investigator who handled both cases. I need some background on the guy before I talk to him. The cases are sex-related and about eight years old, so it's impossible to find a hard copy of the reports in this great and wonderful cop shop on a Sunday."

After a couple of more words, Romano left and I headed for the office. Alone with my thoughts on the virtually empty fourth floor, I looked out my office window, down onto Exchange Street and over toward the new Blue Cross-Blue Shield building. What had been a clear, sunny morning was turning into a chilling, overcast afternoon. And it simply wasn't the change in the weather that made me feel discouraged.

My mind wandered to another time, more than a quarter of a century earlier, when a child killer brought terror to the city. It was back in the early 1970's, well before I even became a cop, that three kids got killed over a period of a couple of years. I had heard stories about the case, of how it had affected the city. Parents demanded protection for their children. During the time following each of the killings, school parking lots were filled with cars of moms and dads who picked up their child from school rather than allow the kid to ride the bus or walk home from school. Well-intended citizens, along with the crazies that such cases attract, overloaded the cops with suspicions, guesses, assumptions, psychic feelings and tiny pieces of information.

The cases wore away at the frustrated detectives, turning them into fanatics who chased every lead and got nowhere. The killings consumed their lives for several years, and when the killings stopped, they became more distraught at not knowing who had committed the murders...and if—when—the maniac would strike again. The killer had carefully selected each of the victims. Each had double initials, that is, the same initial in their first and last name, and each body had been dumped in a town that began with the same letter as the child's initials. Details were set up to predict and protect the next potential victim and, as the research showed, there were hundreds of them. Cops delayed their retirements just to work on the cases. Families either set aside their vacations or went on them without their cop-father. Off-duty cops followed cars or persons who "just didn't look right." Teletypes were sent to every city that had a remotely similar killing. Countless hours of unpaid and uncompensated overtime hours were worked in the hope that one more hour chasing one more lead would bring a break in the investigation. Cops who did eventually take a vacation or a few days off to supposedly be with their family covertly visited other police departments to pick up photos of suspects who had committed crimes against children. Marriages were ruined. Alcoholics were created. Friendships dissolved. But it was all to no avail.

After a period of about two years, the killings stopped. No one was ever arrested. No known suspect died, moved away, or was incarcerated. It simply ended. It was over.

Standing there smoking and looking down at the few cars that traveled along the avenue four stories below me, I imagined the pain, anger, anxiousness, disappointment, and frustration felt by those detectives so long ago. They were now all retired and many of them were dead and buried. My mind asked if they, in the after-life, ever found out who had been the killer. Standing alone in the office on that day, that Sunday morning, I could not begin to imagine the terror this present-day killer was going to throw into my city, nor could I foresee what he would do to my squad.

Back then, during the Double Initial Murders, investigators were called detectives. Somewhere along the line, one of the suits on the sixth floor decided what we really needed to do was investigate more than detect. So now—whenever we remembered the change—we were called "Investigators". That was all that had changed in almost 30 years. Kids were still being killed, detectives—investigators— were still chasing leads, mothers were still crying…and evil bastards were still spreading their special brand of terror and fear.

The sudden noise behind me made me jump. Turning, I saw Walz and Paskell looking at me with quizzed expressions.

"What did you say?" I asked in an attempt to appear unruffled by their presence.

"I said, 'Hey, big boy, do you come here often?'" Walz said with a laugh.

"Bite me, Walz!" I said angrily, but flashed a slight grin.

"I never bite, Lieutenant," she replied in a sexy voice. "At least not on the first date."

With our sarcastic, sexually-suggestive exchange out of the way, I asked, "So what have you got."

"Betty Chilsom received the call at about 9:15 this morning. She says the voice was 'normal' with no accent and nothing definitive. He sounded young, possibly in his twenties, but she has nothing on which to base that opinion. There were no discernable background noises. She thinks he might be white, but that is simply due to the lack of any other noticeable accent. The only phrase she picked up was that he said 'Hey now' a couple of times. Like he would say, 'Hey now, you listen to me', or 'Hey now, you write this down'. She says he used that phrase five, maybe six times in the three-minute conversation…that and he referred to the victim's breasts as 'nubs'."

"What about him telling her there were going to be more killings?" I asked.

"From what she's able to recall, he said there were going to be more kids killed…a lot more kids," Walz said as she opened her blue-hue eyes wide. Flipping through her note pad and finding the place where she had jotted the crucial information, she added, "He said he was going to make everyone afraid of him, and that people would be terrified to let their kids go to school, to go to the mall, to leave their sight for even a minute."

"What about how he killed the victim?" Jimmy Paskell asked.

"That's really frigging weird. He said he 'tasted' her. I don't know if that means he put his mouth on her body, on her vagina, or what the hell. He just said that the victim 'tasted real good'. And, as the mother was dealing with that, he went into a description of how he choked her, actually lifted her off the ground as he choked her, so that she was 'kicking and squirming until she was dead'."

"I want this son of a bitch," I said. "I want him bad!"

"We'll get him, Lute. Don't you worry, we'll get him for you," Paskell said with his head nodding up and down.

"And when we do," Walz said as she pulled off her coat, "I want to be the one to make a soprano out of him…with a very rusty and very dull knife."

If a producer of television commercials were going to typecast the perfect people to play the role of sweet, old, gray-haired grandmothers, baking chocolate chip cookies, Ann Salber and her sister, Josephine Maira, would get the parts.

Mrs. Salber and Mrs. Maira are my downstairs neighbors. They are also the babysitters for Max. He, in turn, viewed the two gentle women who filled him with snacks as his favorite people companions.

At 6:00 a.m. Monday morning I slipped my business card under the door of the Salber-Maira apartment. When one of the two elderly women found it, they would know I was planning on a long day and would go upstairs to fetch the Westie. This had happened so often, I finally had a key to my apartment made for them so that I didn't have to leave the spare key every time I got called out to work or had to remain on the job long after quitting hours. The ladies would spend the entire day with Max, take him for a short walk or two, and make sure he was overstuffed with the human treats that were in constant production in their oven and on their stove.

The day had begun at 6:00 a.m. with a shower. An hour later, copies of up-to-date reports were passed out to offices of Chief of Police Matthew Murphy, Deputy Chief Ernie Cooper and my immediate boss, Major Art "Skip" Winston.

At 9 a.m. the four of us sat around the Chief's conference table as I brought them up to date on the investigation. Murphy took notes as Skip Winston used a highlighter to mark portions of the reports. Our sawed-off Deputy Chief of Operations worked his eyes around the table, trying to determine how he could throw cold water on the investigation.

"What do you need?" Murphy asked.

"Nothing right now," I answered. "However, if he follows through on his threat to take down more kids, we're going to need all the help we can get. For the time being, I would like to be notified regarding any reports of any missing kid and I want the word to go out for the de...the investigators in the patrol districts to jump on every single one of those reports just as if they're the next homicide."

"If the need arises, I can give the Lieutenant a couple of guys from the Check Squad or one of the other units," Winston volunteered.

"We need to chat about how to handle the press on this matter," Murphy suggested after he nodded at Winston and stood to stretch out his six-foot, one-inch, athletic frame.

"As far as I'm concerned, I would like to see the Public Information Officer handle all of it," was my input.

"The PIO is okay for most things," Cooper chipped in. "However, I don't see her handling something like this. We need to keep the Chief or his designee out front on a case like this."

Winston didn't like the Deputy Chief anymore than I did, so he was quick to jump in and surgically cut his legs out from under him. "If this guy goes after more kids, this case is going to go very high profile very quickly. Also, it will *not* put the Department in a favorable light. Whoever is out front on this one better have the right skills and better be willing to risk his career on the outcome." He paused to watch Cooper muddle over the potential for anything negative happening to his career. "In order to keep the lid on everything, I would recommend that Lieutenant Amato brief the PIO daily—and only on what she actually needs to know—and then let her deal with the media. That way we have control on everything that goes out...and nothing slips out accidentally."

Cooper was about to say something when Matt the Chat stated flatly, "The Major is right. That's the way it needs to be done."

Whatever it was that Ernie Cooper was preparing to share with us became lost in a nod as he pretended to agree with his boss.

"There is one other thing," I interjected. "When this printout from DMV comes in, we expect it's going to be massive. We're going to split it up and begin running down the cars in the area of the victim's home first, along with cars in the area where the body was found. If that turns up nothing, we're going to have to spread out and chase down everything. At that point, there's going to be a tremendous need for one hell of a lot of personnel."

"If it comes to that, I'll put *my* Tactical Unit into it," Cooper said as he pointed a finger dramatically from his chest to the window that faced the city.

"If it comes to that, Lieutenant," Matt Murphy said, "The Deputy Chief will see to it that whatever is needed from *our* Department will be made available." Cooper realized his egocentric mistake and cleared his throat as the Chief continued. "Right now the red car is the only lead we have. We need to do whatever it takes to find that vehicle. Major, your division will of course have the lead in the investigation. If any assistance is needed, run it past the Deputy Chief and he will see to it you get the help, any help you need."

As is the case with most cop Public Information Officers, Monica Sheldon is a re-tread from television news who realized she could make almost as much money with the city as she could with one of the local TV stations, but with a lot less hassle. The woman understands her job which, in a nutshell, is to give out the bad news while the Chief or the Mayor get to hand out all the good news.

After I gave her all the information I wanted her to have, we started to say our good-byes. However, because her old job still influenced her thinking and her ways, she tried to pry some details from me.

"You have everything, Monica."

"Bullshit, Amato!" she said with a laugh. "I have everything you're willing to give me, but I don't have everything there is."

"You have everything you need to know," I answered with a wink and a crooked smile.

"I know you want to keep me in the dark on some of this stuff so that I don't give away some precious clue, but I would still like to get the full story."

"Trust me," I said with the same grin. "You have the full story."

We ended the conversation with an exchange of upraised center fingers and I then made my way to the elevator.

I caught a quick glimpse of Gail Walz and Jimmy Paskell as they entered the elevator next to the one that delivered me back to the fourth floor. Making my way to the sea of cubicles, I said to Frank Donovan, "Catch me up. What did I miss?"

"St. John and Romano are on their way out to the Thruway to meet a state trooper who's running the last leg of the relay of the DMV computer printout from Albany to here."

"And?"

"And, Paskell's in the shit with his old lady, and he's taking it out on Walz."

"Why? About what?"

"Jimmy's wife baptized her sister's baby yesterday. Last night and this morning she was all over him about not showing up at the christening."

"Why didn't he say something? We could have let him slip out for at least a couple of hours."

Donovan shrugged. "I told him that but he said his place was here, working on the case." After a shrug he added, "Let it go for now, Mike. He'll get over it. Right now it ain't no big thing, and besides, Walz can handle it."

"Where are they going now?"

"They're going down to the school to interview teachers and then back into the neighborhood where the victim was abducted." Detective Donovan paused long enough for me to nod and then added, "I'm going to get myself down to the Medical Examiner's Office and pick up the final report on the autopsy. He called to say it was ready, and by the way, he confirms there was a reddening around the kid's breasts. After I grab the report I'll be back to give you and the other team a hand with the DMV thing."

As it turned out, the computer run from the Department of Motor Vehicles was a massive amount of information. The almost 100 pages listed 1,947 red, maroon, rose, or rust-colored 1985 through 1995 Honda Civics and similar makes registered in Monroe County. After almost three hours of work, St. John, Romano and I were able to narrow the list down to a mere 316 cars that were registered in the zip codes where the victim was abducted and where her body was found. That meant each team would have to track down about 100 cars, interview the owners, run criminal history checks on them and look for some tiny detail that might tie one of them to the crime. After another hour of work, and with the help of Frank Donovan who had since returned to the office, we narrowed the list down to 94 cars that fit the basic criteria of being a 1988 to 1993 red Honda Civic and were owned by people living near the victim's house or near the vacant lot where her body had been dumped.

Even though the other squads in the Detective Bureau chipped in three guys to help out, it was going to be a long, ass-dragging week.

The week was very long indeed. And the one week grew into two, and two weeks became three. In that time, Rochester experienced the last warm breezes of late summer turning into the coldness of autumn. As those weeks passed, we dug deep into the life of little Becky Chilsom and all those who touched her few years. While the squad accomplished that task, all three teams continued to handle their load of open cases, testifird in court and before the Grand Jury on some of the closed cases, and took on the new investigations that kept coming. The squad was not cut any slack by the bank robbers with guns, husbands with axes, and punks with automatic rifles. Life, death, and crime rolled on while we tried everything we could to get a handle on the killing of little Becky Chilsom.

In less than a month we had gathered reams of information, but were not any closer to identifying and finding the killer. Friday afternoon, three weeks after the homicide of the Chilsom girl, found me alone in the office, gazing out the window and thinking through the information we had assembled after almost 900 man-hours of work.

We knew the victim was an intelligent little girl, with an above-average IQ. She enjoyed math and science and was fascinated with space travel. Her teacher loved her and she had a circle of about eight-or-ten close friends. Although friendly with some of the boys in her age group, she was still at the age when boys were a nuisance and not an attraction. We knew she and her mother were very close and were seen very often walking together in the neighborhood. Betty Chilsom attended every school event in which the child was involved and was very attentive to her daughter's education.

As the first week came to an end, we were able to examine the photos we had taken at the child's funeral, and were not able to identify anyone in the crowds that had a pedophile history, or who even attracted our attention. During the two following weeks, the photos had been discounted as not having any evidentiary value.

We knew by then that Mr. Roberto Garcia had a minor gambling record, but that he could not have abducted the girl. That was because Donovan had verified Garcia was at his grocery store the entire afternoon and evening of the abduction, working with a plumber on a leaky pump that was in danger of ruining the store's cooler, the floor and the water-soaked wall.

The autopsy told us that our victim had ingested a jelly donut less than an hour before her death and that strawberry jelly—most probably from the donut—had been rubbed on the crotch of her pants.

We also had learned there were 16 stores between Jay Street and Scrantom Street where jelly donuts could be purchased. Unfortunately, Walz and Paskell learned that no one at those 16 stores remembered seeing a man with a child, or specifically, the victim, in or near any one of those stores.

Randy Tyrell had also been cleared of any involvement in the crime. At the time Becky Chilsom was being murdered and dumped in the lot, Tyrell had been working with the minister of his church - having been dragged there by his wife - installing a hot water heater.

The weeks had also seen us respond to 13 reports of missing children, and thanks to the Saints in Heaven, all 13 of those kids returned home safely.

In between it all, we had managed to find 92 of the 94 cars on our primary list of suspect vehicles. Each of the owners and operators of those 92 cars had been interviewed and researched through records. During the last week we had expanded the list and were now digging into a fresh pool of 118 additional cars that were registered to owners outside the ten square blocks of the Jay Street and Scrantom Street crime scenes.

All this we knew and none of it did us any good. The weeks had added up to a lot of nothing.

I sat down at my desk and began to go through the administrative crap that had piled up through the week. In with it was the staff schedule I was supposed to have reviewed and approved four days earlier. Looking at it made me laugh. How could a unit this small live by any schedule at all? Crossing out entries and adding my own brand of scribbling, I changed the schedule so that Walz and Paskell could have the weekend off—their first weekend break in almost two months. It was my intention to slip in St. John and Romano for weekend coverage, but with the exception of the past Sunday, they also had not had a weekend off in almost two months.

As I toyed with the mundane, one of the squad members was making a discovery that would blow the case wide open. And, as he did that, our killer was actively stalking his second victim.

CHAPTER FIVE

UNBOUNDED FEAR

Traci Pauline Taylor left Number 38 School on Latta Road with her cluster of friends. The six little girls sat in the back of the school bus so they would be sure to be in position to see all the other kids, especially the girls, who entered the bus. Their placement on the bus was important because it provided an observation platform from which they could—and would—critique who was wearing what, how they walked, to whom they spoke and the hodgepodge of other relevant factors so important to third grade girls.

The bus turned off Lake Avenue at Boxart Street, stopped at the next corner, and a smiling, still chatting Traci Taylor exited the bus alone. Maureen Dunther, her best friend of all best friends, was confined at home with another bout of asthma. In her absence, Maureen had missed the instructions regarding the school's Halloween costume contest and Traci saw it as her duty to brief her friend thoroughly on the matter. Together, over the weekend, they would make two outrageous costumes that would be the talk of Sally D'Angelo and her bratty friends.

Traci Taylor did not mind the block-and-a-half walk from the bus stop to her friend's home, although her parents always seemed uptight about the distance. It was a stroll of less than five minutes—and it would be a stroll never completed.

Frank Donovan and I were finishing our third beer when my pager went off at 7:30 p.m. After a quick call to the dispatcher, we were both on our way to Boxart Street on the city's far north side, less than a mile from Lake Ontario. Along the way I provided the information the dispatcher had passed on to me by way of the sergeant at the scene.

"She's eight years old and gets out of school at three in the afternoon. The normal routine is for her to go to a neighbor's home and stay there with a friend until her mother gets home, which is usually about 4:30. Today, the mother got home, took care of some odds and ends and by 5:30, when the kid didn't show up, she called over to the neighbor's house and learned that the girl, ah, one Traci Taylor, hadn't gone to the neighbor's after school. The mother called the cops; the cops checked with the school; made a few calls. Our cops subsequently found out the Taylor kid got off the school bus at her usual stop at the usual time and hadn't been seen since. The uniform guys did a neighborhood search, contacted some of the friends, and the bottom line is that no one had any contact with her after she left the bus."

"Is she in trouble at home or got some problems at school that she's afraid to see mom and dad about?" Frank asked.

"As far as the sergeant is able to determine, there's no reason for her to run away or be leery about going home."

Once past the windowless buildings where Kodak processes film for most of the world, we were out of the heavier portion of the city's traffic. I gunned the motor and was cruising at 60 miles-an-hour as we approached Holy Sepulcher Cemetery. Slowing for the curve near the old, four-story, granite block building that had once been Saint Bernard's Seminary on the right—a place which my mother had prayed would be my destiny—I made a quick sign of the cross and nodded to the large tombstones on my left. It was a habit drummed into me so long ago. The small gesture was a sign of respect for my parents, a couple of aunts, an uncle, and Danny Martin—a friend from the old neighborhood—all of whom were buried in the place. I slowed back down to 40 miles-an-hour as we passed the attractive, multi-colored wooden sign that announced, "Welcome to Charlotte" and then drove into the deep dip in the road as the avenue intersected with Cherry Road. I knew Boxart Street was coming up soon, but wasn't quite sure where it might be. It's probably a good thing for the people in this area of the city that homicide cops were unfamiliar with the territory.

Rochester's strange pronunciation of words extended from my old neighborhood where they said "gooms" when referring to the gums around one's teeth, to here, where the neighborhood is called "Shar-LOT" with the accent on the second syllable, but spelled the same way as Charlotte, North Carolina.

Finally seeing the sign for Boxart Street, I made a right-hand turn, traveled a hundred yards or so under an archway of trees that provided a summertime canopy of leaves over the entire width of the roadway. The street curved left and back to the right. Our battered car moved slowly as we passed the red brick building of the Weyerhaeuser Company on the left side of the street. The neighborhood is a series of comfortable, two-story homes placed back from the street on well-shrubbed, neat yards. There in the midst of middle-class comfort was the home bearing the number 201.

Donovan noted that beyond the home, at the end of the street, is a densely overgrown area of wild bushes that lead down a steep bank to the Genesee River flowing lazily north to Lake Ontario, about a mile away. "If she's hiding down there, we'll never find her."

The Taylor home showed evidence of a family that was very particular about the appearance of their yard and residence. The grass along the edge of the sidewalk had been fastidiously trimmed and the brick steps showed signs of recent repair and upkeep.

Sergeant Carl Kosloski had been promoted relatively late in his career, so the new, stiff chevrons on his blue coat belied the experience he brought to his supervisory role.

"Lute, Frank," the Sergeant acknowledged to each of us as we walked into the home. "This here is Jackie and Luther Taylor. The missing child is their daughter." Then after introducing us to the parents, Kosloski gave us virtually the same rundown the dispatcher had provided. Next, he brought us up to date on the extent of the search, the number of blocks that had been combed, each one of schoolmates, friends and relatives who had been called. Finally he provided us with a picture of the thin, black girl with the gapped-tooth smile.

"Is there any reason your daughter might delay in coming home, Mr. Taylor?" I asked.

"No, none," he said in a baritone voice that was emphatic, but not angry.

"Has she ever been late before?" Frank asked.

"Not unless she called first. She's very responsible, very considerate of her mother and me."

The list of routine questions continued and Luther or Jackie Taylor answered each directly. After Donovan had gotten Mrs. Taylor to show him Traci's room, I sat down in the small, comfortable living room with the father. As I delved into his relationship with his wife and daughter, I knew Frank was upstairs doing the same with Jackie Taylor. Later we would compare notes and decide if it was necessary to bring the parents in for a more direct line of questioning.

"We, my wife and me, that is," Luther Taylor explained, "were both raised in the inner-city, over around Joseph Avenue, and we worked hard to buy this house out here where we thought it would be safe for us and Traci." After I nodded and grunted a sound that meant I understood his plight, he continued. "We don't drink, don't smoke and consider ourselves to be very active Christians." Then nodding to me in such a way that I took it to mean he understood *my* plight, Luther leaned forward on the couch, put his muscular arms on his knees, and confided, "I know you have to consider me and Jackie as suspects, Lieutenant. I know that. But, I'll tell you right now in the presence of these here other officers and with God as my witness, me and her mother have nothing to do with Traci's disappearance. We'll take any test you have, do anything you ask. You do what you have to with us, but you find my baby, and you bring her on home to me and her mother."

If honesty has a face, it was that of Luther Taylor. I didn't want to believe him. I wanted to remain more objective, more open at this point. However, the fact is, I believed him…and I felt sorry for him.

While Donovan called the driver of the school bus to arrange an interview, I went to the home of Maureen Dunther. Although the girl was already in bed, her mother woke her and we talked for about ten minutes. Neither Frank's telephone call or my visit gave us anything new.

It was close to ten o'clock at night before Frank and I left the home and headed back to the center of the city. We talked about the parents, about our interviews with the two people, and concluded they were not—at this point of the investigation, at least—suspects in the disappearance of the young girl. We discussed the idea of calling in another team, but decided against it. If the child was not found by the next morning, we would bring in the entire squad and comb the whole neighborhood door-to-door.

"We need to get a trap put on their phone A-SAP," Donovan noted, almost as if talking to himself. "If our guy is behind this and the bastard calls the family like he did with the Chilsom woman, we'll have to be ready for him. I'll get it done when we get back to the office."

Then there was silence in the car as we made our way back to the central part of the city. Again, as we passed Holy Sepulcher Cemetery, I made the sign of the cross. Donovan remained wrapped up in thought as he drove the five or so miles until we entered downtown. Only then did he break the peaceful silence and say what I was thinking.

"We've got a fresh one, Mike. The son-of-a-bitch just hit again."

"I'm afraid so," my lips acknowledged as my stomach churned.

Saturday morning found us without any news about the missing child. The bad news was that she had not returned home. The good news was that her body had not turned up anywhere. The killer had dumped the body of the Chilsom girl in a matter of a few hours. The Taylor child had already been missing almost 17 hours. Hope being what it is, I for some reason, found encouragement in that fact. Maybe we would get to her before our killer unleashed himself a second time.

After my call to Major Art Winston the previous night, and his subsequent conference call with Chief Matt Murphy and Deputy Chief Ernie Cooper, it was agreed the squad would once again have all days off cancelled.

By eight o'clock in the morning, the telephone trap was in place at the Taylor home. The six of us from the Violent Crimes Unit, along with five police officers and three investigators from the city's northern Lake District, met up with ten cops from the Tactical Unit and assembled in the midst of the Detective Bureau's maze of cubicles. After everyone was briefed regarding the disappearance of Traci Taylor—and the possible connection with the murder of Becky Chilsom—assignments were made.

The plan was simple. The Lake District cops would cover the heavily wooded areas at the end of Cherry Road and Boxart Streets, including Turning Point Park. The cops from the Tactical Unit would go yard to yard, looking on top of, below, and behind everything they encountered. Every shed, garage, tree house, and anything else big enough to conceal the girl would be opened, turned upside-down and inside-out. While the search was in progress, my people and the three additional Lake District investigators would go door to door to talk to everyone and anyone. The two main questions would be, "Did you see this girl yesterday?" coupled with, "Have you noticed anyone hanging around lately?"

"All of you have a picture of the missing victim along with a clothing description of what she had on yesterday. If you find anything—anything at all—you call for one of my people right then and there! Don't rush it and don't take any short cuts," Donovan warned. "If we don't get what we're after this time, we're only going to do it all over again. So, take your time and get it done right the first time."

Bobby St. John tossed in a reminder that if anyone of the cops encountered a red car, possibly a Honda, they were to contact one of the Violent Crime Unit's detectives.

Donovan and I then fielded a few questions and then advised the group we would meet at noon, at Turning Point Park, to de-brief and set up our next sweep.

"Lieutenant?" Investigator Guy DiGennaro of Lake District asked as he waved a hand. "It's a lot colder than I expected and I'm not really dressed for this door-to-door crap." He paused to give me a wink and a smile. "How about if I baby-sit the parents, you know, in case they get contacted by the suspect?"

"Tough shit, Guy. You must have gone through at least thirty Rochester autumns and if you haven't figured out by now that the weather sucks, you probably shouldn't be a detective. You hit the bricks with everyone else." Then winking and smiling back at him, I added, "It's a dirty and thankless job, but you've taken the oath. So, go be a crimefighter."

The request had been greeted with a few snickers and the sudden urge of several of the uniform cops to cough and clear their throats. The response brought forth a few laughs and heavy coughs that did a poor job of concealing their catcalls of "Asshole!"

"That was a vintage Mike Amato answer," Donovan said as he slapped my back with one of his ham-sized hands as the troops cleared the room.

The big Irishman and I covered the victim's home street while Bobby St. John and Tommy Romano headed for Cherry Road and Weston Street. Gail Walz along with Jimmy Paskell targeted Harding Road and Felleson Road. One member of each of those teams covered the north side of their assigned street; the other member covered the houses on the south side. The three plainclothes guys from Lake District took on Leander Street and the employees working the weekend shift at the Weyerhaeuser Building.

Twice during the morning the media interrupted our trek. They had missed the twilight hours of the Chilsom homicide but were not about to let that happen on the Taylor case. Was the disappearance of Traci Taylor related to the murder of Rebecca Chilsom? Was there a killer preying on our city's children? What was being done to find the killer? Were more killings expected?

In turn, my responses were short and nebulous. We didn't know if the cases were related. The Chilsom case was a homicide; this was a missing person case. There was no firm indication there was a child predator loose in the city. The Rochester Police Department was very concerned about all missing children and that is why my squad was asked to come in and assist Lake District with the search. Everything that could be done was being done. We surely hoped and prayed there would be no more killings.

As the morning ended and the sun tried diligently to penetrate the thick, gray clouds of an impending winter, the police radio was silent and it became obvious our efforts were accomplishing little, if anything at all. By 12:30 in the afternoon, the last of the cops dragged themselves into Turning Point Park. Tommy Romano, always the conniver, had arranged for six large pizzas and a case of soda to be delivered to the park. I was tempted to ask how he had finagled it and who had paid for it, but on second thought I decided I really didn't need—or want—to know.

One by one, the teams summed up what little information they had come across. The uniforms went first. In a nutshell, none of them found anything of value. There was no sign of the missing girl, her clothes, books or backpack. There had been two close calls. One had occurred when a dead dog was first smelled and then found. A second alarm was sounded when a large doll had been discovered partially buried under some fallen leaves.

Investigator Ted Woffman, an up-and-comer from Lake District, had come up with one lady, over on Leander Street, who saw a black van stopped just off of Lake Avenue on Boxart Street.

"She says it was about 2:30 Friday afternoon, but she didn't make too much of it. But later, when she saw it go past her house twice more, she began to wonder if it was someone looking around the neighborhood to do a burglary. Naturally, she didn't call the cops, but she does think the police need to do more around here to prevent the burglaries."

"Typical citizen," one of the cops said through a mouthful of pizza.

A falsetto voice cried out from one of the picnic tables, "Oh, Officer! I don't want to get involved. I just want to piss and moan." The cop doing the impression stood up to take a bow when he received a round of applause.

"Did she see the driver?" Walz smiled as she asked.

"No. Nothing on the driver," Woffman responded.

One by one, I called off the streets that each team had covered. In response to the name of the street, came the answers, "Nothing there, Lieutenant...We got nothing...No hits...Nothing to report...No leads...No nothing."

"Okay, ladies and gentlemen," I announced loudly. "We extend the search and the door knocking." Checking the map I had pulled out of my overcoat, I ticked off assignments to the men and women assembled in the small park.

"Hey, Ted, about this van the lady mentioned," Romano spoke up. "Did she have anything more on it? Any type of description?"

"Black, older model, or at least pretty beat up," Woffman answered. "She doesn't know anything about make, model, year, et cetera. Only that it had some gray paint on it. I asked her if it was primer paint, but she didn't know what the hell I was talking about. All she could say was that it had some spots of gray paint on the right side over the wheel wells."

When Tommy simply nodded and didn't ask anything more, I bellowed, "We meet back here at four o'clock."

I was almost back to my car when I felt a hand on my left shoulder. It was Tommy Romano accompanied by his partner, Bobby St. John.

"Lieutenant, we may have something," Bobby said. Not waiting for me to ask what it was that we may have, he explained. "On my list of red Hondas that we have to run down, there's one guy over on Weaver Street who has a black van with gray primer all over it. I've been there twice now, but there's no answer at the house. The Honda hasn't been there, but the black Chevy van is in the driveway. It's got gray primer paint on all four-wheel wells and on the lower edges of the back doors. I know most of the cars in Rochester that are more than three years old have primer on wheel wells due to the salt crap they spread on the streets all winter, but what the hell. It's probably some wild-ass coincidence, but yet it might be the same van. Right?"

It only took me a second or two to mull over the revelation. "You guys arrange to get a car from Clinton Section to go over to the address and sit on it. As soon as the red Honda or the van shows up, you get your ass over there and talk to the guy. In the meantime, go over and re-interview the woman Woffman talked to."

Maybe I was wishing for too much, but for the first time in several weeks a feeling of accomplishment was seeded in my mind. "This may be nothing, Bobby…probably is nothing, but if it turns out to be a hit, I'll kiss your ass at high noon on the corner of Main Street and State Street and give you half an hour to draw a crowd."

I stood there in the park, my hands resting on the old metal railing that protected pedestrians from falling down the steep, cliff-like embankment that led down to the river's edge. My eyes looked down the hundred-foot drop to the Genesee River. The area was serene and therefore it helped my mind work the problems that were milling around within it.

If Traci Taylor had been abducted, killed, and then had her body disposed of in this area, it would take months to find her. Turning Point Park was so named, because it was a wide spot in the river, wide enough for Great Lakes' barges to turn around after dropping off tons of goods and then head north across Lake Ontario and back to Canada. East of where I stood was the heavily wooded drop to the river. On the other side of the flowing water stood the suburban town of Irondequoit. If the kid's body hit the river, it was gone until it washed up somewhere…almost anywhere from here to fifty miles away in Canada. Behind me was a parking lot that was meant to hold about a dozen, maybe fifteen cars. And beyond the parking area were a few acres of woods, brush and wild vines that provided food and shelter for the chirping birds that seemed to be everywhere around me…but were nowhere to be seen.

The trail on which I was standing ran parallel with the river and was meant to be a source of quiet recreation for the families and lovers who walked along it in the summer months. It was also a means for the killer to walk north or south with his victim, molest her, choke her to death and then discard the body in undergrowth so thick only the squirrels would find her.

I thought about calling back some of the cops and concentrating the search in this area that surrounded me with hopelessness, but then decided against it. What they were doing now—finding witnesses, any one with a speck of information—had more potential. Besides, when the troops finished their present task we would all go into the thicket of bushes and trees to look for the body we hoped we would not find. If the killer had used a car or truck, there would have been little motivation for him to drive to the park, get out of the vehicle and carry the body into the dense overgrowth. No, I reasoned, this guy isn't a snatch-and-dump murderer. He was one who coveted his abducted prize and enjoyed playing with it until he decided to destroy it. The thoughts about what he might be doing to the Taylor child at that very moment, as I stood there with my thumb up my butt, angered me and made me feel all the more useless.

Becky Chilsom had been missing about four hours before her body turned up. That homicide was our killer's first venture into his dark side. If the Taylor kid is his second victim, he would keep her longer and would then dispose of her remains in another almost public, easy-to-be-found, spot. If he took the time to buy the first victim a donut, and then spread the jelly over her crotch, he would take even more time to savor this victim.

It was a sick thought...but we were dealing with a sick bastard.

Twenty minutes into my thoughts, St. John called me on the radio.

"Clinton Section called. The red one's there," was his cryptic message.

"Do it!" was my condensed response.

An hour went by. I rejoined Frankie Donovan on the canvassing effort and briefed him on St. John's mission. An hour-and-a-half passed. I kept an ear toward the radio to pick up any transmissions from Detectives St. John or Tommy Romano, but there was nothing. Two hours and fifteen minutes went by. Finally my cell phone rang.

"You better come in here, Boss," Bobby said almost in a whisper. "We've got the owner of the van *and* the Honda in the office. You aren't going to believe this, but he works for the Rochester Public Schools, and, get this, he works at all the schools, including Chilsom's and Taylor's schools."

"Do you get any inkling from him? Do you think he's our guy?"

"I can't say. His story sounds like B.S., but yet he comes across believable."

"I'll be in the office in about 20 minutes."

George Capwell was a large, solid-built, 48 year-old, black man. He had been born and raised in our fair city and had never been in trouble with the law. I stood outside the interview room watching him talk to Bobby. From what I could see, he appeared to be direct but non-confrontational with the detective who was listening to him. My heart and soul wanted to enter the room to become a part of the conversation, but my mind kept me in check and waiting in the hallway until my detective came out. That took almost another 90 minutes.

Donovan and the rest of the squad had already returned to Headquarters. They briefed me on what they had learned. In a word, it added up to "nothing". Almost 170 man-hours had been spent on the neighborhood check. With the exception of the lady who saw the black van, it had yielded nothing. Maybe, just maybe, Capwell was going to make it all worthwhile.

The clock was creeping toward five o'clock in the evening when I told Paskell, Walz, and Romano to leave for the night. All of them muttered an affirmative answer, however, none of them left. They sifted through their desk drawers, straightened things on their desk, pulled out some files, and put some others away. Administratively they were off the clock, but their curiosity wouldn't allow them to leave while they wondered if the killer was sitting thirty feet away from them in a small, stuffy interview room.

Finally, Bobby St. John entered my cubicle and tossed his notebook on his desk. Everyone drifted toward the two of us.

"He's not our man," he said with his head tilted down. Looks of disappointment and disbelief were exchanged around the room "I can't say for sure," Bobby added, "but I think this guy is giving me the straight scoop. I don't think he did the killing, but," and then he smiled broadly, "I think he knows who our man is."

Eyebrows now raised and smiles broke out around the room. St. John didn't wait for the round of questions.

"When we got to the house," Tommy Romano continued as his partner filled his empty coffee cup, "the red Honda was there, but the black van was missing. I knocked on the door and gave him a line of crap about us investigating a hit-and-run accident and how his car was similar to the one we were looking for. He was 100 percent cooperative from the go. Capwell took us out to look at the car to see if there was any recent damage. When I asked him if anyone else drove the car, he said 'no' but he got a little nervous. Anyway, we asked him to come down here to the building with us so we could check on some information. When we got him down here, we went through it all again. I told him we had some witnesses to the alleged accident and I wanted them to take a look at him. He said that was fine with him because he hadn't been in any accident. When I got him in the room and started to get a little more direct with him about who else drove his car, he just clammed up. When Bobby told Capwell he and his car were suspected of being involved in a *fatal* pedestrian accident, that's when he began to roll over."

"Will you guys cut to the frigging chase," Paskell interrupted.

St. John threw Jimmy a scolding look before he continued. "Capwell works for the school district. He comes under the Maintenance Department, but he's primarily responsible for grounds and landscaping. There's a young kid about 22-23 years old, who works for him as a laborer. The kid, one Wayne Graham, borrows Capwell's car or truck from time to time. And, here comes the beautiful part," St. John said as he gave Donovan a thumbs up sign. "Graham has had the car, the red Honda, on and off—but most of the time—over the past month. The only exception is that the Honda has been having battery or alternator problems, so Graham brought it back to Capwell on Wednesday. Capwell fixed the alternator problem but still had to get some parts, so when Graham said he needed a car on Thursday night, Capwell gave him the van! This Graham guy has had it ever since."

"Is he sure that Graham had the Honda the Friday that Chilsom got killed?" Paskell asked.

"He's not exact on his dates, but he says that Graham usually takes the car from Thursday until they go back to work on Monday. Oh, and get this! They don't work Fridays because their hours have been cut back," the detective said with a noticeable smile.

The next question came from Walz. "Where's Graham live?"

"That's the problem! He doesn't know. He's never been to the kid's place. And, he doesn't know any of the guy's hangouts, friends or relatives. Also, the reason he didn't want to give us Graham's name at first is because he's fairly sure the guy doesn't have a driver's license."

As more questions were thrown out to Bobby St. John, Frank Donovan was on the phone with the Records Section of the Department.

"There's a Wayne Graham who has a juvie record only," Frank announced to the room as he hung up the phone. "And, being that those records are sacred and locked away, there's no way we can get into them at this time. Graham has no driving record and he has no driver's license, at least not in this state."

A couple of ideas were kicked around and it was finally decided to set George Capwell loose for the time being. After he was gone, Paskell and Walz would concentrate on finding out whatever they could about our unknown Wayne Graham. When Tommy Romano volunteered to get in contact with his aunt—a Rochester Public School administrator—to see if he could get a line on Graham, he was greeted with a round of cheerful sarcasm.

"Is there anyone in this city you do not know?" Donovan asked.

"No, don't contact her, Tommy," Gail said with a grimace. "Just sit there with your finger two knuckles deep in your nose and we'll wait for the guy to come in and surrender himself."

"Can this so-called aunt of yours change my grades from high school?" Jimmy Paskell quizzed as he wrapped an arm around Romano and gave him a powerful squeeze. It was the first time in three weeks I had seen Investigator Paskell emit anything that even closely resembled a smile.

Romano smiled at the question and asked, "Well, do you want me to call her or do you just want to cast aspersions on my hard working family?"

"Cut the crap and call your aunt, Tommy," I suggested with little humor.

It was getting past 6:30 p.m. when Bobby St. John returned to the office from ferrying Mr. Capwell back to his residence. No one had left the office. We were all waiting for the miracle that Romano's Aunt Rose was going to pull out of her hat.

At 7:15 p.m. Donovan made a run to Nick Tahou's and picked up a dozen greasy white hotdogs loaded with the works. The hot dogs were being ingested when Aunt Rose Tomasso called. Tommy took the call as we all waited to hear the other half of the conversation, for all we heard from the detective was, "Yeah…uh-huh…why? Is there a way? Uh-huh…Okay…Why? Yeah…yeah…okay." Finally he acknowledged, "Thanks, *Zi,*" and hung up the phone.

"She checked, but can't come up with anything," Tommy volunteered without waiting for us to jump him with questions. "The school district has cut back on manpower, so they farm out a lot of routine, laborer-type jobs to private contractors or to labor pools. Although Capwell is a city employee, some of the guys who work under him are from employment agencies. The school district pays the agency under a contract and the agency pays the worker. Consequently, when she got into the computer and ran the payroll, our boy, Wayne Graham, doesn't show up. He could work for anyone of a half-dozen contractors or labor pools, so my aunt can't even point us in a direction right now."

Several obscenities were muttered and I joined the chorus. The squad was chomping at the bit to get a lead and then pursue it. In a matter of minutes the only significant lead we had mustered had fizzled. All we could do now was wait until Monday morning and try to pick up Graham when he returned to work.

Frank Donovan asked, somewhat in jest and somewhat as a plea, "So, Tommy, do you have any relatives who work for labor pools?"

"Sorry, Frank," was the response. "The Romanos and Tomassos favor civil service jobs."

Assignments for the weekend were discussed. Donovan volunteered to pull duty on Sunday in order for the rest of the gang to get in a day off. He would use the time to reach out for an old-time detective friend who had worked the Juvenile Unit a few years back and see if she could grab something out of her memory about Mr. Graham. Other than that, there was nothing for us to do but to go home and get some rest.

That was the plan. However, the killer had other plans for us. In three hours all of us would be standing under an old-fashioned, attractive gazebo, looking down on the positioned body of Traci Taylor, seated on a park bench…with jelly smeared over her sad, dead face.

CHAPTER SIX

THE SECOND VICTIM

A homicide cop tries very hard to avoid any sensitivity when it comes to victims and suspects. Maybe that's why our wives and lovers, family and friends, see us as being callous. It's a trick of the trade. One learns not to be too impressed with death; not to allow it's finality attach itself to our emotions; not to let it penetrate our thickening skin. I knew the concept well and had taught it to the younger detectives. If you start getting involved—emotionally involved—with every victim, you quickly lose your perspective. From there, it's a downhill tumble and you end up sucking the end of your gun. A good homicide cop views the body as a broken piece of machinery and then focuses on finding out who broke it. Black humor, sick jokes, feigned apathy, sarcasm, and cynicism become the drop cloths to protect the mind from reality…and the detective's own feelings of mortality.

I knew all this and I understood it. But even so, the sight of Traci Taylor reached inside me, crawled under the drop cloth, gripped my heart and made my jaw quiver. It took only seconds to walk the few yards from the curb to the body…and in those seconds sadness turned to shock, and shock became disgust, and disgust ebbed to loathing, and the loathing bred anger and hatred for the animal who had done this, this act of cruelty, this sick, bastardly act of inhumanity.

The call came in at 11:30 p.m. Saturday night, almost 36 hours after Traci Taylor had turned up missing. The body had been found in the Cornhill neighborhood, seated on a park bench near a gazebo.

I had the dispatcher call in Donovan, St. John, and Romano, and in less than 20 minutes I was crossing West Ridge Road and entering the expressway that would get me to Cornhill within another five minutes.

Cornhill is one of Rochester's smaller neighborhoods, but nonetheless, one with an interesting history. The neighborhood name came about because, allegedly, in the early settlement days, those traveling the fast-flowing Genesee River could see a large-sized rolling hill covered with corn which had been planted by the immigrating Scots and English who had taken hold in the area. By the late 1800's and well into the 1920's, Cornhill was home to some of the city's wealthiest families. Situated on the southern edge of downtown, the neighborhood allowed for a short carriage ride—or on warmer days, if the mood struck one, a walk—to the banks and businesses of New York State's third largest city.

When the automobile allowed the residents of Cornhill to move farther away from the center of town, the oversized homes were divided into apartments, and with the apartments came the less economically advantaged. By the 1940's, Cornhill was at the lower end of Rochester's range of income. With the advent of drugs and gangs, it evolved into the dirty meaning usually associated with the term "inner-city." The 1964 and 1967 riots that tore Rochester apart almost totally destroyed Cornhill and soon it became a wasteland of deserted buildings and rat-crawling alleyways.

Only when the wrecking ball of what was laughingly called "Urban Renewal" was on its way to destroy most of the old town's charm, did someone in City Hall get a brain fart, and then a very interesting thing happened to Cornhill. The city began to offer low interest loans if a family would take over the broken down mansions, fix them up and live in them for five years. The homesteading idea was brilliant, for in less than ten years the deserted homes became showplaces occupied by yuppie families. The re-birth of Cornhill was considered good public policy by some and viewed as a miracle by others. The bricks of the homes once again showed their bright red and colors; the rusted wrought-iron fences were brightened with glossy-black enamel; and, the ornate wood that made up the eves and trims of the home went from a bare-wood brown to colors of blue, tan, and yellow.

With the facelift on the homes, the city streets were widened, new curbs were added and a brand new elementary school sprung up Phoenix-like on the corner of Fredrick Douglas Street and Adam Street. Just as urban decay is cancerous, Cornhill and its new-borne spirit proved that urban rejuvenation is also cancerous. The home improvements spilled out of the tiny eight-block area and began to creep up Clarissa Street, Troup Street, and to some extent, along parts of Plymouth Avenue. Only one thing needed to be done, and that was to decide if the neighborhood was to be called "Cornhill" or "Corn Hill"…an argument that still hasn't been settled to this day.

The showplace of Cornhill/Corn Hill is its small, brown gazebo with a steep, peaked roof, (much like a dunce cap) situated on a traffic circle in the center of Fredrick Douglas Street where Glasgow and Edinburgh Street meet up with Cornhill Place to form spokes to the wheel-like circle. The neat, always clean, gazebo sits in the middle of a small grassy circle that forms the hub for the six spokes of streets that enter and leave the hub. And, it was there, in that spot that was a tribute to a city's guts to live and regenerate itself, that Traci Pauline Taylor's sad looking, lifeless body had been deposited.

The inner part of the gazebo is lined with wooden benches attached to the railings of the structure. Around the outer perimeter of the gathering spot are a number of black, wrought-iron benches, and it was on one of those benches the child had been placed in a seated position. Her arms had been raised almost shoulder high and then draped over the back of the bench so as to hold her in the pose that had been created by the perverted son-of-a-bitch who had killed her.

The beam of my flashlight played over the child's face that had been smeared with jelly. The light ran down her buttoned blouse, plaid skirt, white socks, and black loafers.

"There's got to be some sick animals in this world of ours, eh, Lieutenant," Investigator Carlos Krueger asked from behind me.

The young detective was assigned to Genesee Section as a general assignment investigator. In that role he handled all the rapes, robberies, assaults, burglaries and other assorted felonies that came in during his shift. Due to the number of crooks and dopers in this section of the city, Krueger and the five other investigators assigned to the area had more than enough job security to see them through their careers. Because of his workload and his ability to solve a good percentage of the cases thrown at him on a daily basis, the kid had earned a damn good reputation in the department.

As the story went, Krueger's strange blend of first and last names came from his native-born Cuban mother and his German father, a descendant of missionaries who had traveled to Cuba at the turn of the century.

I was glad to see Carlos at the scene, and said so. His presence was an assurance the location had been protected from any foul-ups or unnecessary trampling.

Opening his notebook, the young investigator began his briefing. "Genesee 243 and I had just finished booking a burglary suspect at the PSB. I was coming back from the cop shop when I decided, you know, just for the hell of it, to take a spin through Cornhill. We've had some dirt bag breaking into cars around here for a month or better. My headlights caught the kid as I began to go around the circle." Krueger stopped long enough to draw a breath and let it out as a sigh. "I guess while I was sitting in the Public Safety Building doing a couple of reams of paper to make the District Attorney and senile judges happy, the bastard was over here doing this shit."

"Any idea how long she's been here, Carlos?"

"Genesee 233, Kenny Jasper, took a family trouble call over here at 9:35 tonight. It was a routine call, so he talked to both of them and sent them on their way. He cleared from the call about ten o'clock. I found the body at 11:25."

"Is Jasper still around?" I asked as my eyes covered the small gathering of cops and citizens.

"No way, Lute! It would be overtime! My captain would rather have his scrotum ripped off by a wild pit bull than spend a dollar on overtime."

I smiled at his observation before asking, "Is there any chance the body was here while Jasper was dealing with the domestic call?"

"I called Kenny and went over that with him. No way. The couple that was arguing was right over there in the corner of Glasgow and Freddie Douglas. Jasper said he had his car and headlights pointed directly at the gazebo. Then, after the two lovers boogied out of here, Kenny said he parked right next to the gazebo, just about where we're standing, and caught up his car log sheet for the night. He swears the kid wasn't here when he cleared the scene." The young copper in the off-the-rack sport coat and loosened tie added, "Jasper told me if you need him, he'll come back in. He says he doesn't want the overtime pay if he can do anything to help catch this prick."

Donovan had pulled up and was exiting his car as Bobby St. John and Tommy Romano pulled around the corner. Donovan shook his head when he saw the body. Bobby stopped dead in his tracks when he caught a glimpse of the child's body. Romano's whistling cut off in mid-note and he, too, stopped in his footsteps upon seeing our latest victim and made the Sign of the Cross. Once all four of us were together, I gave them a quick synopsis. Krueger filled in the blanks.

"We'll get started on the neighborhood check," Donovan volunteered.

"Right," I said. "But first, let's get a car over to George Capwell's place and see what cars are there."

"Already done," St. John said. "I had a car go over there while I was heading in. The red Honda is in the driveway but the black van is missing. The house is dark so I had the cop go to the door. Capwell and his wife are home and were already in bed when the cop got them up."

"This scene is going to take us all night, so first thing in the morning…" I started to say when Romano interrupted.

"First thing in the morning, Bobby and I will reach out for Capwell and find out if the red car was used tonight and why the black van is nowhere around. And, if I were gambling man, I would lay you eight to five our boy, Mister Wayne Graham, has got the van."

"Let's hope he does," Donovan offered. "That will move him way up on the hit parade."

We began to divvy up the neighborhood for our initial sweep when Investigator Krueger offered to give us a hand.

"I can't authorize the overtime, Carlos," I said quite honestly.

"Screw the overtime. My love life isn't, by any stretch of the imagination, what one would call exciting. I've got nothing but an empty apartment and Jay Leno to go home to."

"I would appreciate the hand."

"I thought you would, Lieutenant," Carlos said with a smile. "But really, all I'm doing is sucking up so maybe someday you'll pull me into your squad."

I smiled back at him and nodded at the not-so-bad idea.

Three hours later the four of us from Violent Crimes sat in the squad room along with Carlos wolfing down Greek, sauce-laden white hotdogs from Nick Tahou's joint and recounted what we had accomplished through our efforts. It was a short conversation. The sum total of the night totaled up to a big, fat zero.

Although the area of Frederick Douglas, Edinburgh and Glasgow Streets are totally residential—with the exception of the old Immaculate Conception Church and rectory—not one witness was uncovered. Twenty-one houses had been visited and 34 people had been interviewed, but not one shred of information had come out of the effort.

Donovan had a Clinton Section cop sit on George Capwell's house. That had also netted us nothing. The residence remained dark, without any visible sign of activity the entire night. The only interesting, albeit irrelevant, fact of the night was brought out in the sarcasm of Tommy Romano.

"Here's an interesting, little known fact about our illustrious city," he said with a grin as he wiped off his mouth. "Even when our city fathers try to honor a great man like Frederick Douglas, they screw it up."

"How so?" Bobby asked with genuine interest.

"Where Glasgow Street comes into Frederick Douglas Street, Douglas is spelled D-O-U-G-L-A-S. However, on the other side of the circle, where Glasgow goes out from the traffic circle, they have Douglas spelled D-O-U-G-L-A-S-S. Two S's instead of one! Ain't that something? Only the trained eye of an experienced, shining star, crime fighting, urban detective would pick up such small nuances," the dapper investigator commented as he took a bow.

"You're my hero," Donovan commented without any hint of being impressed.

"It was probably one of your relatives that screwed it up, Tommy," Bobby St. John said as he turned back to his report writing.

Once again, there was a scheduling change. Because Donovan had pulled the all-night duty, it was necessary to call Walz and Paskell in to cover the Sunday day shift.

"Walz will be in at seven o'clock," Donovan told me after making the calls.

"And Jimmy?" I asked.

"Gail says not to bother him. She says he's trying to solve some problems at home. She'll cover the shift and will call one of us if she needs help."

With that out of the way, Donovan and I made the trip north to Boxart Street at three in the morning. The Taylors had to be notified that their child's body had been found, and that was my job. It went like all the other death notifications. It was pure hell! The words were said. Gasps were uttered. Looks of disbelief were exchanged. Embraces meant to comfort gave little comfort. Questions asked didn't have answers.

We left them there, praying to their God. On the way back to the city, I wondered what type of God allows children to be murdered. Was it the merciful God the nuns had told us about in grammar school? Was it the omnipresent God? Was it the all-powerful God? My cynicism embarrassed me as we once again passed Holy Sepulcher Cemetery and once again I automatically made the Sign of the Cross out of respect to the dead.

Once back at Headquarters, I dropped Donovan off at his car. We promised each other we would go right home and get a good day's sleep in preparation for Monday. It was a promise made in all sincerity, but with no intention of being kept.

It was just getting to be six in the morning when Romano and St. John headed out to see George Capwell and interview him about the missing black van. Realizing that another hour's lack of sleep wouldn't kill me, I decided to wait for Detective Walz to arrive for her shift. When she came in, I briefed her on the finding of our latest victim and the night's activities.

Ten minutes later Bobby St. John reported in by phone. Our hoped assumption had been accurate...Wayne Graham had borrowed the errant black van for the weekend.

After that, there was little to do but head back to my empty apartment. It was Sunday and the world, except for some shift workers at Kodak and a bunch of fire fighters and cops, would be closed. That gave us one more day of waiting and delay before we could find and pounce on Wayne Graham.

"So what then?" my voice asked the car's interior. Would Graham be our big break in the case? Or, would he be just another dead end? There were two dead children out there with the promise of more to follow. We should be doing more, my mind nagged at me. "Sure, do more." I snickered, "But what?" Without a person to talk to, without a place to go for the next lead, without a shred of tangible evidence to analyze, where do we go? What do we do?

Crunching the pillow up under my head, I drifted off to a restless sleep with one question on my mind. When was the killer going to call the Taylors? When was he going to call? While my mind struggled with the question, my tired body mercifully put it's brain to sleep. It was a good thing that sleep took over, because the answer to the question was that he would not call. Our killing bastard had other plans for the Taylor family.

CHAPTER SEVEN

LUNCHES, LETTERS, AND NOTES

Monday dawned with a hope, almost a promise that the case would now take off. However, it was not to be. The first thing to be encountered after entering the office was a review of the crime technicians' compilation of reports. To the point, not one single piece of significant traceable evidence had been found in, near, or on the corpses. Both of the victims had had their bodies exposed to a lengthy chemical process in an effort to lift fingerprint impressions from their flesh. Only two prints had been found on Traci Taylor's forehead and, for a time, the technicians held out the possibility of a lead, a clue. However, the prints turned out to be those of her mother, a mother who had felt her daughter's head in an effort to see if she was coming down with a fever that had visited other neighborhood children.

The day had started as a flop...it also began with some terse words between Jimmy Paskell and me.

"I want you to tell me why I wasn't called in Saturday night when the Taylor kid's body was found," Paskell damn near demanded as he stepped into my cubicle and made no effort to lower his voice.

This was not the easy-going, somewhat paranoid Paskell that I knew! I decided to cut him some slack and let the mandate slide as if I hadn't noticed it. "You've been working straight through on this case, Jimmy. I thought I would leave you alone and let you get in some family time," I replied as I looked up at him and offered what I hoped to be an apologetic look.

"It's my case. I should have been called in, Lieutenant," he insisted.

"It's *our* case, Detective," I corrected still keeping my tone of voice calm and civil. "The call came in late. I was in a rush to get down to the scene. I had the dispatcher notify the on-call team. That was Romano and St. John."

"If that's the case, why wasn't I called in yesterday when you called Gail? Am I being left out of things for some reason?" There was suspicion in his voice, a suspicion I understood, a suspicion that would have been in my voice if it were me who had not been called in when my partner was asked to report for duty.

"There wasn't much to do, Jimmy. I only needed one of you, so I called for Walz. Her daughter is staying with her ex for the weekend, so I thought she would be able to come in and you, on the other hand, could spend some much needed time with your family."

"You let me worry about my family," Paskell ordered.

"Are you chewing my ass, Detective?" I asked as I stood up and narrowed my eyes at the challenging subordinate. Paskell was pushing the envelope too far. He needed to have his heels cooled.

"All I'm saying is that I don't like being left out!"

"And all I'm saying is that I'm running this frigging squad and I'll call the shots. Is that clear? If I need to overwork your ass, then I'll do that. On the other hand, if I decide to give you a break, then I'll also do that!"

We both stood there looking at each other, waiting for the other man to make the next move.

"What are you saying?" Paskell demanded. "Do you think I'm going over the edge?"

"I didn't say that and you know it."

"I think you did!"

I was halfway between mellowing my words more and ripping into the detective. I never had a chance to decide which way to go. Jimmy Paskell simply shot me a look that was pure poison and walked out.

Fifteen minutes later the squad was standing by for the morning briefing. I figured it was time for me to tighten the reins. After each team caught the others up on the status of their assigned cases, I got up to pour myself some coffee. Stirring the cream and sugar in the cup, I started my speech.

"This case is going to be a long, hard battle for all of us. So we're going to chunk it down. Paskell and Walz will have the lead responsibility for the Chilsom killing. You two will devote your time to running down any loose ends that may exist. Donovan will have the lead on the Taylor case. He'll work the case until it's cold or gone. I'll assist him. St. John and Romano will take the lead in working on Graham. If, God forbid, there's another one of these killings, they will catch the case. From now on, plan on 12-hour days and don't make any plans for your days off. I'll make changes as necessary and I'll be available to help any and all of you. All reports will come to me by the end of your shift. If you can't complete your reports for some reason, then you'll give me a verbal summary of what's going on. We're not banking a hundred percent on Capwell's vehicles being the cars used on these homicides, so each one of you will continue to run down the cars on the DMV printout. I will, from time-to-time, for one reason or another, change your shifts, your partner, and your days off. That's the way it's going to be! If you don't like those rules, you can see me in my office. And, by the way, when you come in to see me about it, have your transfer request in your hand. Now get to work!"

I left the squad room and retreated to my inner sanctum. Donovan joined me a few minutes later.

"What the hell was all that about, Mike?"

"The squad's coming apart at the seams, Frank. They need a little leadership."

"What do you mean?" he asked somewhat cautiously.

"Walz is covering for Paskell. Paskell was in here bitching about not being called in. St. John hasn't said more than a dozen words in the past week. Romano is taking this thing too lightly," I said with my head back in the chair and my eyes closed as I pinched the bridge of my nose. "The case is getting to all of them. I needed to kick some butt."

"It's getting to all of *us*, Mike," Donovan corrected. "I know what you're doing, just don't push it too far, okay? What you said in there was pretty cold."

"As far as I know, I'm still the boss around here, so let me handle it, okay, Frank?" The words came out more sarcastically than I intended.

"Sure thing, *Lieutenant*," he said and then silently withdrew from the office. His words were cool, almost frigid. I knew he meant them to sound that way.

By nine in the morning we had located the labor pool that provided Graham with his job. A half hour later Romano and Bobby St. John had Wayne Graham's address, date of birth and Social Security number. By ten o'clock they had driven by his house, and by ten-thirty they were back in the office with the news.

"We still have the record clerks checking on Graham by name, DOB, Social Security number, and a couple of variations on his name," Romano announced as he came through the door. "In the meantime, while we wait for that, here's what we got."

Pulling up a chair and throwing the calf of his right leg over the corner of my desk, the strident detective started his monologue. St. John gave his partner—and the leg—a chastising look accompanied by an apologetic shrug in my direction.

"Graham is 25 years old and a bachelor," Romano continued without taking the hint offered by his associate. "He lives in a small, cottage-type home on Silver Street. It's basically a dump alongside the old B&O railroad tracks, but hey, what the hell, the man calls it home. Although born and raised in Rochester, he has spent the past four or five years away from our lovely metropolis—which is of great interest to my partner and me—and has returned to our fair city within the past six months or so. He works as a day laborer for a landscape company that holds some city contracts, one such contract being with the Rochester Public Schools. According to our preliminary quest into the bowels of the Records Division, he has no driver's license and no criminal history. However, as we did learn earlier, there is a sealed juvenile record we can't get into…yet!"

"For now, that's all we have," Bobby St. John concluded. "We'll take the rest of the day, the rest of the week if necessary, and dig deeper."

"Dig very deep," I advised. "If he's our guy, we may get only one shot at him and I want it to be our very best shot. We need a full background on the guy, from his birth to his last meal."

With a wink, Bobby added, "Tommy's got a cousin working on getting his credit history, a former neighbor trying to get all of his phone records, and an ex-girlfriend or two looking into his gas and electric bills."

"Is there any place in this damn town where you don't have a connection, Tommy?" I asked as I shoved his leg off my desk.

"It's a curse being this handsome and charismatic, but I try to use it for righteous purposes, in doing God's work. You know, in righting the wrongs that men do, refusing to sheath my sword until crime is driven from our streets, never again to place our citizens in fear or jeopardy for life, property or loved ones."

Getting in my first laugh in the past couple of days, I instructed St. John, "Do me a favor and get him the hell out of here."

Alone in the half-walled cubicle the city says is an office, I made use of the time to go through the departmental mail that had been stacking up for about a week. Some pieces got tossed in the trash can, some got initialed and forwarded, and some got slipped into the "TO DO" basket that was beginning to sag under the weight of the accumulated paper. At noon I thought about grabbing some lunch somewhere, but decided to forge ahead with my administrative tasks.

Ten minutes later, St. John and Romano were back at my desk.

"And the plot thickens," Romano announced while twisting the end of an imaginary handlebar mustache.

Bobby St. John simply shook his head at his whimsical partner and stepped around him. Handing me a neat stack of papers that had been stapled together, he read from his spiral pad as I kept up by looking at the faxes, criminal history reports, and copies of booking reports he had provided for me.

"When we run our boy by 'Wayne Graham' and his social security number, we don't get much. However, running him in a general query as "Graham Wayne' and playing around with his birth date a little, we find that he—or someone very similar in height, weight, hair, and eyes—took a bust five years ago in Springfield, Massachusetts. That same person, the Graham Wayne guy, took another hit in Boston about a year or so later. Both of the charges were related to assaults and one included a deadly weapon charge."

I nodded and raised my eyebrows as I looked over the hard copies of the information that had been faxed to us by the Massachusetts cops.

"Sixteen months later he gets busted in Camden, Arkansas, wherever the hell that is," St. John continued. "That was for disorderly conduct. And then, not eight months later, he took another bust for an assault in some hellhole called Gallup, New Mexico."

"If it's the same guy in all these places, I would say that he's one angry young man, and that he sure gets around," I commented. "Are any of these cases related to grabbing kids, to sexual assaults?"

"Oh, it's the same person, Lieutenant," Bobby said. "Look at the last couple of pieces of paper. They're the fingerprint classifications from Boston, Springfield, Arkansas, and New Mexico. We had Clancy down in ID look at the fingerprint classifications and some of the faxed prints, and he says they're all the same." St. John flipped through some more notes and added, "The one assault in Boston was on a 16-year-old female, but it's not clear if it was sexual in nature. We'll call the Boston cops on that one. The one in Galluping, New Mexico, or whatever the hell it is, probably was sexual. He grabbed a 12-year-old girl out of the back of her father's pick-up truck. Some relatives were nearby and they beat the crap out of Graham before the cops rescued him. He got charged with a minor assault charge, came up with the bail and skipped. And, before you ask, no, they won't extradite him back there on the bail skip."

"Be nice to me, Bobby, and tell me there's a warrant outstanding for him in one of these places."

"I wish I could, but I can't. He has no wants, no warrants, and only the one bail skip in New Mexico. Basically, the man is free and clear."

The room went silent for a minute as I looked over the reports that St. John had provided. The time wasn't spent in reading the information, but rather to think over our next move. We needed to get the prints of *our* Wayne Graham and make absolutely, one hundred percent sure he was the same one as the Boston-Springfield-Gallup Graham Wayne.

Tommy Romano read my thoughts when he asked, "So, do we get to pick up Mr. Graham and squeeze his head?"

"For what? On what information? What the hell do we have on him other than he travels and gets into fights?"

Again there was silence as I moved some papers around on top of the desk. This time Detective St. John broke the silence with the observation, "I don't think we should move on him yet. If we grab him and he lawyers-up, we're dead later on if we do get something on him."

"He's the best suspect we have right now...the best one and the only one," I said. "Stay on his background and let's see what breaks. And start nosing around to see if we have his prints on file anywhere so we can say for sure, without a doubt, that he's the same guy as the one you have there in those reports."

Cheryl Centonze has steel blue eyes that, at the age of 65, create a marvelous twinkle in them and highlight her warm smile and smooth, un-aged, cherub-like face. The woman is a legend in the Rochester Police Department, but her matronly appearance hides the legend well.

She had become a nurse at the age of 21, married when she was 23, and widowed by time she was 25. In 1962, at a time when police*women* were officially—according to the department's rank structure—outranked by police*men*, she became a cop. In those days female cops had little hope of going into patrol and out on the streets. Consequently, Cheryl was relegated to office duties and eventually assigned to the old Persons Unit, i.e., the kiddie cops, the ones who handle all the juvenile delinquents. From time to time she was asked to take on the task of interviewing a young sex crime victim and it was there she showed her full worth.

By 1980 she had risen to the rank of Lieutenant and commanded the Sex Crimes Unit in a more enlightened and modern Rochester Police Department. Lt. Centonze had done her job well. She had developed a reputation for being one who could leave one office after crying with and comforting the victim with a soothing, patting hand, and then walk across the hall to shout and make the most disgusting rapist pull back in fear. There were many stories about her cunning and conniving ways with rapists, pedophiles, exposers, and other assorted creeps. She was not above showing a little cleavage, if that's what it took, in order to trip up a suspect who let his penis do his thinking for him. Nor was she one to deny a battered wife the opportunity to stay at one of Rochester's nicer hotels for a night or two…at Cheryl's expense.

Although some of the Jane Wayne cops of the present day look down their noses at Centonze's era of Police*women*, and their deference to a male-dominated job, it was she and Joan Mathers, Margaret Phuntner, and a few others, who paved the way for the modern-day female Police *Officer*.

Other than by reputation and a couple of cases she helped me on way back when I was a young copper, I hardly knew Cheryl. However, Frank Donovan had spent better than a year working with the woman when he was on assignment in the Sex Crimes Unit. Therefore, it was he who arranged our Tuesday afternoon lunch date.

"Hello, Mike," she said as she stood to shake my hand. "I'm still hearing a lot of good things about you."

"It's good to see you, Cheryl," I said. "But you know you aren't suppose to believe everything you hear."

She and Donovan then kicked around a couple of old cases as we ordered lunch and waited for our meals to arrive. With the preliminaries aside, Frank channeled us into the purpose of the meeting.

Turning to me, he said, "When I called and asked Cheryl about the Graham kid, she was pretty sure she remembered an incident with him. So I asked her to dig up what she could. I know how meticulous she always was with her cases, and sure as snow, she pulled out some old files and notes that are going be a big help, Lieutenant."

The preface to the discussion was not needed because Frank had already given me the background. However, it was necessary, as a courtesy to the woman, that he pay her respect and honor her reputation.

"I'm just an old pack rat, Mike," she said as she waved off Donovan's commendation. "When Frank called me and asked me if I remembered the Graham boy, I thought his name rang a bell, but I wasn't too sure. Then, after he gave me a fairly good idea of when the lad might have been arrested, it was just a matter of getting to the right box in the garage and finding the right notebook."

For the next twenty minutes, between, neat, quiet, slurpless spoons of hot soup, retired Lieutenant Cheryl Centonze painted us a picture of who—and what—was the person we knew only as a name...Wayne Graham.

Within two years of his birth his mother had, for whatever reason, abandoned Wayne Grankovski. After kicking around from one foster home to another, he was adopted at age seven by two schoolteachers, Martha and Lewis Graham. Once settled in with his new family, Wayne Graham began to flourish as a student. For the next ten years, the boy functioned well in his suburban home while his adoptive father climbed the ladder in the Rochester Public School System. After holding a couple of positions as principal of a middle, and then later, a high school, Lewis Graham moved on to become the right-hand assistant of two successive school superintendents.

Although Wayne was scholastically capable, he lacked friends, and remained an outsider. Suddenly, in his senior year, without any warning, the quiet kid began to get into small scraps with other students. Then, one month before graduation, he committed an act that shocked everyone—classmates, teachers, and the school board.

On a Saturday morning, just before a varsity high school baseball game, the school mascot, a falcon, was found hanging by its neck from the backstop of the baseball diamond. The bird's stomach had been slit open and its entrails were left to dangle from the belly of the mutilated fowl.

With only three students and two teachers at the school who cared for the mascot, it was only a matter of time before the suspect was identified and charged. That suspect was Wayne Graham.

"It took me no more than a half-hour to break him," Centonze said after she pressed a napkin to her lips. "The boy was a mess of emotions, hysteria, and passions. He would cry for two minutes and then laugh for thirty seconds. Try as he may, he couldn't explain why he had done that terrible thing to the school's mascot. However, I think he did it to strike back at his adopted mother and father...especially his father!"

"What gave you that impression?" Frank asked as he furrowed his brow and leaned back to observe and absorb the woman he obviously admired.

Cheryl licked a thumb and flipped through a couple of pages from an old, worn notebook she had pulled out of an enormous handbag. "When I told him he owed his parents some explanation for his actions, he said, and I'm quoting him here, 'They deserve whatever they get out of this…they deserve it and they know why'."

"What was that supposed to mean?" I asked.

"I can't swear to this, Mike, but my best guess is that the boy was abused. There were things about him, things he said that he did, that made me think he was abused in some way. Maybe beaten, perhaps sexually, maybe verbally. I don't really know. All I do know is that I was around that sort of thing for too long, and I can sense an abused child! I even had him remove his shirt so I could see if he had marks on him. He didn't, but it didn't change my opinion. As I said, I had been around enough child abuse to have a good sixth sense about it."

The lunch ended with protests over who should be allowed to pay the bill. The matter was settled when I announced that the meal was on the city. Of course, that was a lie. That privilege was saved for Chiefs of Police who wine and dine citizens who head power groups that hate cops.

The concern about the bill aside, the lunch was invaluable to us in understanding Wayne Graham; and, it would give us an edge if we had to interrogate him…if we ever got to interrogate him.

As soon as Frank Donovan and I called back in service from our lunch date, Jimmy Paskell called on the radio to advise us that he and Walz were on their way back to the cop shop and we should make it a point to meet them. The words were routine; his voice was not.

Back in the squadroom, we could see Walz was visibly shaken although she offered a weak smile and a nod. Paskell made no attempt to conceal his emotions.

"The dirty bastard sent a letter to the Taylor kid's parents," he began loudly. "He told them how she begged to be turned loose, cried for them, and then how he choked her to death. He put it all down for them just to…to…fuck with them."

"Where's the letter?" Donovan asked calmly.

"We've got to get this son-of-a-bitch, Frank. We have got to get him!" Jimmy went on, probably not even hearing the question.

"We dropped it off at the lab, Frank," Gail answered Donovan's question after clearing her throat. Then standing up, she offered him two sheets of paper. "The technicians made us a copy for the file."

As my partner read the letter silently, I stood at his side reading the same neatly typed words. Hearing his deep breaths and short snorts, I knew we were sharing the same hate for the animal who had written the letter.

Late in the afternoon, Bobby St. John was led into the morgue-like homicide offices by his whistling and dancing partner. Met with four sets of mean, serious eyes, Romano stopped in his tracks and asked, "What?"

Walz supplied the happy jester with the news of the letter. Then, even Romano, shared the look that the rest of us wore. St. John, always the quiet one, simply sat at his desk, pulled out some blank reports and began documenting the team's activities for the day.

"So, what have you guys got for us?" I asked Tommy who was still standing motionless in the middle of the room.

"Bobby and I went down to Ladera Landscaping and spoke to the boss. I passed us off as Immigration and Naturalization agents and told him, Gus Ladera, the owner, that we were looking at the possibility of him having hired some illegal Canadian immigrants."

"Who the hell ever heard of illegal Canadian immigrants, Romano?" Paskell asked angrily. "Why the hell don't you use your head?"

"Did you expect me to tell him Graham was Mexican?" Tommy shot back sarcastically with a light laugh. "That would have been a good move, huh? Yeah, you're okay, Jimmy. I should have told Ladera we were looking for a Mexican National by the name of Wayne Graham!" Romano chuckled as he looked around the room at his audience. "That would have been real smart!"

"Everything's a big joke with you, you asshole!" Jimmy said as he got up from his chair.

"Screw you, Jimmy," Romano answered back with a wave of his hand.

Paskell took a step toward his shorter, thinner antagonist. "Unless you really want a good ass-kicking, Jimmy, you better sit down!" Romano cautioned.

"Alright, cool it. Cool it!" I commanded with a bark. "Both of you shut the hell up, sit down, and let Bobby give us the briefing."

The offending detectives both gave each other glaring looks and then sat down to pout.

Somewhat exasperated by the scene, Bobby St. John picked up the recap of the visit to Graham's work place. "Like he said, we scammed the owner of the place that we were from Immigration and asked him to open up his records on Graham. He told us the kid came to work for him back in June. Ladera says Graham is a good worker, keeps to himself, comes in on time, does his job, et cetera, et cetera, et cetera. While Graham was with him. he received one complaint on the guy from a homeowner who accused him of slacking off and spending too much time talking to her kids. So, to keep peace with the customer, he switched our guy over to the labor pool crew that's working on the school contract."

"Graham's putzing around with some customer's kid, so they send him to work at the schools where there's thousands of kids?" Walz asked incredulously.

"Our feelings exactly," St. John confirmed. "But we didn't want to burn any bridges with the guy, so we let it pass. Anyway, he has nothing but praise for our suspect. Ladera says he's had teachers and principals compliment Graham on the way he gets along with everyone, does his job and even plays with the kids. To make the point, he told us that a few weeks ago, Graham had raked up a bunch of leaves at one of the schools—it just happens to be the one Rebecca Chilsom attended—and the kids started to play in the mound of leaves. Instead of getting mad, Graham jumped in with the kids and started to throw the leaves around with them. Later on, he stayed over on his own time and raked up the leaves again."

"He's a regular peach of a guy," Tommy commented to his desk. "The shithead was probably taking the opportunity to cop a feel or two."

"Is this Ladera guy going to keep his mouth shut about this inquiry?" Donovan asked.

"No problem there, Frank," Bobby answered. "He has a cousin on the State Police, and besides, Tommy made it clear to him how pleased his government would be to have his cooperation…and how angered they would become if he blew the whistle on the investigation. He got the message. I got the impression he doesn't want the feds digging around in his tax records."

"Nice job," Frankie Donovan commented.

"It gets better," St. John said. "While we're going through Graham's work file at the place, we find a slip of paper that has a list of personnel actions. One of the items that's checked off is 'Fingerprint'. When we asked Ladera about that he says the School Board has a policy that requires anyone who works at the schools to be fingerprinted! It turns out the Sheriff's Department took Graham's prints, and yes, they most definitely are the same as the Wayne Graham and Graham Wayne that came up earlier when we were pulling his criminal history in Boston, Arkansas, and New Mexico!"

There were smiles all around. The case was moving.

That evening, after the office cleared, I hung back and pushed some administrative stuff from the In-Basket to the Out-Basket. Finally, after standing to stretch, I poured the last of the rotten coffee into my cup, added a couple of ounces of *Sambuca* to the mug, and looked out onto the lights of the city's west side.

It was one of those many times on this job when you feel useless. You know who the bad guy is and you know where to find him, but there's no sense in going there, because you have nothing on him. We were going to have to do something about Graham. I knew that; the entire squad knew that. However, the question was, do what? If we picked him up now, we didn't even have enough to bluff him into a confession, and without the confession we had nothing.

What is this guy's problem? I've seen a lot of bodies and I've heard a lot of reasons about why people kill other people. I understand rage, anger, hate, passion, hot flashes, greed, jealousy, distrust, mistrust, pathos, pride, prejudice, and the other hundred reasons why man kills his fellow man. Even the killings we call "senseless killings" have some sense to them, some thin scrap of reason. But killing a child? Why would one…how could one…kill a child in cold blood? Sex was not the answer. There were signs he had molested the two little girls he killed, but it was not necessary to kill in order to fondle. And, as if the brutality of the killing is not enough, why does our animal find it necessary to torture the parents with the details of his deed?

Standing there, looking out over the city I call home, I wondered these things and my mind delivered not one single answer. My brain did not understand these things so it was incapable of bringing me the understanding I sought and the answers I needed.

For those answers I would have to go elsewhere. I would have to go into the mind of Graham, a mind that understood these things and could explain them to me.

The cup was drained and I stood there looking into it as if the stains would deliver me an answer to the most important question, the one and only salient question. Who was next? What child out there had been marked for murder? What parent had been targeted to suffer the insufferable…the loss of a child?

Unfortunately, our killer did not have that question bothering him. He had already selected his next victim.

CHAPTER EIGHT

THE MIND IS A TERRIBLE THING

Zachary McGill should have been a cop instead of a psychologist. His father was a cop. His grandfather was a cop. Even his sister Mackenzie was a cop...of sorts. Zack McGill considered his younger sister the black sheep of the family because, after completing her Master's Degree in Psychology, she had joined the FBI. Even now that she's a member of *The Bureau's* elite Behavioral Science Unit, Zack would often joke about his make-believe shame over his sibling's choice of employment as he would wipe his brow and say, "I'd rather have a wife in a whorehouse than a sister in the FBI!"

Dr. McGill is a big man, standing well over six-feet tall. He has the upper body of a weightlifter and moves like an accomplished athlete. That, together with his full head of rumpled blond hair and thick Fu Man Chu mustache, does well to conceal from most people that he's a respected psychologist. By the time he was 30 years of age, the man had established an admirable private practice, but the truth of the matter was that he loves cops more than he aspires for the wealth that such a practice could bring him. Consequently, when the Rochester Police and Fire Departments sought to hire a Public Safety Psychologist, Zack McGill sought and was awarded the position. However, long before he ever held the official position as the cop and fire shrink, his unofficial—and usually uncompensated—work with our breed had already earned him the respect of the men and women whose minds had been pushed to the edge of sanity by the sights and sounds of their life *on the job*.

Although I don't take easily to such men of higher learning, "Zack", as the cops and firefighters knew him, was a man I truly liked. Not being one to let his book learning go to his head, he had been a frequent attendee at our Almost Monthly Poker Games and earned himself the reputation as one who could tip more than a few beers with the best of partying cops. Consequently, it was easy for me to approach the man and ask him to join me for a long lunch.

After the introductory light conversation, I got down to business. Knowing I could trust his promise not to breath a word about what I was about to tell him, I laid out the entire cases of the Chilsom and Taylor homicides for the man. I gave him a full, detailed description of how the bodies were found, the jelly smeared on the clothes and face, how Traci Taylor had been displayed on the park bench, the nature of the call to Betty Chilsom, and finally, showed him the letter received by the Taylor family. He absorbed it all with a few nods and an occasional note on the notepad in front of him. When I told him we were narrowing in on a suspect, he stopped me.

"Let me stop you right there, Mike. I want to get all this straight first, and then, before I become biased by who you're looking at for these killings, I want to take some scientific wild-ass guesses at what the killer may be like."

McGill asked a few questions about the victims, the presence or lack of signs of violence on their bodies, how the bodies and heads were positioned and a couple of other details. When he had all the information, he took a few minutes to internalize the information and scribble a couple of notes. He then drew in and blew out a long breath of air.

"The first thing you need to know is this entire thing needs to go to the FBI's Behavioral Science Unit. I know your thoughts on the feebs, and you know, in spite of Mackenzie's position there, I share most of those beliefs. However, crime lab forensics and behavioral science is what they do best. They're the experts in this area, and there's no denying it." Then, with a grin he added, "Not that I'm admitting or even hinting that Mackenzie is a better psychologist than I am, but they do have the corner on the market when it comes to psychological profiling."

I nodded and begrudgingly agreed.

"Now, with that said, I'll tell you this, I have done a lot of work and study in the field of forensic psychology and I'll be more than happy to share some thoughts with you on the subject." He paused and signaled to me with his eyes that he sought my agreement on what he was about to say. "However, you need to assure me that you'll go to the feds with this. You're only getting one man's, local-yokel opinion from me. However, with the FBI's people, you're getting one hell of a lot of experience based on cases from all over the world."

"It's being packaged for them now," I stated truthfully. "Bobby St. John is going to be getting it out to them by the end of the week. But, I can't wait a couple of months for a response, Zack. It's been almost two weeks since we found the Taylor kid, and I'm afraid...hell, I know, this guy is getting ready to strike again. When he does, we have to be ready for him. I need some help, Zack, and I need it now."

McGill looked at me with patience in his eyes and nodded. "I'll call Mackenzie for you and see if she can push it along a little." After taking a sip of coffee, he set down the cup and leaned forward. "Okay, Mike, get your pad out and take some notes, because I'll give it to you the way I see it."

"Shoot," I replied as I clicked the ballpoint pen into the ready position.

"What I'm giving you is off the top of my head. I'll need to know a lot more, even see the crime scene photos, that is, if you don't mind."

"I have no problem with that, Doc."

"Based on what you've just told me, my guess is the guy you're dealing with is what we refer to as 'anger retaliatory'. He's got a hell of a lot of anger stored up and I suppose that anger is directed at the parents and the victims, or, more probably, at his own parents or authority figures he has encountered in his life. What he's doing is not about killing kids. No, not at all. What he's all about is striking out at the parents. He's grabbing the kids, keeping them a while, and then killing them. But that's not his point. His point is made when he calls or writes the parents and details what he did and how he did it. He's punishing the parents, Mike."

After I had time to put down a note or two and comment, "Go ahead," the shrink continued.

"This guy is going to get more and more bold over time. Each new killing is going to be more shocking than the last. When you consider that he dumped the first kid in an empty lot and then put the second one on display over in Cornhill, I have to guess he's really going to go out of his way to display the next body. The son-of-a-bitch might even put the body on Main Street or on Exchange Street, right in front of the main doors to the Public Safety Building. If you don't catch him, he's likely to send the next parents an audio or videotape of the child being killed. And, my good friend, if you do catch him, you better be able to put him away for good, because if he does get out, he'll be back with a vengeance. If he gets off, he'll go all out, maybe like taking an entire school hostage and killing kids left and right."

The thought sent chills up and down my spine. I covered my emotions with the question, "So tell me about the killer, Doc. Who are we looking for?"

"Who? I don't have the foggiest idea *who* it might be. However, I can tell you *what* you're looking for." McGill paused, finished his coffee, and then went on. "This guy will look and act as normal as anyone of us here in this restaurant. He's probably working at some menial job, but doing well at it. His house and his life are neat, organized, structured. The guy is no rocket scientist, but by the same token, my guess is that he is fairly smart with a decent IQ. Somewhere in his background you'll probably find he was abused or misused as a child. There's a couple of things about him that suggest his parents were probably upper-middle class and might have held some responsible position...maybe like a bank president or an executive position at one of the big companies."

The big man came up for air and gave me a minute to catch up on my note taking. Then he asked, "So, how does all that fit with the guy you're looking at for these killings?"

"It fits," I said with a few short nods. "A lot of it fits like a glove."

"Are you going to pick him up, Mike?"

93

"I wish we could, Doc. However, the fact of the matter is that we don't have squat for evidence. But, if…when we do get him in, how do we handle him? What's going to make a guy like this bastard want to roll over and 'fess up?"

"The good news is I don't think he'll be that hard to break. This guy wants the world to know he did it. He wants it made public. That's the only way he has of retaliating against his mother or father, or whoever it is that he sees as having done him an injustice."

"And, the bad news is…?" I questioned.

"The bad news is that he will only confess to someone he sees as his equal. You see, this bird views himself as a pretty smart dude, much smarter than the average Joe, and definitely a lot smarter than a cop. He's only going to confess to someone he sees as being superior in their job, just as he is superior in finding and killing these children! I'm guessing he'll want to—probably demand to—talk to the Chief of Police or even the FBI."

"Ain't no way that's going to happen!" I said emphatically.

"You might have to let him do it, Mike…or learn to live with the fact you'll never get that confession you need." Zack McGill leaned back in his chair closed his eyes, and ran his large hands through his hair a couple of times. When he came back from wherever his thoughts had taken him, he said, "However, there may be a way he'll talk to you."

"How? What have I got to do?"

"I'm pretty sure he won't talk to a regular detective. He'll see that as a put down to his feelings of superiority. However, he might talk to a boss, if, and only if, he recognizes that person as someone of importance, someone with superior skills."

"I don't get it," I confessed. "What are you saying?"

"What I'm saying is that you need to get yourself built up as *the* expert homicide sleuth. Get your media people to run a feature story on you and some of the cases you've broken like the poker murder case and the Danny Martin killing. Have them get you a big splash in the paper about those bank robbery cases you guys cleaned up last year."

"None of those cases were mine alone. I would be slapping the squad in the face if I took credit for any one of those cases, Zack."

"Well, that's your call, Mike," McGill said as he grabbed the check off the table. "I'm sure the FBI will give the RPD *some* credit for the case after they arrest him," he said with a huge smile and notable wink.

After giving McGill a ride back to his office, he again had me reassure him I would get the information to the FBI's Behavioral Science Unit. Then, after obtaining my promise, he cautioned, "And don't you ever let Mackenzie know I referred you to her organization. She'll never let me ever live it down!"

Major Skip Winston listened intently as I briefed him on my meeting with Doctor McGill. As a part of the briefing, I hit him with McGill's advice that we make me out in the press as being some kind of super cop.

"It sounds like a plan to me, Lieutenant," he confirmed with a nod. "I'll run it past the Deputy Chief, but for now, plan on working with Monica Sheldon in order to get out some press on you. She's been bugging the Chief that as the Public Information Officer she has an obligation to put out some positive news on the department."

"I really think we should put Bobby St. John out front on this one," I countered. "When we bring this bird in, Bobby should be the one to do the interrogation."

"Why is that?"

"He's got the personality and the background for it. He's calm, educated, classy, and has a good vocabulary. If our mope wants somebody intelligent to deal with, Bobby will fit the role better than me."

"True," Winston conceded. "But he doesn't have the rank. If what McGill said is accurate, Graham will want to talk to the boss. That's you. You have the job."

With that subject out of the way, I moved on to the next matter. "I want to reach out for Graham tomorrow."

"Oh? How so?" Winston asked with noted interest.

"He needs to have his cage rattled a little. I'm thinking of sending St. John and Romano by his place to talk to him about some make believe hit-and-run accident he had in George Capwell's van."

"You're not planning on picking him up, are you?"

"No. I just want the guys to make contact with him and see how he reacts. Besides, we need to see where he lives, how he lives...to see if McGill's suppositions about his lifestyle are accurate." Winston seemed comfortable with the suggestion. For good measure, I added, "Besides, we might get lucky and see something...or he might get stupid and say something."

"Okay," he consented cautiously. "Go for it, but don't make it too heavy. If we try to snatch him now with what little evidence we have, we'll lose the case just as sure as I'm sitting here."

An hour later, near the close of the day, I called down to Monica Sheldon's office. When I asked if she was free for a short meeting, she suggested that we meet over a drink. Not being able to find any fault with the idea, I agreed with her suggestion.

Thirty minutes later we were seated on very high stools at a small round table that seems to be fashionable nowadays at trendy bars that serve too much fruit and not enough liquor in their drinks.

"So what's up, Amato?" she asked with a smile. "Why do you need to see me?"

"Major Winston tells me that you're hammering the Chief about doing an article on some of the cops or one of the units. And, much to my disagreement, it looks like it's been decided that I'm going to be the one they want you to target for your project."

The attractive woman studied her drink as she continued to wear the thin, tight smile. Then, raising only her eyes, but not her head, she said with a tone of amused disgust, "Bullshit, Amato! There's more to it than that."

"Hey," I protested with both hands in the air. "It wasn't my idea. Believe me! I'm not the one who came up with this brilliant inspiration." The statement was fairly close to the truth.

"I've told the Chief I want to do a story on the Tactical Unit, the Vice Squad, the dispatchers or one of the patrol sections...but I never mentioned you," Monica noted suspiciously.

"Yeah, well, be that as it may, it looks like Chief Murphy thinks I need the publicity. Besides, he probably thinks you have the hots for someone in one of those commands, so he is shuffling you off to me."

"And, what if I have the hots for you, Lieutenant?" Sheldon asked with a broad smile.

I shrugged and offered a smile of my own. "I guess we'll have to keep that as our little secret."

"What does Deputy Chief Ernie Cooper think of the idea?" she asked as she continued wearing the smile, although it had shrunk slightly.

"He probably thinks he should be the subject of the story with an emphasis on his plan to be the next Chief of Police," I quipped.

"The man is a legend," the PIO said with a wink to accompany the smile.

"...in his own mind," we said simultaneously.

The woman took a breath and I couldn't help but notice the ample shape of her breasts as they strained the silk of her blouse. She caught me looking and gave me a subtle, suggestive flick of her eyebrows. "Why don't we start the story over dinner?" she proposed.

"That line sounds like I'm being picked up at a bar," I offered with feigned shock.

"You are," was her simple, to-the-point reply. Then standing up and slipping into her coat, and once again pointing her breasts at my observant eyes, she instructed, "Pay the bill and meet me outside. You can follow me to my place. You'll do some steaks on the grill and I'll start taking notes."

Before leaving the bar I called Mrs. Salber and asked her to take care of Max for the night. She expressed her usual concern for my safety and I confidently told her I was going to be fine!

Although there were a dozen or so reasons why I should have turned down the invitation, I couldn't—or didn't bother to—come up with one right then. The night looked promising. And, if all went well tomorrow, we were going to get a shot at Wayne Graham.

As it turned out, I was right on both counts.

It was almost five in the morning when I woke up in Monica Sheldon's bed with the nagging realization that she had worn me down enough that my body questioned why I was even making the attempt to get up so early...or to get up at all.

"One more time, Amato," the very sexy woman said sleepily.

"Once more and we'll need the Medical Examiner down here to pronounce me dead." It was said to be a joke, although my head—and other body parts—believed the statement to be totally accurate.

It took almost two hours to make it back to my apartment, grab a shower, press a clean shirt from out of the laundry basket, and get ready for the day. I missed being able to see Max, but believed if he had known the reason for my nightlong absence, he would have understood.

By 8:30 a.m., the squad had been brought up to speed on the happenings of the prior day…but not the night. Leads on the case had begun to pour into the police department. The sensational nature of the cases had naturally attracted considerable media attention and now the public, usually misers with their information, began to notify the dispatchers and street cops with ideas, suggestion, concerns, and suspicions. Each lead had to be sorted out for some level of feasibility and the more promising ones had to be pursued. We sorted through the information, selected the ones that seemed to be probable, made assignments, and then got back to Mr. Wayne Graham.

St. John and Romano added a few more notes on what they had dug up on Wayne Graham, and that amounted to the fact that many of his high school alumni saw him as kind of freak, geek, loner, or outsider.

"We want to get to his parents, but don't want to do it now. It might spook him," St. John said.

"We'll need to do it, but we'll do it later, maybe after we talk to him," I stated as a suggestion, "however, tomorrow being Friday, and seeing how Graham has off on Fridays, I do want you guys to pay him a visit…kind of an exploratory visit. Let's see how he acts, what he does."

"We'll hit him with the hit-and-run scam we've been running on Capwell," Romano volunteered.

"Shouldn't that be me and Gail doing that, Lieutenant?" Jimmy Paskell asked with a slight edge in his voice.

"No," I answered. "You guys stay on the first victim and run down some of those hundred and fifty leads that have come in over the past couple of days."

Paskell snorted, but I didn't dignify the act with a comment. Instead, the conversation drifted to when and how the suspect would be confronted. We nailed down every last detail of the plan, including what he would be asked, how to insure the interview took place in his house, how the detectives would act and what they would be looking for as they talked to the suspect. It was a good, well thoughtout, solid plan. The only thing wrong with it was that God had other plans…and so did Wayne Graham.

I was getting ready to head home at six that evening when a uniformed cop presented himself at the entrance of my cubicle. I looked up at the kid and waved him in.

"Lieutenant?" he asked cautiously.

I responded with a nod and then verbalized the invitation for him to come into the office. The copper seemed almost afraid of me and I wondered what stories he had heard about nasty, old, Lieutenant Ace Amato.

"I'm sorry to bother you, Lieutenant," he said as he stepped toward my desk.

"No bother. I was looking for an excuse to get out of this paperwork." As the words came out, I stood and offered him my hand and a big smile, hoping that both would help alleviate the young cop's obvious uneasiness. "I'm Mike Amato. What's your name?"

"Francisco Torres. Officer Torres. The guys call me Frankie, Frankie Torres." The rundown on name, official title, and nickname were offered in quick succession as the young cop tried to figure out what form of his identification was proper for me to know.

"Well, Officer Francisco Frankie Torres, what can I do for you?" I hoped my smile would let him know I wanted him to relax.

"I got a guy in here, Lieutenant. I picked him up on a stabbing we had today at one of the downtown stores. He went kind of crazy and stabbed a young woman, a clerk at a record store, right on Main Street, about an hour ago. I picked him up nearby and the clerk identified him, so I'm going to charge him with Assault Second."

"Is she going to die?" I asked, wondering why I was being dragged into a routine assault. "Do you need some help with the case?"

"Oh, no, sir. She's not going to die. She got cut up pretty bad on the arm, the right arm, right forearm, but she won't die…at least the ambulance crew didn't think so."

"Well that's good," I acknowledged with a new smile.

"And the investigators from my section, are on the way up to help with the paperwork and all."

"So how can I help?" I asked, getting a little tired of nervous cop's stammering.

"The guy I have up here, in one of the interview rooms, he says he knows who's killing the kids."

"He what?"

"He says he knows who killed the Chilsom and Taylor girls, and…"

"Who did he name? What name did he give you?" I interrupted.

"Well that's it, Lieutenant. He won't tell me. He says he'll only talk to you. He won't give me his name, address, anything. He just says he'll talk to you and only you."

In two seconds I was headed in the direction of Interview Room 3. In the short distance I got some basic information about the suspect's demeanor and some details about what he had said up to this point.

When I looked in the narrow pane of glass in the center of the interview room door, I smiled. Inside the room, sitting calmly at the table was a chubby, balding man in his late 40's who was familiar to me…and most cops who had spent anytime on a foot or car beat in the downtown area of Rochester.

"Frankie, your man is Charles VanVorhiss. He is better known to one and all as 'Machine Gun Charlie'."

"Machine Gun Charlie?" Torres asked as he took a second look at the unassuming figure in the interview room. "Why's he called that? Does he carry a machine gun?"

"No, not at all," I said with a little smile. "But, have you heard him talk?" I asked.

"Yeah, ah, yes sir. A little. He's said a little bit. Not much though."

I gave the rookie cop the rundown on Mister VanVorhiss. "Charlie is a street guy. He's nuttier than a shithouse rat. The guy's been around for years, maybe fifteen or twenty years that I know of.

He got his nickname from the way he talks, in those short, rapid, bursts of words. Charlie is a whacko from the word go. Usually, day-to-day, he's not dangerous, but every now and then he flares up and hurts someone. About eight, maybe nine years ago, he broke a man's neck. Killed him like that," I said as I snapped my fingers to make the point. "He's been up to the State Hospital's Mental Ward enough times to earn him a place on their board of directors."

"Why hasn't he been put away?" Torres quizzed as if I understood the screwy things our court system does. "If he killed someone why isn't he doing life?"

It was obvious Officer Frankie Torres was still new enough to this convoluted job that he actually believed that justice came out in a courtroom. "Charlie goes to court, the shrinks evaluate him, find him officially nuts and find him not guilty by reason of insanity. Then, he gets put away in a psycho ward for six months, maybe a year. After he's had enough treatment and enough medication, he mellows out. When he becomes nice and normal acting, the doctors evaluate him as being no harm to society, and, having already been found not guilty, out he comes again."

"What about the murder?" Torres asked. "Did you guys nail him on that?"

"Oh yeah. Sure thing. The squad that was up here back then proved he did it, but he was so whacked out, the judge again found him innocent by reason of insanity. Again, he went to the nut house and stayed long enough to get his shit together. When he officially became sane again, he was released and cautioned to go forth and sin no more."

As the young cop tried to figure out where the justice was in that little scenario, I suggested, "Let's go talk to him. I'll introduce you to Rochester's version of the Christmas fruitcake."

As soon as I opened the door, the chubby little, monk-like man reacted with a startled look and stood instantly, shoving his chair back and knocking it over. After he had two seconds to look me over, he moved toward me in one, long step.

"Mike-ie!" he shouted and threw his arms around me, startling my young co-worker. "Mike-ie, how ya doing?" he asked in his rapid clip of words that made it sound more like, "Mike-ie, howyadoin?"

The last word—or, at least the last syllable—of each sentence ended on an upward lilt.

"Mike-ie, it's wrong. Wrong. They tell me I stabbed some innocent girl. She's not innocent, Mike-ie. She was one of them. She was KGB. A KGB double agent. I heard her. She was transmitting." He pumped out the words in staccato bursts.

"Calm down, Charlie. Calm down," I said gently, guiding him back to his chair. "What happened?"

"Got up this morning. Had a bowl of cereal. Drank some coffee. Everything was good. Went for a walk. Could hear them." His short, choppy sentences came in quick, short, clips that dropped pronouns and other incidental words that might slow him down. "Went downtown. That's where they hang out. Told you that! You know that! They were there. She was one of them. She was sending waves to them. Tried to disguise it. Make it sound like music. I could hear them, Mike-ie. She was using the music. Code. All code."

"Music?" I asked with a suppressed grin.

"It's a record store, Lieutenant," Torres volunteered. "They pipe music out to the street."

VanVorhiss shot the rookie a look of suspicion.

"It's okay, Charlie," I said as I patted the man's right hand. "Officer Torres is cleared for this information. He's working with us on loan from the CIA. He has a clearance rating of Excessively High Top Secret. As you know, that's the highest clearing you can get." The crazy man seemed to be evaluating my information, so I added, "I've personally trained him. He's been assigned to downtown patrol so he can work on this exact case you've just busted wide open."

"Should have told me. Didn't know," Charlie admonished Torres.

"Well, I'm not at liberty to expose my true identity unless Lieutenant Amato authorizes it," Frankie Torres played along.

Charlie seemed to accept the reasoning, and then looked back at me. "It's big, Mike-ie. Big! International. Oh yes! Goes all the way to Moscow. Havana too!"

"The girls, Charlie. Tell me about the girls who are getting killed." I wanted to get to the meat of the discussion and quit wasting time with something that was, in all likelihood going to go nowhere.

"Same thing, Mike-ie. The girls are ours. We train them. All their life. They're our agents, Mike-ie. Goddamned KGB. They got their names. I don't know where. Don't know how, when. They got the names. It's a new agent. New KGB agent. He's hunting them down. Killing them."

"Who's the agent? What's his name?" I asked, somewhat playing along.

"Don't know, Mike-ie. Don't know the name. Gonna get it for you. It's a matter of time. I'll get it. I will. Code name is Shadow. Shadow. Don't know that for sure. Pretty sure. Shadow. That's him."

What I really wanted to do was to get out of here, go home, and take Max for a walk. However, it was obvious Charlie had had another relapse, and as I had suspected when I walked into the room, this was going to be another one of his KGB versus CIA scenarios. Taking a few minutes with him, I convinced my screwy friend that the secret agent who was killing the girls was now snooping around the State Hospital. In order to further the case, I was going to have Special Agent Francisco Torres arrange to have Special Agent Charlie VanVorhiss get inside the State Hospital so he could learn the identity of the secret Russian agent.

"Good, Mike-ie. Good there. They know. Should stay there. Live there. Learn all the agents. All the double agents. I like them, Mike-ie. Assign me there. They like me. Good place. Protected there. No voices in my head. No one yelling! Please, Mike-ie. Put me there."

"You're the only man I can trust, Charlie. I know it's going to be hard on you, but I really, really need you to handle this for me." I was standing when I finished my request. "Now you give Agent Torres the information he needs in order to slip you into your undercover assignment." With that, I slipped out of the room.

"Machine Gun Charlie, again, Lute?" Detective Robert Bishop of the Downtown Patrol Section asked as he and I met in the hallway.

"You got it, Bob," I confirmed. "He's on his way to another six, maybe ten months at the State Hospital."

"It's going to be a hell of lot longer than that, Lute," Bishop said with a notable amount of confidence.

103

"Why's that? Do you have pictures of the judge having sex with a chicken?" I asked with a grin.

"It's the victim. She's Councilwoman Tillery's niece…and daughter to our favorite liberal, bleeding heart, New York State Legislator Roland Nugent. Old Charlie is going to go away for a long, long time on this one. I'll bet my retirement on it!"

"Ah yes," I acknowledged. "Politicians do swing a bigger sword than Lady Justice."

I was in the process of shaking hands with Bishop and saying good night, when Officer Torres came out of the room and announced, "The guy won't talk to me, Lute. He says he has to hear the code first. Do you know the damn code? Do you have any idea what he's talking about? I'm stalling him. I told him I had to get the okay from you in order to use the code."

"You're finally learning to bullshit, Torres. I'm proud of you, rookie!" Bob Bishop said as he gave the kid a hardy pat on the pack. "Bullshit is where it's at, kid. If you can't bullshit 'em, you can't lead 'em to the path of righteousness."

"The code is always in three parts with Charlie. You have to say something like, 'There's rain in the forest'. He'll come back with something about there's snow someplace or another. The first two exchanges are always about weather. Then you have to come back with something not related to the weather, but something more man-made, maybe something about a car being on fire. That's the code. You say something about the weather; he answers with a weather thing; you come back with something about fire, or smoke, or an accident."

"Okay," Torres said with a tone that let me know he was wondering if maybe I was a little nuttier than Machine Gun Charlie.

When the young cop went back into the room, Bishop had him leave the door open so we could listen from the doorway.

"Look, Charlie, Amato said I could use the code, but if I do, you better own up to what happened today. Okay? Do we have a deal?" Officer Torres asked.

"Ain't saying nothing. Nothing to say," VanVorhiss responded in a smug response.

"Well you better because there's rain in the forest, Charlie."

There was a pause and I could only imagine Charlie coming to the realization that he was perhaps in the midst of a new, super-spy. "Don't know about that. Not my business. Just a lot of snow on the lake."

"That's interesting, Charlie," Torres said before adding, "And there's fire in the house."

"Frank-ie!" Machine Gun Charlie exclaimed to his new-found friend. I smiled to myself and left the building for the night.

That cold evening, as I took Max for a well-earned walk around the neighborhood, I found myself angry at what we laughingly referred to as our criminal justice system. Charlie VanVorhiss had never really received the attention he needed so badly. But now, based on the fact that he had picked the wrong victim—a politically connected victim—he would surely get the attention he needed, and he would be getting it for a long, long time.

I tried to shift my thoughts back to Wayne Graham and the pending attention he needed, but my mind drifted back to a chubby, short, crazy man begging me to send him to the place he knew he needed to be. My brain would not let me separate the two instances, and as much as I steered it to Wayne Graham, it veered back to Charlie VanVorhiss.

At nine o'clock in the evening, I poured my last cup of coffee for the day and spread the newspaper open on the kitchen table. Max was under the table not six inches from my feet. All I wanted to do was scan the sports section, but my attention was drawn to the front page and the headline, "How Safe Is Your Child?" The *Democrat and Chronicle* story focused a good chunk of space on murders of Becky Chilsom and Traci Taylor.

The reporter recounted the Alphabet Murders of the 1970's and related the fear that had spread through the city those 30-some odd years ago. To make the connection between then and now, the story was sprinkled with an ample amount of quotes from parents who dreaded to have their children leave for school each morning, who were panicked when their child came home a few minutes late, and who refused to let their sons and daughters play anywhere out of their sight.

The fear that had crept into the community was beginning to spread and I knew the story would escalate that fear into panic. Tomorrow the police phones would light up with hundreds of calls; calls asking for assurances, calls demanding protection…and maybe a couple of calls that would give us information, information that pointed to the murderer, information to support Graham was our man, information we needed so badly.

Before flipping to the sports section, my eyes caught one paragraph that said the police were baffled by the case and didn't have any leads to pursue. I snorted at the words and said out loud, "Oh, we have a lead, my friend, and we're going to move on that lead tomorrow, and then there won't be anymore panic, anymore killings."

Time would prove me right on the first statement and wrong—totally wrong—on the second.

CHAPTER NINE

HE KNOWS WE KNOW

Life did not stop because we had two murdered children on our hands. Other criminals continued to ply their trade on the streets, inside stores, and in the privacy of their homes. Hefted on top of the normal flow of new crimes the teams continued to handle *and* the assigned investigations each one of them already carried in their briefcases were the hundreds of leads that now came regarding the Chilsom-Taylor homicides. Chief Matt Murphy assigned six cops from the Tactical Unit to us so we could cover the leads flowing in by phone, through the dispatcher, detectives in other squads, and the street cops. Then we were given three more investigators from the Vice Squad. Eventually we had—including my squad—22 cops assigned to cover the leads that kept pouring in.

The public was being gripped by fear, fear that was being perpetrated by a psycho and peddled by the news people...each with their own mission and agenda. The public responded to the fear with the only tool they had—the police. They called in reports about suspicious cars that drove too slow or too fast. They reported their weird neighbor who had lived next door to them for 15 years and had always been weird, but now they suspected he was a child molester. Women who sought revenge against their ex-husbands, ex-boyfriends and ex-fiancés, threw them into the hopper. An equal number of men who sought to eliminate husbands, boyfriends, casual lovers, and other competitors also called in their phony suspicions. It took four cops just to separate the possible leads from the improbable ones. To be on the safe side, all leads were followed up, but priorities were assigned to each lead. The suspicion about, "a guy in the neighborhood who walks kind of weird," went to the bottom of the pile. However, a tip on a, "former lover who always liked me to dress up like a little girl and call him daddy…even after he got out of prison for molesting children," was handed directly to an investigator for immediate follow-up.

That's where we were Friday morning when the squad—minus Frank Donovan who had been assigned to supervise the evening shift of support help that had been allocated to us—showed up for work. The plan that morning was for Bobby St. John and Tommy Romano to hit Wayne Graham with an unannounced visit.

The plan went to hell shortly after 10 o'clock Friday morning when Tindell Steele entered a small neighborhood grocery store on Clifford Avenue and announced his intention to rob the store. Instantly, Mister Stevie Chung, a handsome, young Korean lad who was the proprietor of the store, announced that he, on the other hand, was the proud owner of a new .45 automatic…and promptly sent three rounds of ammunition in Tindell's direction. All three rounds struck their target and did a wonderful job of rehabilitating Mister Steele from his life of crime.

It was the type of homicide we actually enjoy covering…one where the good guys win and the bad guys end up dying with the thought that they would have been better off pursuing other endeavors.

By one in the afternoon, we had the investigation under enough control so that St. John and Romano could be cut loose to run down Wayne Graham for a casual, but very critical, interview. With things finally calming down, I took the time to relate the story about Machine Gun Charlie VanVorhiss to the squad. Everyone got a good laugh out of the KGB-CIA connection to the case. It was good to see the teams loosening up a bit, now that we had a real suspect and some focus on the investigation.

It was going on four in the afternoon before the St. John-Romano team returned to the squad room. Although both had much to say, it was Romano, in his highly animated fashion, who began.

"He's our guy, Lieutenant! This frigging Graham dude is our man."

"Oh really?" I asked with a note of suspicion over the proclamation. "Did he confess?"

"He might as well have!" Tommy said as he uncharacteristically tossed his sport coat over the back of a chair. In a calmer moment, he would have taken the time to carefully place the jacket on a hanger, smooth it down and then hang it on the clothes bar behind the squad room door. "He was having a great time frosting our balls. The creep was damn near laughing at us."

"Give it to me in English, Tommy," I instructed, somewhat frustrated by his rambling.

"We got it all on tape," he announced for Walz, Paskell, and me. "We taped the entire thing. You aren't going to believe it! The arrogance of the man! He was smiling at us, almost challenging us to bust him. I'm telling you, I should have busted him in the mouth."

"Thank you for that enlightening briefing of your interview with Mr. Graham, Detective Romano," Gail Walz said sarcastically. "Now then, Bobby, can you give us any *facts and details*?"

Robert St. John is a proper man of few words who is often disturbed by his partner's uncouth behavior and high-energy, whimsical ways. Today, as usual, he was calmer and more staid than Romano. Seeing that Walz, Paskell, and I were getting tired of Romano's non-descriptive briefing, Bobby took over the orientation.

"Lieutenant, he knows that we know he did the murders. Graham is our guy, and he knows we know it. The weird thing is—and this guy *is* weird—it doesn't bother him. In fact, it's quite the opposite! He seems delighted by the fact that we're on to him." After stirring his coffee, he continued. "We asked him questions about his whereabouts—in relation to the supposed hit-and-run accident—and he just smiled at us. He even asked if there weren't some other crimes we wanted to ask him about." Slipping into his chair, Bobby summed up, "He did the killings…and he's going to do more. He enjoys what he's doing to the kids, to us. He's our killer. Take it to the bank."

"How sure are you?" Paskell asked with excitement in his voice.

"I've never been more sure of anything in my life, Jimmy," St. John said flatly. Then he added, "Listen to the tape. It's all there. You can almost hear the smile in his voice. And, pay special attention to the little phrase he uses three, four, maybe a half-dozen times."

As Tommy pulled out the tape recorder and set it up, he gave us the background on the tiny microphone he had built into a tie clip for instances such as this, and how he could personally guarantee the recording would be high quality.

The tape began with some loud banging noise and Gail Walz voiced my concern that the tape would end up being garbage.

Romano gave her a disgusted look and explained that was him knocking on Wayne Graham's door.

"How you doing, Mr. Graham?" Romano's voice came over surprisingly loud and clear on the tape. "I'm Detective Romano and this here is Detective St. John. We understand you can help us with something were looking into."

"Sure. Come on in detectives. Come on in and get out of that cold weather."

There was some small talk about the nastiness of Rochester winters, and some gratuitous comments from Graham about the hardships of being a cop. With that coming to an end, Romano instructed all of us to listen carefully.

"I've been expecting you fellows to stop by," Graham's voice commented.

My eyes caught Bobby St. John's eyes, and I nodded at him. He was right—you could hear the smile in the suspect's words.

"Oh really?" We heard Tommy ask through the speaker of the recorder. "Why's that?"

"*Hey now*, with those two children being killed, I just figured the police would want to talk to everyone who works at the schools."

Bobby St. John pointed to the recorder and non-verbally asked me with raised eyebrows, "Did you hear that?"

His partner verbalized the same question as he exchanged a high-five with Walz. "Did you hear it? Did you hear the 'Hey now'?" Romano asked excitedly.

"Just like the Chilsom woman reported," Walz noted with some satisfaction.

And," Graham continued with some emphasis, "I do work at each of the schools those two girls attended."

"Well, that's very interesting Mr. Graham," St. John joined in. "However, we're here to talk to you about Mr. Capwell's cars that you drive."

Romano hit the machine's pause button and said, "We should have pursued that, Bobby. Why the hell did you get him off the subject?"

"Because," St. John answered, "Graham was too comfortable going in that direction."

"Bobby threw some shit in Graham's game," Walz noted as she gave Romano a stiff slap to the back of his head. "It was a good move."

It was a simple exchange of opinions among members of the squad, but I was concerned about the smile and look of satisfaction on Jimmy Paskell's face. He was happy, too happy, that Romano had been put down.

Once again, the sound of the tape recording filled the corner of the room where the five of us and three Tactical Unit cops were gathered in a huddle as Graham asked, "Hey now, cars? What about the cars?"

"Well, it appears that Mr. Capwell's red Honda Civic may have been involved in a hit-and-run accident with a pedestrian back about…"

"I don't know anything about that," Graham interrupted, notably upset by the unexpected direction of the interview.

St. John then went into a short monologue about the fictitious accident. Next, he shifted gears by asking Graham about the times when he used the car or the van. When the suspect offered up the exact days he had used one of Capwell's cars, he fed the two detectives the exact dates our two victims had been abducted and murdered.

Bobby pointed to the recorder and said, "He's smiling at us again. He looked me dead in the eye and smiled when he gave the dates."

At that point Romano re-entered the interview and began questioning our suspect about his work duties, locations, working hours, days off and related information. Graham answered each question clearly, eagerly…and again, one could almost hear the smile in his voice.

Bobby's voice was then heard on the tape commenting about all the books in the suspect's home as he asked, "Have you read all of these books?"

"I am rather well read, detective. I've read all the classics, from Chaucer and Homer, to Hemmingway and Steinbeck." There was pause. And then our antagonistic suspect asked, "And you, detective? Do you read?"

"Oh yes, yes I do," St. John answered as if he wasn't bothered by the sarcastic, demeaning question. "I just be po' black folk, but yes sah, I does read."

Graham was obviously irritated by the demeaning question being turned on him in returned sarcasm. "My question was not a reflection on your race, Detective St. John," he said politely, but yet gratuitously. "However, I apologize if I may have worded it poorly. What I meant was, do you read the classics?"

"Personally, I find Homer boring, although there is some brilliance insofar as he was somewhat progressive for his day in the way he crafted *The Odyssey*. However, as far as I'm concerned, one cannot even begin a discussion of the classics without first mentioning Shakespeare. Hemingway is, of course, in my humble opinion, the premier contemporary author and I share your enthusiasm for his works."

Again there was a pause and I could only imagine Wayne Graham absorbing the fact that he was not talking to an uneducated man.

Finally, it was Bobby who broke the silence. "Well, in any event, we do appreciate your time and candor, Mr. Graham. I shall look forward to engaging you in conversation once again, when the need arises…perhaps sometime in the not too distant future."

"You are truly a gentleman, Detective St. John," Graham said politely, but the smile was gone from his voice. St. John's "not too distant future" remark had evidently struck Graham.

"Have a nice weekend, sir," Bobby stated in a pleasant voice.

"Oh, *I will,*" Graham responded and the smile had returned very clearly to his words.

The three words, "Oh, I will," sent a chill through me. And, in looking up at the squad members, each of whom exchanged looks with the others, I knew they also understood the message behind the three, simple, short words.

"He's going to do it again this weekend," Paskell announced loudly. "He might as well have said it right out. He's going to do it!"

"I'm not so sure," Bobby St. John threw into the conversation. Then he added, "Listen to this next part. He may be teasing us and then again he may be warning us."

Wayne Graham's voice came from the recorder. "I just bought a new computer and I plan on spending the weekend surfing the net, searching out some information I need, and downloading some of that information."

"Well, we hope you…" St. John began to say something before he was interrupted.

"Hey now, if you run a surveillance on me, you'll see I'll be here all the time."

"Now why would we want to spend a lot of time setting up a surveillance on you, Wayne?" Romano was heard to ask suspiciously.

When there was no answer from our suspect, I looked to Romano to provide an answer.

"He just smiled, Lieutenant. A big, stupid, smile," Romano said.

The tape ended with a round of good-byes. When it was shut off I said to the team, "Tell me about him, about his house."

"It was just like Zack McGill told you, Lute," Romano said. "It's a little dumpy cottage down at the end of Silver Street, right near the railroad tracks, but inside it's neat and clean."

"The books I referred to are set up in alphabetical order by the author's last name," St. John stated. "He has bookshelves made out of concrete blocks and planks of wood, but they're all equal in height, width and length. The main room, the living room is neat, very organized, very structured."

The impromptu squad meeting then shifted to what needed to be done. It was decided that Romano would personally contact George Capwell and get his assistance in notifying us if—when—Graham borrowed either vehicle. All of us would work the entire weekend on a round-the-clock surveillance of Wayne Graham. Shifts were assigned for the surveillance.

"It's going to be a difficult surveillance, Lieutenant," St. John advised. The portion of the street that Graham lives on is right near a dead end. Before it gets to the dead end, it bends sharp to the left. We're going to have to sit up the street, probably out of sight of the house, and just look for the car leaving."

I nodded at Bobby's observation. It was just one more difficulty to overcome.

The last event of the day was to brief Major Winston. After I played portions of the tape-recorded interview for him, he was as convinced as was the squad that Wayne Graham was a child killer. When Skip Winston suggested I utilize the Tactical Unit to supplement the stakeout, I refused the offer, telling him the squad needed to have the lead on this latest break.

"They need some rest, Mike," he cautioned. "They've been running hard on this thing for well over a month. They need a little breathing room."

"They'll get all the breathing room they want when this asshole is locked up. Until then, this is what they get paid to do."

"You're pushing them too hard, Mike," Winston cautioned. "Ease up a little."

I let the words go without comment.

Back in the squad room, Tommy Romano hit me with some bad news.

"I called Capwell to tell him me and Bobby were coming out to see him. When he asked why I told him I wanted to ask him about the van and the car. I'm still going down to talk to him, but he already told me the van is in the shop for repairs—something about the alternator—and he isn't lending out the Honda to Graham because he, Capwell, needs it."

With that turn of events, the plan shifted emphasis. We would still keep a surveillance on Graham. His veiled comment that he was planning on having a nice weekend was too close to a threat, and I didn't feel comfortable leaving him free to do whatever he wanted to do. After all, he may have access to more vehicles than just George Capwell's two family cars.

It wasn't a brilliant plan, but it was a good plan. If and when Graham moved on a kid, we were going to be on him like white on rice, like stink on shit, like ugly on an ape. We were going to nail him in the act. Things were finally going well in the investigation. If our suspect hit this weekend, the bust would pull the squad back together, and by Monday morning things would be back to normal. If, on the other hand, Graham didn't make a move all weekend, well, at least it would be one less dead kid.

That was the plan as I drove to my apartment looking forward to seeing Max and even more so, getting a good night's rest. Although somewhat pleased with the progress the case was making, I was daunted by an old saying that went something like, "While man plans, God laughs." Maybe my cynicism was going unchecked again, but then again, maybe I was just being a realist. Only time, the great truth-finder, would sort that out for me.

After Max and I took our walk—and he had the opportunity to sniff at and urinate on every bush in the three-block area—I returned to the apartment to be greeted by the annoying ringing of my telephone.

"Lieutenant Amato?" the woman's voice asked in response to my greeting.

"Yes."

"This is Jane Paskell, Jimmy's wife."

"Hi Jane," I said in a cheery voice…all the time wondering why Paskell's wife was calling me. "Is there a problem?"

"Please don't tell Jimmy I called, but I need to ask you to do something." There was a pause, but when I didn't fill it, the woman continued. "You need to take Jimmy off this case, Lieutenant. It's killing him…us."

"What do you mean, Jane? What's going on? I mean I understand what you said, but I can't just take a man off the case at this point."

"I'm afraid he's cracking up, Lieutenant. He doesn't sleep, won't eat. I can't carry on a decent conversation with him without getting into an argument. He's like, like a bear. He paces constantly. He won't let the kids out of his sight when he's home, and when he's not here, he calls constantly asking me where they are. Then, when I ask him what's bothering him, he tells me it's nothing."

"He's just under some pressure now, Jane. We all are. It'll be okay. We're getting this case put together nicely. It'll be maybe another week or so, but you'll see. Everything will be back to normal in just a little while. Okay?"

"No! No, it's not okay, Lieutenant," she almost shouted. "You don't understand what I'm telling you. Jimmy is losing it! He's headed for a nervous breakdown! He won't let the kids out of the house without him or me personally escorting them. He won't even trust me to take them to my mother's house."

We talked another few minutes, but covered virtually the same ground. She wanted her husband taken off the case and reassigned. I tried to explain that doing that would only make matters worse. If I dumped Jimmy now, he would think I had lost my confidence in him.

Again I asked her for one more week. "Jane, Jimmy gets ticked off even if I don't call him in when something develops. If I take him off the case now, it'll be even worse. Believe me. We have a good idea who the killer is, and in a week, maybe two, we'll have this thing put together and then…"

"I don't think he's going to last that long, Lieutenant," she said a little calmer but just as firm. "This case is ripping him apart…and it's pulling us apart." There was a pause and then she threw the ball into my court. "Okay. One week. One week and then I go to the Chief with this. I may lose Jimmy by doing that, but at least he won't end up in a mental ward."

The phone went dead.

I grabbed a bottle of Scotch out of the cabinet over the stove and poured myself a stiff shot. I was on the second shot when the phone again came to life.

"How are you doing Amato?" the voice asked, and immediately two questions went through my thick head. The first one was, What the hell is this, ladies night? The second one was, Who is this?

"I'm doing okay for an old man," I responded, still wondering to whom I was speaking.

I guess my failure to recognize the voice carried through the phone lines, for it was then the caller identified herself. "This is Monica."

"I knew that," I lied unashamed.

"Liar!" she said so as to shame me. Then not waiting to carry on the argument, she said, "I'm going to make you a hero, Lieutenant. You're going to be in Sunday's *Democrat and Chronicle*, in a feature story about what a wonderful detective you are."

"Really?" was all I could come up. "So soon?"

"Is that it, Amato? Is that all you can say? How about, 'Gee, what a wonderful job you did, Monica.' Or you could say, 'I'm really impressed by your hard work for me, Monica'."

"I'm saving that until I see the story," I chuckled.

"Well, in the meantime, you could come over here and take me to bed while you interrogate me about what I may have said about you."

It was an offer I didn't want to refuse, and yet, it was an offer I wasn't up to accepting. "I'm going to have to beg off on that, Monica. It's been a terribly long day and I have to go in early tomorrow. Can I get a rain check?"

"You're breaking my heart, Amato. I'm a devastated woman, but I can handle the rejection…for now."

We talked another minute or so before saying good night. Ten minutes later I was in bed. With Max snuggled up at the foot of the bed, I looked forward to a good night's sleep. Jimmy Paskell's wife's words played in my mind, and my last thought before drifting off to sleep was about how I could save the detective's marriage, his sanity…and his job.

With a deep sigh, I tried to push the thoughts out of my head. I hoped for a good night's sleep, but it was not to be.

CHAPTER TEN

BAD DREAMS AND BAD WEEKS

The fears and trepidation that live in the mind are safely kept locked away during the activities of waking hours, but in sleep they are free to roam...and become alive in the silence of dreams. That was the nature of the dream that haunted me.

It was only a dream. I knew it was dream. It was the same dream that had crept into my nights every now and then for the past four or five years. That night, that Friday night, it came again.

It's late at night, well after midnight as I walk down one of the long, business-district streets on the city's east side. Perhaps it's Joseph Avenue, maybe Clinton Avenue, or Hudson Avenue. There's rain in the air...the sweet wet-street-smell of a summer rain after a long, dry, hot spell. I have no business being in that neighborhood. A glance over my shoulder reveals there are a dozen, maybe even 15 or 20 people in a small, closely clustered group that follows my path and matches my speed with theirs. Fear becomes panic as I feel for my gun and my hand touches an empty holster. Could I be so stupid as to go walking this late at night, in this neighborhood, without my weapon?

I quicken my pace and so do they. My fast walk becomes a jog, and the jog turns into a gallop. I'm breathing hard and fast in short gulps of air as my mind curses the cigarettes I inhale with such frequency. I run into an alley, somewhat confident they have not seen me. However, as I turn to look over my shoulder there they are, moving quickly behind me, not running as hard as I am, but yet gaining on me. Just as I turn to look forward, my body is walloped with a blow that knocks me flat on my ass. I've run into a brick wall! The alley is a dead end! There's nowhere to go!

I slump back with my back and shoulders against the unyielding bricks. Although I make every attempt to cover my face, I can see them advancing on me, moving slowly, deliberately. At a leisurely pace they bend over my cowering body, lowering their faces to mine. Only now do I realize they have no faces! There is hair and heads, bodies and torsos, arms and fingers, but no faces. What should be a face is covered with smooth skin, absent of eyes, nose, cheeks and mouth.

The old one, the one with the gray hair, leans in close to me and reaches for his own throat with his right hand. Slowly, arduously, he pulls up on the smooth skin from below his chin, pulls it upward, up toward his mouth, nose, and eyes. Pulling the skin away to show his features. I know this man. I never met him, but I know him. I know his face, his body. I know of his death. I know his name. Bernie Katz, a storeowner shot and killed six years earlier. His murder has remained unsolved, and he reminds me of this as he asks, "Where's my killer, Amato? Why haven't you found my killer?"

A young woman advances on me and pulls the skin up, off of her face, revealing the features of Marie Denwaldt, a young mother raped and stabbed to death with a screwdriver over five years ago. "What about me, Amato?" she asks. "Where's my killer?"

A short, stooped-over woman pulls off the skin covering her face and I see the wrinkled, kindly face of Josephine Cindelli. "Why have you not found my killers, Amato?" she asks through a busted up mouth and her swollen eyes testify to the wounds she suffered as three purse snatchers kicked her to death in a struggle for her purse containing less than four dollars. "You promised me, Amato. You promised me you would get them."

One by one, the members of the group approach my fetal-position body. One by one, the unsatisfied victims of unsolved murders, pull the skin from their faces and reveal their identities to me.

Jeff Gibson, a high school athlete who had been murdered for no reason in a senseless drive-by shooting; Isaac Jordan, stabbed and killed in a mugging; Bertha Halloway, beaten to death with a two-by-four; Roberto Diaz, beheaded with a machete for some unknown reason by an unknown maniac; Gloria Steiner and Elizabeth Manderelli, two teenage girlfriends, raped, tortured, and later dumped into an abandoned quarry; Gilbert Yancy, who was run over repeatedly by an irate driver who thought the old man took too long crossing the street; Stefana Rosetta, shot to death at a bus stop for the wedding ring her deceased husband had placed on her finger 54 years earlier; Bobby Martinez, a teenage clerk in a convenience store, killed when a ball point pen was shoved into his brain through his ear by an unknown robber; Kirk Devon and Patty Nichols, parked on a lover's lane in Durand-Eastman Park and shot to death by an unknown suspect for an unknown reason.

They each come forward one at a time, and each asks the questions.

"What about me, Amato?"

"When are you going to find my killer, Amato?'

"Did you forget about me, Amato?"

"Why haven't you solved my case, Amato?"

And finally, two new characters in this long-running, repeated dream come forward, and they also pull away the smooth skin. However, even before they have it removed, I know who they are...Becky Chilsom and Traci Taylor.

I am crying now and begging for forgiveness, promising to work harder, to dig deeper, to labor longer. Through my tears I see the group part in the center, and from the back there comes a new victim, a short, young victim. He...maybe she...stands in front of me and makes no attempt to remove the skin covering the faceless face. Although the identity is not shown, I know who this child is.

It's the next victim!

I woke in a desperate attempt to suck air into my deprived lungs. My heaving, rapid, deep-breathing chest causes the tiny streams of perspiration to move quickly down my face and drip off my nose and chin.

Out of bed I curse the dream...and the night...and the killers. Max lifts his head, looks at me with serious regard and then rests his chin between his paws. He has seen the results of the dream before and he knows there is nothing he can do.

Saturday morning began with a quick drive down Silver Street. Bobby St. John's warning about the difficulty of the surveillance became instantly apparent. The street is narrow, and as it travels east from the area of the Bulls Head shopping area for about five blocks, Silver Street suddenly makes a sharp curve to the left, where it narrows even more. Once the street passes Wayne Graham's residence, it then turns sharply to the right, runs parallel with about six or seven pairs of railroad tracks on the left and a couple of homes on the right; it climbs a small hill, and then abruptly ends where a bridge over Saxton Street had once existed.

"Do you see what I mean?" Bobby asked me. "If we go around the bend so we can see his house, we're almost on top of him."

"And," Romano interjected, "if we sit back here, we can't see his house."

"No doubt about it," I acknowledged. "But, on the other hand, he can't leave the house in a car without us seeing him. If he comes out of the driveway and turns left, he hits the railroad tracks and there's no way a car is going to make it over those tracks. If he goes straight, he hits the dead end where Silver Street used to cross over Saxton Street. Therefore, he has to turn right and come out this way, straight at us."

"But he can leave on foot, cross over the tracks over to Maple Street, and we'll never see him," Romano observed.

"Right you are, Tommy," I conceded with a healthy slap on the back of the shorter man. "But I don't really think he's going to walk away from here, snatch a kid up, and run down the street with her...do you?"

For the teams it was a long, boring day that turned out be a long, boring weekend for the entire squad. As far as any of us knew, Wayne Graham never left his home. Each of us took a turn at the surveillance and each of us felt stupid and useless sitting there, waiting for...for what?

On Sunday morning, I caught a glimpse of my mug on the front page of the paper, alongside a caption announcing, "The Rochester Police Department's best-known detective is featured in today's

Rochester's People feature on page B1 of the Sunday *Democrat and Chronicle*."

My groan attracted Max's attention and he cocked his ears as he turned his head to one side. "The squad and the rest of the frigging department will be busting my balls for a month over this," I explained to the dog who seemed somewhat perplexed that I was trying to explain human social interplay to him.

The article, no Pulitzer Prize winner, did a nice job of pumping up the entire squad and reassuring the citizenry that we were hot on the trail of the killer who was tracking and abducting their children. It also—with some degree of overkill—did its intended job of painting me as a superior detective who was more than the equal of any killer. To me it reaffirmed what I had already told Max...I was going to take a lot of ball breaking over the article.

A couple of hours before being relieved on the Sunday surveillance, I made some excuse to Donovan about me needing to leave early. Once out of the area, I called Detective Gail Walz.

"Hi, Gail. This is Amato," I announced into the tiny mouthpiece of the cell phone.

"How you doing, Lute?" she asked almost cautiously. "Do you need me and Jimmy to come out early and relieve you and Donovan?"

"No, no need for that. You can come in at your regular time. But I need to talk to you, and I was wondering if maybe I could stop by and just see you for a few minutes, a couple of minutes." I felt uncomfortable making the call to my female subordinate, and then felt more uncomfortable when I realized I wouldn't feel this uncomfortable if I were calling one of the guys. Then, like an idiot, I added, "It's about the job. It's not personal."

"Oh good, Lute," she kind of laughed into the phone. "I was wondering if maybe you were hitting on me."

As I took directions on how to get to her place, I realized I was blushing over my stupid babbling about my visit being official police business.

Twenty minutes later I was being greeted at Detective Gail Walz's door by a kid about eight, maybe ten years old.

"Hi," the little girl said to me cheerfully. "You must be Lieutenant Amato. I'm Wendy. My mom will be down in minute."

"Hi," I responded in similar cheer. "I'm Mike. You can call me Mike."

Wendy Walz corrected me and, with some chagrin on her part, let me know that her mother didn't allow her to refer to grownups by their first names. "So, it has to be Lieutenant Amato, or Mister Amato. Which one do you like?"

Before I could answer, Gail presented herself at the top of the stairs apologizing for keeping me waiting. Although dressed in a pair of jeans and a sweatshirt—one that did little to conceal she had not bothered with a bra this early afternoon—I was struck by the beauty of her person and her manner. After I apologized for interrupting her off-duty time, she assured me it was perfectly fine, and we moved into the kitchen where I was offered coffee. In the meantime, the kid, Wendy, disappeared. As Gail assembled cups, saucers, sugar, cream, spoons, and some cookies, we made small talk. And, as we talked, I found myself acknowledging the fact that if she didn't work for me, I would very well be hitting on her.

Once coffee was poured, Gail put her elbows on the table, laced her fingers together and rested her chin on the backs of her hands. Her cocked eyebrows told me she wanted me to tell her why I was there, in her kitchen, having coffee.

"It's about Jimmy," I said as I raised the cup to my lips. "His wife called me and she's, ah, she's very concerned about him."

"About what? Why?" Gail asked with noted concern.

"She thinks he's coming apart. She says he doesn't eat, can't sleep, and that he spends every waking moment talking about these murders." I saw that Walz wasn't going to volunteer anything that may have compromised her partner's place on the squad, so I asked the question. "What about you? Do you see it too?"

Rather than answer without thinking, the experienced detective took a sip of coffee, placed the cup carefully back into the saucer and only then looked at me eye-to-eye.

"The case *is* having an impact on Jimmy. He's into it too much." Realizing that last statement may have hurt her partner, she back-pedaled a little. "I don't think he's going off the deep end or anything like that, but it's been eating at him." Without waiting for the question, she explained. "The first victim, the Chilsom kid, looks very much like Tamara, Jimmy's youngest child. He can't get past the fact that it could have been Tamara laying there in the vacant lot on Scrantom Street."

"Then his wife is right?" I asked.

"Mike, I'm going to lay it out for you this way. Jane Paskell doesn't like Jimmy and me working together. The bottom line is she thinks we're screwing each other. And, before you ask, no we are not! She's been pressuring Jimmy to get a transfer and get out of the squad just so he'll be away from me."

"So, are you telling me that she's blowing smoke up my butt about him being close to a nervous breakdown?"

"Jimmy is taking this case very, *very* much to heart…maybe too much. But, what I'm saying is his wife may have had other motives in calling you."

We talked a little about some of the things Jimmy was doing, and whether or not he was putting himself, the case, or his partner in danger. Gail summed it all up by saying, "Yes, he could crack. I don't think he will. I *really* don't think he will. He's just going through a lot right now. His wife is leaning on him. Becky Chilsom's similarity to Tamara rocked him. He thinks you don't like him or trust him. It's all just hitting him hard right now."

"But, the only salient question here is, do I pull him off the case? Is leaving him on the case going to hurt him—or the case—in the long run?"

Gail began shaking her head in the negative before I finished the question. "Taking him off the case is just going to make things worse," she offered solemnly. "He'll think you don't respect him, trust him, whatever, and it will probably put him over the edge. I'll keep an eye on him, and if it begins to look like he, well, if it seems that he can't handle it, I'll let you know."

"But for now? Do you think he's handling it for now?"

"For *now*…he's okay."

Monday came and went without any new developments on the case. Romano and St. John went looking for Graham's parents, and although they obtained an address for the couple, they didn't find them at home. Tuesday also was uneventful…right up until 4:30 in the afternoon. It was then, as we were about to call it a day, the phone rang. It was George Capwell calling to say that Graham had borrowed the red Honda for the evening.

"He just told me he had to have it tonight, that there was something he had to do ever since the weekend, and he had to take care of it tonight," Capwell told Romano.

"What is it that he has to do, and why the hell couldn't he do it this weekend?" the detective asked the caller.

"I don't know what he has to do tonight, but this past weekend I had one car tied up with repairs and I needed the other one," Capwell answered. "All I know is he just said he had to have some wheels for tonight. He said he had some unfinished business from the weekend, and he had to take care of something tonight."

That short call threw the squad into overdrive. Arrangements were quickly made to watch Graham all night long, from the second he got home from work, until the minute he left for work the next morning. Donovan hammered out a schedule and immediately afterward the squad began to make calls home. One by one, they advised their families that whatever was planned for the night needed to be modified because the cop in the family was either going to be working late or catching some sleep to relieve the ones who were going to be working late.

We needed to cover the suspect for about 14 hours, that is, if he went to work the next morning. If he stayed home on Wednesday, the surveillance would have to cover over 36 hours. It felt like Graham was yanking our chain...and by the next day we would find out that was exactly what he had done.

During the entire night, Wayne Graham never left the house. The red Honda remained parked in his driveway throughout the evening, nighttime and early morning hours. At 7:22 a.m. he got into the car and drove directly to work.

At eight in the morning, the squad assembled in the squad room to assault the absent suspect with a stream of venom in the form of curses and obscenities. He had once again let us know he knew we were on to him...and once again, he had had fun doing it.

The parents of Wayne Graham made their home in the Town of Irondequoit, a suburb to the northeast of Rochester. The house was an older, but very stylish residence on Kenmore Lane, which sat back off the roadway in a covey of trees. What the detectives had learned in the interview was relayed to the rest of us as we sat around the squad room Thursday morning.

It had been Wednesday evening—after normal work hours and before they pulled their turn on the surveillance—when Bobby St. John and Tommy Romano finally had an opportunity to talk to the Grahams, the adoptive parents of Wayne. Now the squad needed to know how they fit into the killer's life…and his mind.

Florence and Lewis Graham had met during their first teaching assignment at Wilson High School. They dated for a few years, were engaged for two more, and finally married just as Lewis took on the role of a vice principal. Their attempts at having a family were unsuccessful, so after seven years of marriage, they finally sought to adopt a child of their own.

Wayne Grankovski entered their lives as they approached their early-30's. The boy was almost five at the time, and although he had developed some poor personal behaviors, the nurturing of the Grahams eventually put him, as Florence labeled it, "…on the correct path for life." Lewis Graham made it a point to describe how he had prompted, encouraged, and scolded his young charge to do well in school and to mold him into a respectful adolescent who always obeyed and showed respect.

By the time their son started high school the relationship between father and son was becoming hostile. It opened up into a wide abyss when Wayne was found to have been the one who killed the school mascot. Although the elderly woman saw the act as a "boyish prank," she felt it totally crushed her husband and it forced him to retire earlier than he had planned. The father, on the other hand, saw the act as "open rebellion" that was meant to embarrass him in front of his colleagues and force him to give up his chosen career.

"How often do they see him?" Paskell asked.

"She says she hasn't seen him in more than three years and has no idea where he might be," Tommy Romano responded. "The old man told us basically the same thing…and he also doesn't care where the kid is."

"Did you find anything pointing toward abuse?" I asked.

Bobby St. John spoke up. "There's no doubt in my mind there was mental abuse. The father made no attempt to conceal the fact that he berated the child, scolded him in public, and humiliated him in front of his playmates because of his poor grades."

"They came right out and said that?" Walz asked with disbelief.

"The old fart bragged about it," Romano stated flatly in his less than charming manner. "He told us he would make Wayne wear a cardboard sign around his neck that read, 'Stupid.' He had the kid wear it even while he was on the school bus, both to and from school."

That evening I called Doc McGill and gave him a rundown on the background information the team had gathered from the Grahams.

"It's consistent, Mike. I would think there's probably more in the suspect's background as far as abuse, even sexual abuse, but this here, this stuff you learned today from the parents, is consistent with the type of murderer you're looking for."

By the time Friday night rolled around, I—along with the entire squad—felt a begrudged relief that the week was over. It had been a miserable week of waiting, hoping, and expecting. The seven miserable days and nights had amounted to a big, fat zero. Other than the background information we had obtained from the Grahams, nothing had been accomplished. Twice our suspect had teased us, had dangled the carrot in front of our eyes, and twice we had lunged…and fallen flat on our faces.

I took my solace in a bottle of Scotch. Alone in the apartment, with only Ella Fitzgerald, the Dorsey Brothers, and Glenn Miller for company, I found I couldn't rest, couldn't sit still. The cold weather outside forced me to remain inside. Although the comfort of a bar would have been a welcomed change of scenery, I knew I was bent on getting mind-numbing drunk and didn't relish the thought of driving in that condition.

We needed something to break this case loose, to jar it from the benign stillness in which it had settled. We had to come up with something that would push the case forward. My brooding mood reminded me I was, in essence, hoping for the killer to strike again— and I hated the thought and myself for thinking it. At this point, with what we had, there was nothing we could do to reach Wayne Graham and drag his ass into court. We would need more, and in order to get more he would have to do more.

Half a city away the killer shared my thoughts. He knew that if he was to attract the attention he needed, the attention for which he lusted, the attention he coveted, he would have to kill again…and he was more than willing to do so.

CHAPTER ELEVEN

FAST AND FURIOUS

The phone's ring forced me out of a deep sleep. The instant pain from too much Scotch ran across my forehead and throbbed behind my eyeballs as I raised myself off the couch and made a valiant effort to stand with a steady balance.

"Lute, this is Jimmy. I think Graham just snatched a kid!"

"What? When? How do you know?" I asked in rapid succession.

"It just came over the radio. Some guy in a van, a black van, grabbed a kid off the sidewalk over on Lozier Street."

My mind couldn't decipher the information. Paskell and Walz were supposed to be on a day off. How did he get this information off the radio? Why didn't we know that Graham had George Capwell's van? What the hell was going on?

Although I couldn't formulate any of the questions into a complete thought, Paskell interpreted my mumbling and explained.

"I was out, kind of just checking. I was going to take a ride past Graham's place and see what was going on. Just as I got around Bulls Head, I heard the call go out for a possible abduction on Lozier Street. It's right off of West Avenue, about five-or-six blocks from where I was, so I headed up here. The call is righteous. A little boy, about seven-years-old was grabbed right off the street while he was walking with two other friends."

I had a fleeing thought about admonishing Jimmy for coming in on his day off—after all the bitching his wife was doing about the hours he was assigned to work—but let it go. What he had done had demonstrated his loyalty to his job and to the members of his squad.

The sun coming in through the open blinds and a quick glance at my wristwatch told me it was almost 10 o'clock in the morning. I just wasn't clear on whether it was Saturday morning or Sunday morning. Without trying to resolve the question, I advised Paskell I would be at the scene in less than a half-hour, and then gave him instructions to call in the entire squad.

After a one-minute shower and enough time to throw on some slacks, a shirt and sweater, arm myself, and make sure I had the necessary tools of the trade, Max was shuffled down to his babysitters, Josephine Maira and Ann Salber, and I was on my way. Once the car hit the expressway, I called Major Winston and gave him the news.

Lozier Street is in a middle-class section of the city's west side. The homes sit back, about 30 or 40 feet off the street. The deep front yards compliment the large two-story homes, many of which are topped by an attic that give the homes the appearance of being three-story residences. With the exception of five marked cars and three unmarked cop cars clustered around one home, the tree-lined neighborhood offered no evidence that it had been marked by violence. Number 74 Lozier Street fit in well with the other large, wooden, clapboard homes.

As I exited the car I looked down the street to my left and was struck by the irony that a child had been abducted less than a couple of hundred steps from the light brown, brick sanctuary of Saint Augustine's Church.

Once inside the home I grabbed Paskell aside and instructed him to get down to Graham's house post haste. "If the van is there, let me know and I'll get down there. If we have to, we'll drag the son-of-a-bitch out of the house."

Lt. Mark Moran filled me in on the details. "The kid, one Timothy Bidwell, was walking south on Lozier Street with two of his friends. Their destination was a grocery store on Chili Avenue. When they were only three houses south of the Bidwell home, a black van quickly pulled into a driveway, blocking the sidewalk in front of the two boys and a girl. A man—no real description yet—got out of the van, darted around the front of it, and suddenly grabbed the little girl. The kid pulled away and started to scream. She got away and began to run along with the other boy. Our victim must have froze, because he just stood there. When the victim's friends looked back, they saw the man dragging the kid into the van."

"Do we have a pick-up out for the van yet?"

"Yeah," Moran confirmed. "But, it isn't much. All we have is an older black van. No plate, no make, model, nothing specific."

"Here's what you're looking for," I said as I jotted down a complete description and plate number for Capwell's van. "My guess is the suspect's going to head for the east or north side of the city."

With that out of the way, I called the dispatcher and had a car sent over to George Capwell's home, with instructions for the car's driver to call me as soon as he made contact with the man. As I handed Lt. Moran's radio back to him, I saw Frank Donovan pull up to the curb. Detective Walz opened the passenger door before the car came to a full stop.

"I guess Paskell's already in, so I slipped by and picked up Gail on the way," Donovan said. In the same breath he asked, "So what have we got?"

I gave the two a one-minute briefing, and then repeated it again as Bobby St. John and Tommy Romano joined us at the curbside meeting. With all of us caught up on the morning's events, it was time to pass out assignments.

"Jimmy is covering Graham's house. I want you, Frank, along with Gail, to stay here. Frank, you get everything you need from the parents. Gail, I want you to hit the parents of the kid that was grabbed and broke free. Let's make sure this isn't a case of attempted custodial abduction. If that's the case, maybe when the suspect couldn't get the kid he wanted, he grabbed the next available kid. I'm damn sure that's not the case, but let's cover the angle anyway. When you two get done with that, I want you covering the neighborhood all the way up to Chili Avenue, and all the way down to West Avenue. I'll get Moran to kick in a few guys to help out. I want someone to give us a better description on that van." I took a breath and then turned to the next team. "Bobby, you get over to Capwell's place and find out if Graham borrowed his van, and, by the way, if Graham does have the van, find out why the hell Capwell didn't call us like he promised he would do! Tommy, you get in the office and type up a description of the van from this morning's snatch, and then add in the fact the suspect may be driving the black and primer van owned by Capwell. Put in every damn detail you can on the van, including— and especially—the plate number. Don't hold back a damn thing. Get that info faxed out to every blessed police agency in the county and all five bordering counties, including the State Police. Do not, I repeat, do not put out anything over the radio. I don't want the media jerks picking it up. Do everything by phone or fax. Also, make sure the departments you talk to understand we want a tight lid on the information regarding the van. Once you're done with that, get back here and help cover the neighborhood."

"When do you want to meet up again, Lute?" Romano asked.

"We'll meet back here in two hours unless you're onto something hot. In any event, stay in touch." Checking each head for an affirmative nod, I added, "I'm going down to meet with Jimmy, make sure he's squared away, and tell him to sit still and advise us if Graham shows up. However, and listen up to this, I don't want one, single, goddamn word going out over the radio about Graham or Silver Street. If Jimmy sees the bastard, I told him to call me for a 'coffee meet'. Then, I'm heading for the east side of the city and look for this van."

"Where on the east side?" Bobby asked. "Do you have an idea where he might be?"

"No ideas, only hunches," I admitted. "He grabbed the Chilsom girl on the west side and dumped her on the east side. After he abducted the Taylor girl way up north, in Charlotte, he put her over on the south side of the city. This Bidwell kid got grabbed almost on the damn border between the south side and the north side of the city, but well into the west side. My guess is that he's going to put him over on the east side…maybe around George Capwell's place."

Just as we began to disburse, Major Skip Winston showed up with Deputy Chief Ernie Cooper right on his bumper. Once again I went through the briefing, adding what assignments had been made. When Cooper asked how much he should tell the press, I shot him a look that was meant to question his sense of priorities.

"You can tell them anything you want to, Deputy. Just don't mention Silver Street, don't confirm anything about the van, and don't mention Graham."

"What if they ask if this is connected to the other two abductions?" the pseudo cop asked.

"Tell them that every possible lead is being explored." I paused and added, "I'm just afraid that sooner or later the media group is going to hear some transmission going out for the van on some damn police department's radio system. If that comes up, tell them the van was seen in the area and we're not sure if it's involved but we're playing it safe by trying to locate the van because it may contain a witness. Just don't mention Graham or Silver Street. If you do, we're going to be in front of Chief Murphy tomorrow morning, he's going to want one of our asses...and Deputy, I swear to God, I'll hand him yours!"

With that said, I left the two bosses standing there. There was work to do.

Almost three hours later, the squad, minus Jimmy Paskell, met in the parking lot of St. Augustine's Church. The neighborhood check had come up with two people, luckily on opposite sides of the streets, who saw the van pulling away at a fair rate of speed, slow down at the corner of Chili Avenue, and then turn right, toward the west. One was sure there was gray primer paint on the van; the other witness wasn't sure. The best description we could get on the driver from any of the witnesses, including Tim Bidwell's two small friends, was that the guy was white and kind of young, but not too young...whatever the hell that meant!

Bobby St. John provided us with the Capwell story. "He says he was home this morning and around seven-thirty our boy Wayne showed up at his door. Graham told him he had spent the night with a young lady who lived in the area and that he was now on his way home. Our guy gives Capwell a song and dance about needing to do some laundry and a little food shopping, and asks to borrow the van or car for a few hours, up until about noon or so. Capwell gives him the keys to the van, and because his old lady is harping at him about taking her down to the Public Market before everything gets picked over, he goes ahead and takes her, but neglects to call us."

"Screw him," Tommy Romano commented casually. "He was a contender, but now I'm not putting his name in for the Good Citizen of the Year Award!"

Gail Walz looked at the smiling detective and said coldly, "Shut the hell up, Romano. I'm getting tired of your crap!"

"Alright!" I said with notable exasperation over the bickering that was becoming all too routine for the squad. "We don't need that shit right now!" With everyone's attention now solidly back on the case, my next instruction was for Romano to sit on Capwell's house and wait for Graham to return with the van.

"And, if he shows up…?" Tommy asked.

"Pick his ass up and get that truck secured for the evidence people!" I said with some disbelief that the detective even had to ask the question.

In response to a radio call from Paskell, I ran a fresh cell phone battery down to his location. Once there, we discussed the possibility that Graham was already in the house.

"I was thinking," Paskell said pensively. "Maybe he took care of the kid, dumped the van, and came back here on foot…maybe over the railroad tracks from Maple Street."

I gave the proposal some thought and conceded it may be possible, but unlikely.

"I'm going over to the Maple Street side of the tracks and cover that area myself," I said. "But, Jimmy, right now I smell gas, natural gas. So, in 10, maybe 15 minutes there's going to be a hell of a lot of fire trucks showing up here. When the uniform cops get here, pull one of them aside and make sure they evacuate about four, five houses…Graham's house included, of course. That way we'll know for sure if the bastard is in there or not."

I left the detective and made one stop at a phone booth. With the anonymous call having been made to the fire department, I drove up and down Maple Street and every cross street for eight or ten blocks. There was no black van to be seen. However, just as I completed the check of the first side street, I heard sirens—a lot of them—coming from across the tracks.

Ten minutes later, Jimmy Paskell's voice came over the radio and advised me, "Nobody's home, Lieutenant."

It was turning out to be a miserable day! And to make matters worse, it was starting to snow.

The day that had begun like a heart attack ended with a murmur. Wayne Graham, the black van, and Timothy Bidwell were nowhere to be found. The repeated broadcasts for the vehicle produced nothing. Because the man we hunted had no known friends or even passing acquaintances, we had no place to look for him. Although he had not visited or talked to his parents in over three years, Bobby St. John stopped by to see them. It led to nothing. Without any place to go or anything to do, the squad ground to a halt.

Not bothering to be coy about it at this point, we had even canvassed Graham's neighborhood. As far as the other residents of the street were concerned, the man was a ghost. No one knew him, few could even picture him, and everybody agreed he must be a nice guy because he never bothered anyone.

Tommy Romano was quick to point out, "After we bust Graham, each and every one of his neighbors will be thrilled to put their puss in front of a television camera and say how well they knew him, and how shocked and amazed they are now that they've learned he was a killer."

At ten o'clock Saturday night we had dropped back to the twenty-yard line and prepared to punt. We were out of things to do, however, no one was prepared to leave. Each one of us wanted to do one more thing…anything, but we had no idea what to do. A child was out there, somewhere in the cold night; the child was with a killer and we were supposed to cage that killer.

Paskell and Walz were ordered to go home and get some sleep so they could pick up the Silver Street and Capwell surveillance in the morning. While Romano and St. John maintained the stakeouts for a few hours, I picked the lock on Major Winston's office door and curled up on his couch for a few hours of sleep.

From two in the morning until Detective Paskell relieved me at eight in the morning, I sipped coffee, smoked cigarettes, and sucked sweet, hard candy. I'm sure I must have nodded off a few times—I was getting too old for this shit—but Graham and the van never showed. To fight boredom and sleep, I twice left the warmth of the car and walked in the cold night past the place Wayne Graham called his home. Once I even went into his backyard and peeked into the windows, but there was nothing to see in the darkness.

At 6:10 a.m., just as the false dawn was stealing into the night's darkness, I stepped out of the car once more and lit one more cigarette. The thought I was holding in my head angered and annoyed me, for I knew that as I was standing there with my thumb up my ass, Wayne Graham was very likely killing an innocent child, playing with the corpse…and preparing it for public display. The mental pictures galled me and made my stomach queasy.

Even though I was but a lowly lieutenant, in cases such as this I could demand—and get—a small army of cops, cars, dogs and a helicopter with the snap of a finger. On my say-so alone, I could spend thousands, even tens of thousands of the city's money if it led to the capture of the killer. I had the power and authority to do that, and yet, as the night was bearing witness, I was powerless to stop one man…or to even find that one man.

Sunday was more of the same. Except for taking Max for a long walk, I watched football or dozed all day. I kept the phone by my side, but it never interrupted my day to tell me it was over, to let me know the animal had been caged, and then to sooth my conscience so I could find peace.

Again, late that night I took my share of the surveillance, and again smoked cigarettes, sucked candy, and drank coffee. Again, false dawn stirred and again it found me angry and disillusioned. Again, Jimmy Paskell pulled up behind me, killed his headlights and moved in to take over the mindless task of waiting for a killer to show up.

"It's Monday, Lute. Something has to break today," he said and I wondered if he was trying to cheer me up or convince himself.

"Why, Jimmy? Do you think this prick is worried about losing his job?"

"Not that," he said with a hint of hurt in his tone of voice. "It's just that he's never kept a kid this long before."

Then, like lightning out of the gray morning sky, came the news we wanted and feared, hoped for and wished against. It came in the form of a short message over the radio. The dispatcher simply, without emotion or passion, requested of me, "Call Dispatch by landline, A-SAP."

"Amato here," I said into the cell phone's folding mouthpiece after the Emergency Communication's Operator identified herself with a three-digit identification number that meant nothing to me.

"Lieutenant, we received two calls from citizens about a boy's body being found over on Driving Park Avenue. We didn't put it out over the air but we had a car check it out. An officer is there now and he has a body." The woman's cool, professional, *I-can-deal-with-anything* voice broke a little when she added, "It's the boy. He says it's the Bidwell boy."

In thirty seconds I obtained the location of the body, told Jimmy what was going on and ordered him to stay put. With the cell phone in one hand to call in the squad, I made a wide U-turn right where Silver Street forks off to Dengler Street, and pushed the car west, back up Silver Street, zigzagged up to West Avenue, past Lozier Street where the victim had lived a normal, happy, healthy life, and onto Buffalo Road. I almost lost the ass end of the car going under a narrow underpass, then gunned the motor again, blowing the red light at Glide Street, and turned right onto the wide six lanes of Mount Read Boulevard.

Once on Mount Read, I accelerated again, slowing only for the red lights encountered along the way. The car bumped and thumped over spotty, broken pavement which had been opened up by winter freezes that had been repaired often, but—in true Rochester fashion—had never really been fixed.

As I approached Driving Park Avenue, I had to break hard in order to negotiate the right hand turn. Slowing to a reasonable 30-or-35 miles an hour, the car glided past about 400, maybe 500 feet of chain-link fence on my right and small brick buildings, loading docks, and empty trailer trucks on my left.

There, directly opposite Newberry Street, on a seemingly endless stretch of seven-foot chain-link fence, right next to a white square sign with black characters announcing, "North Lot #4", hung the limp, dead body of Timothy Bidwell.

Stepping out of the car, I looked up at the face of the boy. The collar of his jacket was hooked on the top of the fence. His arms were pulled out to the sides and the sleeves of his tiny jacket were carefully placed over the very top of the fence line. His head was tilted to the left and his face—the innocent face of boyhood—held a look of peaceful sleep.

I knew it right then. I felt it in my heart. I could kill, *would kill*, in merciless cold blood, the son-of-a-bitch who did this.

"Christ on a cross!" I said to myself not in exclamation, but rather in remembrance of another limp, lifeless body I had knelt in front of so often when I had been an altar boy at Saint Lucy's Church, three-quarters of a lifetime ago.

A marked cop car blocked the driveway and the driver of the car sent the arriving workers to the next entrance, farther west along the fence line. Two other cop cars blocked the sidewalk, each one about 100 feet east of where my victim hung by his jacket. Yellow crime scene tape stretched from one car to the other, to the other.

Lt. Laurie Shannon, the uniformed commanding officer at the scene, approached me and I thanked her for the job she had done in protecting the scene. As I spoke to her, I realized I couldn't take my eyes off the face of the boy hanging on the fence.

"I've got some good young cops working for me, Mike. They always do a nice job, but I know they would appreciate hearing it from you."

I nodded at her request and asked for the rundown of what had transpired at this hellish scene.

"I got a call from Dispatch to call them on a phone. When I called they told me they had a report from an unknown citizen that there was a body hanging on a fence out here. I was about five minutes away, responding with lights and siren on as I called Officer Gonzorelli—they call him 'Gonzo'—and told him to meet me at this location A-SAP. He got here a half-minute before me. When I saw what we had, we closed down the scene. That's about it, Mike."

"Do we have the caller?"

"Yeah. He's the guy in the blue jacket, over there by Chris Tucker's car. I don't think he knows anymore than he already told us. Basically, he's worked here about three years, always uses this gate, and drove in today just like he always does. As he made the turn off the street, he caught the kid in the corner of his eye, stopped, and couldn't believe what he was seeing."

"Lieutenant?" a voice over my right shoulder asked. "Can we take him down now?" I turned and saw it was the young, monster-sized copper Laurie had called, 'Gonzo'.

"Not yet, kid. We have a lot of tech work to do. Once the technicians get here and go over the place for tire prints, shoe prints, fibers on the fence, all that stuff, then we'll take him down." I saw the young cop's face, and it was a look I knew well. It was the look that accused me of being a heartless bastard, one who cared little for the dead and worried only about the investigation.

"Well, if I'm real careful about it, can I go over to the other side of the fence and put a blanket over the kid?"

"No," was my instant reply. And then, in answer to the cop's cold look, I explained, "Let me just take a quick look around first. Okay? It's a good thought, but any blanket you put on the body will weaken our case later. If we find fibers or hairs on the body, the defense will say it came off your blanket."

"Sure, Lieutenant," the cop said earnestly. "Go ahead, but don't leave him up there much longer. Okay?"

"I'm sure Lieutenant Amato appreciates your permission to take his time," Lt. Shannon said to Officer Gonzo with a wink in my direction over the brashness of her young subordinate. Before the wink disappeared, she gave the uniformed hunk a hefty smack on his back.

The snow on the ground was at least twelve hours old. It had snowed the day before and the temperature had stayed below freezing. That kept the snow loose to move around in the constant Rochester wind. Some of it packed along the base of the fence line below where the victim hung. Less than six inches from the fence the ground was clear of the white stuff that could have been very helpful in registering some tire marks.

My best guess was that Graham had pulled his borrowed van up to the fence, pulled the body out of the car, and then carefully arranged it. As high as the body was off of the ground, I guessed the murdering piece of shit must have had to stand on the hood of the van. Maybe he pulled up alongside the fence and stood on the floor of the van as he reached up from the side door to get Bidwell's jacket caught on the twisted top of the fence line. I didn't know how he did it and I didn't care. There was no need for me to care, because in a few hours, maybe a day, Wayne Graham would tell me how he did it. He would tell me because he wanted to…or maybe he would tell me because he would no longer be able to stand me squeezing his balls. However, one way or another, the animal was going to tell me.

About that time, the first of several crime scene technicians arrived at the scene. As I began to discuss what was needed from the crime scene cops, Detective Paskell called me on the radio.

"I've got company over here, Lute," Jimmy said.

"Switch over," I said into my portable radio, not wanting to talk to him on this open frequency.

Once we both got the tiny knobs on the radios turned to a secure frequency, I asked guardedly, "Is it our guy?"

"It is, and he's got the wheels."

Knowing that every other member of the squad had automatically switched over, I asked, "Bobby? Are you with us? Gail? Tommy?"

"Go ahead, Boss," Walz said with some excitement in her voice.

"Get over with Jimmy right now. Quick. I want both of you to sit directly in front of his house. One of you park your car right across his driveway. Make sure he sees you. Now I want *him* to know that *we* know!"

"We're going that way too," Romano's voice almost screamed over the radio.

Assuming that he and St. John were already together, I ordered, "Negative! You two get down here to Driving Park, just east of Mt. Read Boulevard." Then, with silence restored, I asked more calmly, "Jimmy? You still on this side?"

"I'm here, Lute."

"If he stays in the house, just leave him be. But, if he comes out of the house, pick him up."

Those last three words would come back to haunt me next summer. However, right then, they sounded oh so sweet.

Fifteen minutes later St. John pulled his car in behind mine. Romano jumped out of the passenger side before Bobby brought the car to a complete stop. Looking at the form on the fence line, the detective silently made the Sign of the Cross.

"Bobby," I said before either of them had a chance to ask anything. "You and I are going to get into the building and start cranking out a search warrant on the van and the house. Tommy, I want you to stay here. You make sure the technicians get everything we need and make sure the ghouls from the Medical Examiner's Office handle that body with care. I don't want to lose one single hair or fiber. Also, get with the guy who found the body and dig out all the information you'll need in order to get into his background. Then meet us in the building."

"Lieutenant," St John said as he held up a hand to signal me to slow down. "I already have most of the search warrant for the van completed. The one of the house is about half done. I banged them out on my laptop yesterday while I was sitting on the surveillance over at Capwell's place. In an hour I'll have it done."

"Good!" I said. Then as an afterthought, I asked, "Laptop?"

"It's mine, my personal computer. I figured as long as I was sitting there, I might as well get a jump on it."

Ever the ball breaker, Romano lent his two cents. "It's kind of like a typewriter, only smaller. It's all electronic."

Man, I thought to myself, you got to love these guys! Instead of vocalizing the compliment, I told Romano to bite me and also advised him to get a ride back to Headquarters with one of Lieutenant Shannon's officers.

When I was five minutes from the office, Paskell called me on the radio and instructed, "Switch over."

Once on the tactical frequency, I heard my detective asking, "Are you here?"

"I'm here."

"He came out. I got him in the car."

"Is Walz with you?" I asked.

"She just got here."

"Have her stay with the vehicle. You bring him in." Again the three last words made me feel good…and again I failed to realize how I would someday have to eat those words.

CHAPTER TWELVE

WINDOW TO THE SOUL

It was 9:45 a.m. when Jimmy Paskell walked out of the interview room and found me in a the hallway. Although I expected to see a wide smile, I looked up and saw the face of a whipped puppy.

"He wants to talk to you," the detective said somberly.

"Tell him I'm not here."

"That won't work," Paskell said so low I had to strain in order to hear him. "He's insistent on talking to you."

"Jimmy, tell him I'm not here!" I said more emphatically. Then taking it down a tone or two, I explained, "We can't give him his way. He can't control this thing. Just go in and tell him I took the morning off because the case is solved. You tell him that, and tell him he talks to you or he talks to no one."

"He's not stupid, Lute. He'll never believe that you're not in the office after we grabbed the guy who did a triple murder. He'll know I'm lying."

"Good!" was my one word note.

Without a word, Paskell left.

Ten minutes later Jimmy Paskell was standing in front of my desk.

"Look, Lute. I know what you're trying to do, but it isn't working. The guy wants to talk, he just won't talk to me. He says if I go in there one more time, he'll ask for a lawyer and then clam up."

"Fine!" I said as if it was a triumph. "Don't go back in! Fuck him! Let him sit there all alone. Go start your reports, and let the son-of-a-bitch sit there and stew."

Paskell left me without saying a word. I sat in my city-assigned cubicle. I hated sitting there. Every muscle in my body wanted to get me off the chair and move into that interview room. My ears wanted to listen to hear his whining explanation. My heart wanted to have the satisfaction of hearing this maniac talk his way into a death sentence. Graham demanded to be in control. He needed to have the upper hand. That control had to be wrestled from him; ripped away, just as he had ripped those children from their parents. If I was going to get into his head, I had to have control of his head. If he was going to get to talk to me it had to be on my terms, under my control.

It was now 10:05 a.m.

Twice my legs pushed me up, and twice I forced my ass back down into the chair. Finally I went down to the Technician's Unit and picked up a small plastic cup—one about the size of a shot glass—with a lid that snapped snugly on top of it.

I was back in my office at 10:17.

I poured myself a cup of coffee and fixed it with cream and sugar, along with a stiff shot of *Sambuca*. Forcing myself to be casual I checked in with Bobby St. John and learned he was printing out the search warrant for the van and Graham's house and would be heading down to court to get a judge to sign it. I told him to hold off on it and see what we could add to it after I had a confession or at least a partial confession from Graham. It was a good plan…or so I believed at the time.

It was 10:31 a.m.

I moved down the hallway and observed Wayne Graham through a one-way mirror. He was older looking than I had imagined him, but his thin frame and tussled hair fit the mental pictured I had formed of the killer. His slender, narrow face and pronounced thin nose made me think of an actor I had seen playing the role of Ichabod Crane. I sipped the coffee cup dry and then refilled it.

At 10:48 a.m. I slipped the small plastic cup and lid into the pocket of my sport coat, buttoned the top button of my shirt, and pulled up my tie. Picking up my full coffee cup—*sans* the

Sambuca—I walked to the interview room, whistling as I strolled. It was show time!

"**W**ayne, I'm Lieutenant Amato," I announced as I walked into the room. "I hear you want to talk to me."

"Yeah," he said with a thin grin. "Yes, I do. But, I don't like to be kept waiting like some common street criminal. Maybe now I don't feel like talking."

I nodded and put the plastic cup on the table. "Spit in the cup," I instructed.

"What?"

"I said, spit in the cup!"

"Why? What for?" the confused man asked.

"Do you want to talk to me?"

"Yes, but I…"

"Then spit in the damn cup!"

"I don't want to!" He was trying to be belligerent.

"Then have a nice fucking day!" I said, and turned to place my hand on the door.

"Wait. Why do I have to spit in a cup just to talk to you?"

"Because I want you to!" I took a step toward the seated, perplexed young man. "You asked to talk to me. I didn't ask to talk to you," I said loudly as I pointed to him on the first statement and then to my chest on the second. "Now if you want to talk to me, you're going to have to spit in the cup. Those are the rules! Live with it or, as I said before, have a nice fucking day."

Graham looked at me and then down at the cup. He then showed that he had an interesting habit, a 'tick' I guess is what you call it. This was the first time he exposed the trait, but it would pop up twenty more times through the day. On each occasion when Graham had something important to say—important to him—he opened his eyes wide and flicked his eyebrows high on his narrow brow.

"Hey now, I don't have to do this," he said with his eyes wide and his eyebrows arched. Then, giving me a wry smile to make it look like he was simply playing along with my stupid game, he reached for the cup, held it up to his chin, lowered his head and spit in the cup the way I wanted to spit in his face.

I picked the cup up, snapped the lid on top of it and put a red piece of evidence tape around the small container. I then scribbled my initials on the cup and stepped over to the door.

"See you in a couple of minutes," I said nonchalantly and left the room. Once in the hallway, I dropped the cup in the first wastebasket I found. Then, like a school kid, I took a few minutes to sneak in half a cigarette in the men's room.

Returning to the interrogation room and not bothering to sit down, I looked at the bastard with indifference. "So, what is it you want to talk to me about?" I asked as I shifted my attention to my right hand and picked at some imaginary dirt under the nail of my right index finger with my left thumb.

"Hey now, cut the act, Amato," Graham commanded angrily as his eyes grew for an instant. "You want to talk to me as much as I want to talk to you."

"I have no need to talk to you," I said without looking up. "And, it's *Lieutenant* Amato, to you, *Wayne*."

"That's bullshit! You *want* to talk to me, got to talk to me. I'll bet you've been dying to talk to me…to get me in here and talk to me."

"Why would you think that?" I asked with a hint of a chuckle in my throat. The words were spoken to him, but my face never moved from my fingertips.

"Because you want to solve the case. You want to arrest me and solve these murders, these kid murders."

"The case *is* solved, Wayne! It was solved almost three days ago. If you think this is some kind of whodunit, forget it! The case was solved the day you grabbed the Bidwell kid. Therefore, I have no need to talk to you." I was pushing hard, and I hoped not too hard. All of my lies and bullshit aside, I needed every utterance this guy made. Without his confession we had nothing!

"If you knew it was me and you had enough to pick me up two, three days ago, then why didn't you pick me up? Huh? Why didn't you arrest me back then on Thursday, Friday, whenever?" I stole a glance at him and saw his eyes widened and his eyebrows hunch up.

"We had you pretty well nailed down Thursday, Thursday afternoon to be exact. However, it takes time to get the paperwork pushed through the DA's Office and then over to a judge, so we never got the warrant approved and signed until Friday, around noon Friday." As long as I was telling a lie, I figured I might as well tell a big, detailed lie. "There were some things that came up Friday afternoon, a husband and wife killing over on the other side of town. So, to be perfectly frank, we got busy. Then you pulled the disappearing act on Saturday. Bing, bam, boom, with one thing and another, here we are."

"But you still need to talk to me. You still need a confession." He said the words, but it was comforting to hear the way he said it. His confidence was ebbing. He said the words but he didn't know if he believed what he was saying.

"Wayne, let me tell you something," I commented, still not having looked up at him. "You may not understand it, but I'll tell you anyway. I have seven witnesses who can put you at or immediately near where two of the kids were grabbed or where two of them were dropped off. Okay? Do you hear me? I also have George Capwell who ties you to the vehicles that were used on all three abductions. Are you getting the picture? There are some other things, forensic things, things you wouldn't understand. As I said, this is not a whodunit. This type of case is what we call a 'no brainer.' In other words, we don't need *you*...we have forensics, scientific facts, indisputable witness statements." Pausing again to remove another imaginary piece of dirt from under my fingernail, I let him absorb what I had said before adding, "So, like I said, you probably don't understand it all, but your lawyer will.

"Oh yeah? Try me. You'd be surprised at what I understand." The killer was testing me. I had opened the door. Now he wanted me to run in so he could learn what I had...and see if I was bluffing. And I was all too willing to oblige him...to taunt his brain and tease his thinking.

"Well, Wayne, let me put it to you this way. It is virtually impossible for you, for any person, to walk into a room and then go out of it without either leaving something behind or taking something with you." I looked up at him for the first time since handing him the plastic cup. It was necessary to insure he was listening, listening intently. He was, so I continued. "Sometimes you leave behind a little thread, or maybe you pick up a fiber. Then again, maybe it's a cat hair, or a dog hair, or a bit of dirt. Do you get the picture?"

He smiled at me. "So you want me to believe I left behind a fiber with one of the bodies?"

"No, no. Not at all! I don't want you to believe anything like that. But we digress. Allow me to continue, please."

"Please do," he said in exaggerated cordiality and a cocky smile that I wanted to knock off his kisser with a good left hook.

"Sometimes a killer gets smart. He plays it very carefully. He dresses the right way, and then throws away the clothes he wore so there won't be any fibers to compare. He's careful and doesn't leave fingerprints, doesn't track around a lot of crap. But then again, sooner or later, some little accident takes place, some weird thing happens, some little thing slips, and well…"

"Such as?" he asked while trying to sound bored, but his interruption was telling. He wanted to know where he had slipped up.

"Oh, I don't know, maybe…" I let the sentence trail off as if I was thinking of an example but Wayne Graham fully believed I was about to give him an idea of where he slipped up…and I wanted him to believe that was the case. In order for him to confess he would have to know, to believe, that we had him nailed dead to rights.

Continuing with the charade, I said, "Such as, he's choking a kid, you know, standing behind her and squeezing her neck. It's an emotional thing for him, for this hypothetical guy I'm talking about. He's squeezing the kid's neck and maybe he's crying, or maybe laughing, or maybe having an orgasm. Who the hell knows what these creeps think of when they're ringing a little kid's neck. Anyway, in the heat of the moment, maybe a little drop of sweat, or maybe a tear, maybe a small drop of drool—who the hell cares—falls onto the little girl's collar. Maybe there's even two, three, four of these little drops. They're really insignificant, those little drops. There's not much you can do with them. You can't analyze those little drops and come up with the killer's name, address, and Social Security number. It can't be done…until you get a guy to spit in a small plastic cup. Then you have something to compare…"

His eyes widened to the size of saucers and his eyebrows crawled up to his hairline as he interrupted, "DNA! You got me on DNA!"

I remained silent.

"You're good, Amato, er…ah, *Lieutenant* Amato."

"I try, Wayne. I really do try," I said with a boyish smile. Then turning my face instantly to a deadpan, I told him, "You wanted to talk to me. I've been talking to you for the past ten minutes. I don't have time to waste with bullshit, Graham! If you want to talk to me, you talk now. Otherwise, I'm gone."

"Sit down," the gaunt man invited as he pointed to a chair and crossed his thin right leg over the other, tucked his right ankle behind the left heel. "Let's talk."

I wanted to dance, to jump up and down with crazy happiness. The son-of-a-bitch bought my bullshit. He went for it hook, line, and sinker! I had him! He was mine. I owned the bastard!

My play had already been made. It was now time for him to make his. Wayne Graham had to think of how he was going to say what he so desperately wanted to say. He needed a moment to decide how he was going to do that. I gave him that moment, then I stood and moved toward the door.

"How was your father with you, Lieutenant?" the man asked as I approached the door to leave the room.

"He was okay. He was strict, but he was okay."

"Well, hey now, mine is a cruel, selfish, egotistical bastard," he said evenly, without emotion, as if he was simply commenting on the color of paint on the walls.

I turned away from the door and walked the two-and-a-half steps back to the chair. Without sitting down, I asked, "So?" The question was casual but my ears were smiling at hearing him again use the phrase, "Hey now," once again.

"As far as my father is concerned, I was never good enough for him. I wasn't up to the Graham standard." He paused for a few seconds, gazed out the window and then continued. "Do you know what he called me, what his favorite name was for me?" It was a rhetorical question, so I merely widened my eyes and arched my eyebrows. It was a gesture Wayne would subconsciously recognize and accept. "He called me 'dummy'. I was his little 'dummy.' Dummy this and dummy that. In front of my friends, relatives, the neighbors, I was a dummy."

I sat down and was looking at him now. With a widening of my eyes and a flick of my eyebrows, I fed him back his own signal to let him know I thought he was making an important point. When he began to speak, I studied his long face that was somewhat shallow without being emaciated. The man had a full head of black hair that was tussled in such a way it made me wonder if he owned a comb.

If the nuns were correct in their teachings—that the eyes are the window of the soul—this son-of-a-bitch had no soul. His sunken eyeballs hid in the shadow of his puffy eyebrows. They were somber and yet cold; sad, but conniving and calculating. I had looked long and deep into the eyes of many homicide suspects. Some of those eyes had been sad and weeping; others were smiling and gladdened; still others had been challenging and confronting. But these eyes, these hallow, concave eyes of Wayne Graham were truly the eyes of a killer.

Returning from my mental lapse, I heard the man across the table from me saying, "When I got into high school, I wanted to go out for the football team. He didn't want me to play football. But, hey, I was a young kid and kind of at that rebellious stage, so I went out for the team anyway. Do you know what he did to me?"

My only response was to look at him without any sign of emotion, without any concern. I needed him to open up and he would only do that if I remained casual and he felt the need to ply me with details.

His eyes bulged under eyebrows that leaped as he said, "He made me wear my football helmet twenty-four hours a day. I had to wear it to bed, to dinner, when I was doing homework, or outside in the yard. He made me wear it on the school bus. That was a real hit with my so-called friends! And then, then when I didn't make the team, he bitched at me for being such a pussy!"

"So, what is it that you're telling me, Graham? You kill little kids because your father's an asshole?"

"Look, Ama…Lieutenant."

"Call me Mike," I said casually. "And, by the way, if you're going to talk to me, I want to make sure you understand your rights. I know a lot of cops don't do that and then later, in court, they lie about it. I don't play that game. I'm going to be fair and honest with you and you're going to be open and honest with me. Understand?"

"Yeah. I'm going to be honest with you. I don't have anything to hide. I know my rights, so you don't have to bother with that stuff."

"Wayne, it isn't that I *have to* advise you. I *want to* advise you." With that said, I went through the stupidity of advising this cold, calculating animal of his rights. He hadn't given those kids the right to life, the right to liberty, the right to the pursuit of happiness, but here I was advising him that he could remain silent and all the rest of that crap.

"Now, Wayne, I'm sure you have your side to the story. I know what the witnesses said, what the evidence indicates; I know what you did, how you did it, and when you did it. The only thing I don't know, don't understand, is *why* you hurt these kids. I don't know what drove you to do this."

I didn't have to wait to see if the ploy to get him to talk had worked. "That's what I'm trying to tell you, Mike," he said with an edge that sounded like he was losing patience with me and all the Miranda crap.

"Okay, if you want to. But first I have to ask you this…do you want to waive your rights and talk to me about this?"

"Yes. Yes! That's what I'm trying to tell you!"

"Okay. Okay! Don't get pissed at me. I just want to make sure I give you every protection you have coming to you." Following a quick breath, I said, "So you were telling me your father was a real, grade-A asshole. Right?"

His nod told me he appreciated the small token I had allowed him. "Mike, I'm here to tell you, the man is a paltry, petty, egocentric, domineering, hateful morsel of sub-humanity." The killer looked at me and I sensed he wanted me to applaud his minimal command of the English language. I raised my eyebrows and fed him a hint of widened eyes.

Graham was on a roll, so he continued. "His favorite quick-time discipline was a smack in the back of the head. If I said the wrong thing, did the wrong thing, sassed back to my dear mother, whatever, I got rapped in the back of the head. For bigger things, I had my head banged against the wall." He stopped long enough to smile. "That was the funny thing about wearing the damn football helmet. He would tell me to take it off, then bang my head against the wall two, three, maybe ten times, and then make me put the helmet back on! I guess he didn't want the helmet to mark the wall," the killer suggested with a crooked grin.

"So your father was rough on you," I commented as if the senior Graham was a normal parent. "So was mine. He didn't mind giving us kids a crack in the head now and then, and he sure as hell wasn't against using a belt across our butts." I said the words and hoped that my father—who had never really touched me in anger—wasn't rolling over in his grave. "He was strict and he was a hell of a disciplinarian," I said with my eyebrows arched high. "Still, I don't go out and snatch kids off the street."

"Hey now, Mike," Graham said softly as he leaned forward and put his palms flat on the table. "Did your father come into *your* room at night, slip into your bed and fondle your prick? Did he try to convince you *you* must be enjoying it and *you* really wanted him to do that because *you* got an erection? Did your old man have *you* give him a blow job?" He saw he had reached into my gut with his words, and then smiled a wry smile as he asked, "Mine did. Did *your's*, Mike?"

I was looking directly into the dark, widened eyes of the madman in front of me and I saw…nothing! Where one might expect to see tears, there were none. Where I thought I might see hate, rage, anger there was nothing…nothing but the vacuous eyes of a crazed killer.

Wayne Graham had taken control of the interrogation and that was not a good thing. Control had to come back to—and remain in—my chair.

"If what you say is true," I acknowledged with a shrug, "and, I have no reason to doubt you, your father is a criminal and a sick bastard. But, Wayne let me ask you something. Let me ask you one, single question, and before you answer, reach down in your gut and pull out the truth."

"Ask," he said without moving an inch.

"Does all that, all the stuff you're telling me, does any of it, for one solitary minute justify you killing three kids? Does it justify you tormenting their parents?"

"*Justify it*? No, it doesn't justify it, Mike. But then again, I'm not here to *justify* it. I'm here to *explain* it. The kids aren't important!

They were simply the vehicle I used to explain this thing and to explain it to you so you can tell the whole world about what a rotten, lousy, no good, sick piece of crap my father is."

The kids aren't important? You want to tell me they aren't important, you slimy piece of human shit!

"So the whole world knows. Then what?" I asked casually.

"Then he'll be embarrassed and humiliated in front of his friends and precious colleagues the way I was all of my life. Then he'll have to hang *his* head in shame."

"But, how will you ever prove it? How will you be able to prove what he did to you back then?"

"I don't have to prove it, Mike!" he said with a wide smile in his sunken, sad eyes. "I don't have to prove a damn thing! All I have to do is say it! That's the way he punished me all my life. He called me names, made accusations, labeled me. He pointed the finger and I had to suffer the consequences. Now I'm the one pointing my finger and he is going to have to live with it!"

"Still, all in all…"

"Hey now, that's the beauty of it, Mike. I'm crazy and people are going to have to figure out if I'm just saying these things because I'm crazy…or am I crazy because what I'm saying is true? It doesn't matter what side of the argument they pick. All that's important is that they'll be talking about it. Everyone will know his name, the oh so proud name of Lewis Graham, and everyone will know what he's been labeled. Fuck him! Let him deal with it! He's the one who gave me my psychosis."

"I see," my mouth said as I thought, *You bullshitting con artist! Psychosis, neurosis, or halitosis, you're going to die for this you piece of garbage!*

So now the cat was out of the bag! Mister hallow-eyed Wayne Graham was going to try to latch on to an insanity plea. That was his game, but it wasn't a game I was about to let him win.

"Let's talk about the kids, Wayne," I said as I bent forward in my chair, getting close enough to the man to smell his bad breath. "If this is going to get out, we have to discuss the nitty-gritty."

"Sure. Go ahead and ask."

"Well, first of all, these kids that you picked up, why did you select those kids."

"Basically," Graham said as he leaned forward and put his forearms on the table, "they were kids I knew from the schools, and because they were young enough."

"Young enough? I don't understand."

Graham smiled and responded, "I mean they were young enough so that their parents wouldn't be too attached to them."

I wanted to kill the son-of-a-bitch right then, right there. How could a human being, even a pseudo-human being such as Graham think that a parent gradually and incrementally becomes attached to their child over a twenty-year period!

I hoped my rage hadn't displayed itself on my face as I continued, "Tell me about the Chilsom girl. What went on there?" It was a simple question, but I hoped to get three things out of it.

First of all, I needed information that only the actual killer would know. That would protect us against the defense that Graham had confessed to a crime he actually did not commit, but only because he's a sick young man who simply wanted to embarrass his father. Secondly, I needed some facts about the case that even we, the police, did not know. That would protect me from the allegation that I made up the confession and then forced him to sign off on it. And third, I needed this human piece of garbage to tell me things he did that would counter a later plea that he was criminally insane. In order to do that, I at least needed some information about steps he took to keep from getting caught. If he were truly insane—at least in the criminal sense—then he would not have any concept of right and wrong and therefore would not see a need to conceal his acts. However, if he attempted to conceal his identity from us, or at least attempted to conceal evidence that would lead us to him, then the District Attorney could argue Graham knew what he was doing was wrong, and on that premise he could beat down the insanity ploy.

In response to my question, Wayne Graham went into great deal about how he had befriended Becky Chilsom at school, and how he used that friendship to convince her to get into the car with him and show him how to find Orange Street. To reward her for helping him, he bought her two donuts. After she had eaten one of them, he pulled

George Capwell's little red Honda behind a car wash on Lyell Avenue and choked the girl to death.

"She went peacefully," he said with pursed lips and a and smug nodding of his head. His eyes that had shown me nothing earlier in the hour now danced with excitement.

While he looked around for a park or someplace to dispose of the body, he decided to spread jelly from the second donut over the girl's body. Not being too familiar with the east side of the city, he ended up getting lost. Coming upon the empty lot on Scrantom Street was just an accident, but as long as the street was a one-way, without a lot of traffic, he decided to take the chance and dump the body there.

When I asked, Graham casually described how he enticed the Chilsom child into his car under the pretext of needing assistance in finding Orange Street. We covered more details, and to each of my one-line questions, he eagerly provided detailed paragraphs of explanation.

"And what about Traci Taylor?" I asked almost three-quarters of an hour after getting him to open up about Becky Chilsom's abduction and murder.

He used the same help-me-find-a-street play with little Traci Taylor and again he bought the little girl two donuts for her trouble. He had almost given up on finding a victim that day, but at that moment the school bus rounded the corner. Although he killed her within an hour of her abduction, Graham decided to wait a while before he disposed of the body. His decision to wait was based on the belief that the anticipation of finding the body would create a better news story when the victim was finally found. He gave me all the details and described how he had set the body on the bench in front of the Cornhill gazebo and had to lay her arms over the back of the bench so she would remain sitting in an upright position.

"What about Timothy Bidwell," I asked. "What happened there?"

Once again, Graham volunteered a detailed account of snatching the boy off the sidewalk after he couldn't hang onto the little girl he had first grabbed. Knowing the cops would be looking for the van, Graham had immediately gotten out of the city. Using small county roads, he concealed the van in an abandoned quarry, strangled the child, and then drove to a small motel. Knowing that we knew who he was, Graham used the fictitious name of Gordon Farrell when he registered at a small motel in the suburban town of Gates, New York. By late Sunday afternoon, when he saw the splash the case was making on the news, he drove the van—with the body in it—to a find a place to display Timothy Bidwell's small body. He said it was about three in the morning when he placed the boy's corpse on the fence on Driving Park Avenue.

"That was a nice arrangement, Mike, wasn't it? I mean putting him up there like Jesus on the cross. That was kind of cool, huh?"

Yeah, cool enough to guarantee you'll die on a prison gurney in the same position, with your arms out and a lethal dose of drugs in your veins.

There was a minute of silence before the suspect said he needed to go to the bathroom. We stood up and walked to the interview room door. I placed my hand on the doorknob and without turning it, asked, "Why did you put jelly on both of the girl's faces?"

The question threw him for a split second. "I didn't put any on Becky's face," he said with some indignation. "I rubbed it on her pants. There wasn't any on her face."

Thank you for that little detail, asshole!

"Even so, why the jelly?" I persisted.

"I thought it might be something the newspapers would like." Seeing the question on my face he smiled and explained, "You know. Like maybe they would start calling me 'The Jelly Donut Killer' or something like that."

Once inside the latrine, I stepped in front of the man and, as I blocked his path to the urinal, asked, "So why no jelly on the Bidwell kid?"

"Hey, fuck him, Mike!" Graham protested. Then, pulling up his right pant leg he explained, "Look what that little shit did to my leg. Screw him. No donuts for that mean little bastard!"

There was a slight, faded bruise on shinbone.

As he stood at the second urinal, I moved to the first one. Then, having him almost literally with his pants down, I casually popped my main question. "So, what did you keep?"

"Keep?" he asked a little confused.

"Keep. You know, most guys keep a little something, something from the victim's body."

"Oh, yeah! Yeah, that's right. I took a little pin, a guardian angel pin. That was off of Taylor. For the first one, Chilsom, I was too nervous to even think about it."

"Anything from Bidwell?"

"His compass. A little plastic compass like you find in a cereal box."

As we did the customary three shakes and then zipped up, I asked where I might find the items.

"In my house," he said with a shrug.

Walking back into the interview room, I stopped and said, "I'm a little dry. Do you want something to drink? Some coffee? A can of pop?"

"Yeah, some coffee if you got it. Cream and sugar."

"Sure thing. I'll be right back."

When I stepped into the squad room Paskell, St. John, Romano, and Donovan all stood up. Already standing was Deputy Chief Ernie Cooper, Major Skip Winston, Lt. Mark Moran, and two young cops I didn't recognize.

"What did you get?" Winston asked on behalf of the assemblage.

"He went for all three killings…in some detail. I still need to get more."

"You didn't abuse him, did you?" Cooper asked.

I shot him a look that told much of my disdain for the little man, and then walked over to the coffeepot. Pouring the two cups of coffee, I issued instructions to the members of the squad.

"I need someone to check the Sleep Well Motel in Gates. He stayed there Saturday night under the name of Farrell, Gordon Farrell. Our boy also says the bus was late on the day he grabbed Taylor. I know we have that somewhere in the reports, but we need to confirm it with a deposition from the driver."

Winston gave the okay to use the extra teams of detectives who were already temporarily assigned to the investigation.

"Great, we'll need them because we have to execute the search warrants on the van and house." Then as an afterthought, I asked Bobby, "Did you get them both done?"

"Got them and they're ready for a judge to sign. The one on the house is kind of weak."

"Okay, then add this to it. Graham says he took a small, gold-colored guardian angel pin off the Taylor girl and a small plastic compass off the Bidwell boy. He says they're both in his house. Put that in the search warrant." Turning to Major Winston, I asked, "We also have to get investigators over to both sets of parents to confirm the fact that the items were missing from their children's bodies when they recovered the bodies from the ME's Office."

As I got a confirmation from my boss, I heard from behind me, "Nice job, Mike." It was Lt. Mike Moran. "My two guys had the report on the Bidwell child," he explained as he nodded to the two young coppers to his left. "They heard you had a suspect in and they wanted to come up."

"Jimmy set the guy up pretty good for me, so it was kind of easy," I said and hoped Detective Paskell felt better about being shoved out of the interrogation by Graham. The detective acknowledged my comment with a polite smile, but there was no heart in it.

Returning to the interview room, I found Wayne Graham with his head resting in his arms that were folded on the table. At first I thought perhaps he was crying, but quickly realized he was merely napping. For him, the game was over, so now he could take time out to rest. It was good that he felt comfortable, for it made him more vulnerable. During the first round of the interview he had supplied me with more than enough information to find him guilty. There was no way his attorney, try as he may, would convince any jury Wayne Graham had made a false confession and was not the real killer. In telling me about the one-night stay at the motel in suburban Gates, and admitting to taking a plastic kid's compass off the Bidwell boy as well as taking the guardian angel pin off of the Taylor child—all things that we cops didn't know—Graham had closed the door to any defense that I had provided all the details to the confession and then had forced him to sign it.

What were missing were the things I needed him to say so he would also be closed off from an insanity plea. There was no way I was going to let this guy go to a psycho ward for a year, maybe two, and then have a miraculous recovery that would put him back on the streets again. That was not going to happen!

"Wayne!" I said sharply as I entered the room. "Here's your coffee."

He looked up and smiled at me with a warmer smile than had been offered by Jimmy Paskell a minute earlier. "Thanks, Mike." Before taking a sip he asked, "Now what?"

"Now we go over it one more time to make sure I have it right...and we fill in some of the holes."

"Holes? What holes?"

"Miscellaneous things, some odds and ends," I said casually. "You tell me you want the whole world to know what you did, but if that's so why didn't you tell Detectives St. John and Romano, you know, when they stopped by to talk to you, that you were responsible for Becky Chilsom and Traci Taylor?"

"It would have been too easy, Mike. Hell, I didn't want to get caught then, not that soon!" His eyes widened and the eyebrows arched high again. "Besides, I wanted to get in another one...another kid...before I retired." Again, that stupid grin emerged.

"What are you saying?" I asked inquisitively. "Are you telling me that if they would have asked you, that you would have told them, you would have admitted it?"

That was the first nail—a small, thin nail—in the coffin of his insanity defense.

"But didn't it bother you, Wayne? I mean, you do know what you were doing was wrong, that it was hurting a lot of people, right?"

"Hell yes, I was breaking the law, breaking one of the Ten Commandments, breaking common rules of morality. So what? It was all for a good cause!"

That was another nail, but it was still a weak one. With the line of crap that lawyers have, one could twist that last statement around. I had to go for the main points from here on in.

"So, then you were just jerking our chains a little when you told St. John you had big plans for last weekend, huh? And that little deal you pulled on us on Tuesday, what was that all about?"

Graham smiled broadly. "Yeah, yeah I was pulling your chain. I knew when you got me you would probably be pissed about that."

"I'm not pissed, Wayne. After all, that little stint of overtime did some healthy things for my paycheck." I raised my hand in the air as a swear-to-God gesture, and in doing so, offered him my own silly little grin...and the son-of-a-bitch high-fived me! I wanted to kick his skinny, scrawny ass all over the room! He was admitting to taking three innocent lives, to killing three little kids that had done nothing to him. He was bragging about cold-blooded murder and he wanted me to congratulate him as if he had scored the winning touchdown in the homecoming game!

That was another nail banged into his coffin.

"What I don't understand here, Wayne, and maybe I'm missing something, is why did you stay at a motel on Saturday night? And, why use a phony name?"

"I didn't want to get caught, Mike! It's that simple. There wasn't anything devious in that. Hell, I just didn't want to get caught!"

Bang! Bang! Another nail. A big one!

"But this morning you drove right up to the house, right? You knew we were going to be waiting for you. Am I right? Weren't you afraid of getting caught then?"

"Mike, the difference is that on Saturday I hadn't had the chance to put out the body for viewing the way I wanted to. Sure, I knew I was going to get caught, but first I wanted to make that last, big statement."

"Wayne, I need to ask you something. It has nothing to do with the case." I lied. "It's just something I have to know, something I have to make right in my own head."

"Ask away."

"Did you know that what you were doing was wrong?"

He remained silent for almost a minute, and then, when he looked up at me there was just a trace of moistness in his eyes. "Sure, Mike. I knew it was wrong. I'm not some animal. I knew it was wrong. That first little girl, Becky, I even sort of liked her." He paused to look at the ceiling. "That's one of the main reasons I bought them donuts. I wanted to make them feel like everything was going to be okay. I didn't want them being afraid when I...I made them die."

Making some lame excuse for leaving the room, I trotted back to the squad room. Once there, I told everyone to clear out because I was bringing Graham down for a statement. Although St. John, Romano, and Paskell had left to take care of assignments, Monica Sheldon had now joined the small crowd.

"Lieutenant, you need to give me something for the media people."

"An arrest is imminent, film at six," I said as I looked around the office for a convenient computer on which to take Graham's confession.

"What about his confession? Can I use that?"

"If you say one damn word about any confession, you're going to screw up this entire case. Don't you dare even allude to the possibility of a confession."

With that I made my exit and returned to Graham. He was standing and staring at the wall.

"Wayne, there's one more thing we need to talk about," I said softly.

"What's that, Mike?"

"The girls. Why did you play with them?"

"I never raped them, never did that to…"

"I'm not talking about rape," I said quickly. "However, you did play with their breasts. That was evident in some things you communicated to their mothers, and it was obvious when the autopsies were performed."

"That? Oh, I just did that for effect, Mike. You know, just to make the parents suffer. I didn't get off on it, if that's what you mean."

Just to make the parents suffer? What kind of fucking animal is this?

There was no doubt in my mind. The guy was truly nuts…100% whacked out, stock-raving, squirrelly, warped-minded, loony, nuttier than a fruitcake, nuts! He killed kids to make the parents suffer because the kids suffer too much? He killed the kids because they suffer? Yes, he was crazy…but he wasn't criminally insane! He could go through this charade of his, play-acting at being insane, but I was going to deprive him of any shot at an insanity plea.

My internal dialogue finished, I said, "Wayne, we need to move out of here and go down to my office now." The man began to move in my direction, but never questioned why. As he got up to the door, I threw out one of the questions that had been burning a hole in my brain ever since the first day of the Chilsom investigation.

"Wayne, where the hell did you get time to buy donuts?"

"What?"

"I mean you have a kid in the car, right? You have to get out of the car to buy the donuts, right? How did you know the kid wouldn't get out of the car and just run away?"

"Well, Mike, the truth of the matter is that I bought the donuts before I picked up the kids. I kind of used them to entice the girls into the car. You know, by saying, 'Show me that street and I'll give you one of my donuts'. Kids love donuts," he said with a few quick nods of his head. "They really do. I even bought some for that last little jerk...the one that kicked me. He just didn't get to have one after that!"

The two of us moved into the massive, less than private Criminal Investigation Division squad room designed by bureaucratic chiefs and consultants who know nothing about police work. Strolling over to the far corner of the room, I sat down, turned on the computer, and instructed my guest to have a seat next to me.

"What are we doing, Mike?" he asked with obvious confusion.

"I'm going to take down your story for you, Wayne," I responded with wide eyes and arched eyebrows.

"I don't want to do that, Mike. I'm not going to sign a confession."

"You don't have to sign anything, Wayne. However, I *am* going to put down what you said to me, and I *am* going to have you read it to make sure it's correct. That protects you from me later adding anything you didn't really say, and it protects me from any false accusations from you."

"Hey now, I'm not signing it, Mike."

"Don't sign it, Wayne...but I am typing it up."

I started moving my fingers across the keyboard in a cop's typical look-and-leap style, when he stopped me. "Bring me to the jail and book me, Mike. I told you everything I'm going to tell you. There's no need for me to sit here if I'm not signing that...that thing you're typing."

I turned to face him and leaned forward with my elbows on my knees. My demeanor changed, and he saw it. His eyes searched my face for some meaning, some clue as to what was going on. I let him search *my* cold eyes.

"I don't have to do this," he said somewhat emphatically.

"You're right," I confirmed. "But the fact is you *are* going to do it because you *want* to do it!"

"Want to? Why would I want to? If you put down everything I told you in the other room, it's going to make me sound like a...a...a monster or something."

You are a monster, you fucking idiot!

"Look, Wayne. You just spent an hour or more telling me what you did and why you did it. That's why you told me everything just the way it happened. Right? You want your story told because you want to punish your father. Am I right?"

"Yes, but..."

"But the only way you're going to get your story out is if I release it. So, the bottom line, Wayne, is you need my cooperation."

"But, the press, the TV reporters will want to know. They'll demand to know."

"You're right, they will. However, your lawyer isn't going to tell them, and he sure as hell won't let you tell them. Consequently, the news guys only get what our Public Information Officer tells them. And, she only knows what I tell her. So they can beg and moan, and cry all they want to, but they aren't going to know jack shit unless I decide I want to tell our information officer."

He sat silent, processing the information to see if it made sense in his mind.

"The other reason you need my cooperation is that you're going to go to jail in a little while. Now then, once you get there, you're going to be with robbers, rapists, murderers, drug dealers, and other assorted dredges of our society. Even though they themselves are basic vermin, there is one thing they all hate...and my friend, that one thing is a child molester."

"But I didn't molest those kids. I never used them sexually!"

"Ah, that may be true, but how will they know that if you don't have a signed and sealed confession? You see, when you go down to jail, and later, when you go to Attica, they can put you in one of two places. One place is in general population where you will have the snot beat out of you every day. At night you're going to find yourself kneeling down while an inmate in front of you feeds you a liquid high-protein diet, and another one, behind you, bores your asshole out to a size that will serve as a carport for a '57 Caddy. Do you get the picture, Wayne? Now then, the second place they can put you is in protective custody where you won't be exposed to the abuse your own father committed on your body." I allowed a few seconds to pass so the picture would sink in. "So the question here is this, do you want general population or do you want protective custody? Now then, if you decide you want the PC instead of general population, then you need me, because I have to make the recommendation."

With my speech out of the way, I turned back to the computer. After an hour-and-a-half or so, twelve pages of Wayne Graham's confession were spilled out, including the name of the donut shop where he made his purchases before killing Chilsom and Taylor.

"Is there anything you want to add?" I asked as I completed the last paragraph.

"Can I?"

"Sure," I said in an upbeat way. "It's your statement, told your way."

"I just want to say that my father drove me to do this. I had nothing against those kids. In fact I was very nice to those kids. I just wanted to show everyone what my father did to me, what he drove me to do. He's the one that drove me crazy…crazy like I am now."

I included the gratuitous, self-serving statement. When the printer finished belching out the typed confession, Graham read it, made a few minor corrections and without a whimper, he signed each page.

It took almost until midnight for the squad to put the finishing touches on Wayne Graham's arrest. Around five o'clock in the evening each detective had made a phone call to their respective spouses or significant other to advise them the case was closed and that they would be late—very late—in arriving home. The coolness, disappointment, and sarcasm on the other side of the phone was ignored. I made my call to Josephine Maira and asked her and her sister to keep Max for the night.

In the twelve hours since Graham's arrest, the squad had tested most everything he had told me. Timothy Bidwell parents confirmed the little boy had a blue plastic compass he carried with him, just as Traci Taylor's parents confirmed the tiny golden guardian angel that had been pinned on her coat. Both of the items had been found in Wayne Graham's house when the search warrants were executed. The search warrant on the van had turned up little, but lab tests would have to be made on the tiny fibers that had been lifted off of the floor of the vehicle. We ran down the cop that had handled the family trouble call in front of the Cornhill Gazebo on the night that Taylor's body showed up there, and took a written statement from him. The records at the motel Graham had visited on Saturday night had been seized and were now safely in the evidence vault. The only loose ends remaining were to run down the bus driver who took Traci Taylor to her home the afternoon of her abduction and locating the owner of the donut shop. Those final leads would be looked into the next day...but as for this late hour, it was party time!

We finally made it to the Robe and Gavel about 12:30 in the morning and by closing time we were well on our way to being totally wiped out. Toasts were made and cheers were shouted. Laughter and sarcastic comments abounded once again in the squad. Jimmy Paskell toasted Bobby St. John's legal brilliance in preparing the search warrants for the van and house. Bobby toasted Paskell and Walz for hanging tight with the case. Walz admitted that she was so drunk that even Tommy Romano looked good to her...but not that good! He responded to the back-handed comment by assuring that, beg as she may, she was not getting into his pants anytime soon. I got toasted for wrangling the signed confession out of our suspect, and in return I toasted Jimmy Paskell and the entire squad for developing the case that made the confession so easy to get. We then toasted the bartender, the owner of the bar, the guy who cleans up the place after closing, the Queen of England, Santa's eight tiny reindeer, Mickey Mouse, Frank Sinatra, a couple of rock bands I had never heard of, the Crime Scene Technicians, the forensic lab's staff, cops everywhere, and police horses.

In reference to a saying that had originated back in the late 1960's by Major Anthony Fantigrossi, a former Chief of Detectives, past Commander of the Violent Crimes Unit, and still a Rochester Police Department legend, Frankie Donovan cried out, "If you bring me the bear…"

I shouted the response, "…I'll make bear soup!"

In a loud, drunken chorus the entire squad shouted, "SOUP'S ON!"

It was a great evening!

When the bar closed we bought a few six packs of Genny Beer and adjourned to the lower level of the Public Safety Garage where the festivities continued until after four in the morning.

Riding the crest of the Graham arrest, we were as close that night as we had ever been. We had bagged the suspect, tagged him, and buried him…and felt damn good about it! And, the best thing about the entire case was that the suspect had no defense. There was no way he could beat the case…

PART TWO:

JUSTICE SCORNED

LOU CAMPANOZZI

CHAPTER THIRTEEN

A HINT OF TROUBLE

Almost six months had passed since the arrest of Wayne Graham. Now spring was taking a foothold in Rochester and trees from Genesee Park Boulevard on the city's far west side to Winton Road on her far east side were beginning to show tinges of green. The snow—a mere 92 inches that year—was gone. Grass lawns that had been brown and laid flat with layers of snow only a week or so earlier were now beginning to turn emerald once again. It's a good time of the year, the best time of the year as far as I'm concerned. Rochester winters are too long and too cold. The summers are hot and muggy with near 100 percent humidity. And, as for autumn, well, it simply means another cold, nasty winter is coming. But spring…well, spring makes me feel resonant and alive.

The squad had bounded back from the churlish combativeness that had taken hold of it in the days prior to Graham's arrest. Things were back to normal now…whatever the hell *normal* is for a homicide squad. We took in stride the five suicides that rained down on us from Thanksgiving through New Year's Day. The usual battery of spousal and girlfriend-boyfriend homicides, along with robbery-murders, drug gang murders, stupid reason murders, and suspicious deaths came and went with their normal frequency.

During the last few weeks of a determined winter, we were hit with a killing of a well-to-do suburbanite. Being that she was rich, white, and killed while returning to her car in a downtown parking ramp, pressure came at us from all directions. City Hall, the news people, citizen groups, business associations and a slew of other righteous bastards crawled out of the woodwork to take a few cheap shots at the squad.

All that not withstanding, it was spring, and as far as I was concerned, all was right with the world...until I took a stroll with Lethal John!

John Niemeyer is probably around 40 years old, stands about five feet-nine inches tall, weighs in at about 160 pounds, and sports a full head of curly, light brown hair. Although he appears unimposing—I think he looks like he should be teaching high school history somewhere—he's a man who is greatly feared by the defense attorneys who service the robbers, rapists, and murderers of Monroe County, New York. Niemeyer is known to one and all around the County Courthouse as "Lethal John." It's a tag given the diminutive Assistant District Attorney because he's responsible for ten or so very unhappy guys who are presently marking time at Attica and Sing Sing Prisons before they exhaust all appeals and end up having their asses fried.

On this particular day in late May, I accompanied the prosecutor for an invited lunchtime walk through downtown. The topic of our conversation remained dormant until we left the Hall of Justice through the heavy-glass doors.

"I think there's a problem with the Graham case," he said matter-of-factly as we turned from Exchange Street and went east on to Broad Street.

"What kind of problem?"

"We're down for trial on June tenth. You know that, right?"

"Yeah, sure. The squad got notified."

"Jeff Longler, Graham's attorney, called me yesterday afternoon to give me the list of witnesses he's calling for the Huntley Hearing. He's only calling two witnesses—you and Detective Paskell."

"That's kind of strange," I commented. "What do you make out of it?"

"What I make out of it, my friend, is that we have a problem."

"Why should there be a problem?" I asked. "The case sailed through the Preliminary Hearing and the Grand Jury."

"Mike, need I remind you the Prelim and Grand Jury are a cake walk? At the Prelim all we have to do is show probable cause that a crime was committed and probable cause that he's our guy, or our 'bear', as you guys say. It's a no-brainer. And, my friend, the Grand Jury is basically the same shit packaged in a prettier box."

"John, please, at this point of my career I don't need a lecture on what we laughingly call our legal *system*."

Niemeyer stopped as we began to cross the bridge spanning the Genesee River. Facing the water below us, he looked out at the river. "Okay my court-smart cop buddy, let me run something by you."

"Shoot."

"Why do we have a Huntley Hearing."

I sighed. "It's a hearing right before trial to see if the confession is admissible at trial. It's a routine suppression hearing so the lawyer can glom more money out of his client, or in the case of a court-appointed attorney, to see if he can screw the State for a few more coins."

"Such a smart friend I have!" the Assistant DA said in the imitated Jewish accent of his paternal grandparents.

As we started to walk east once again, he raised a finger and asked rhetorically, "And, the Huntley Hearing is done in front of a judge only, without any jury around so if the confession is ruled inadmissible, the jury never hears any testimony about it. Therefore, they're not swayed by any inclination that there even was a confession."

Now it was my time to pause our walk. "Come on, John! Why are we doing this freshman year jurisprudence review?"

"Be patient. You'll see!" Lethal John was taking a long time to make his point, but I was enjoying the walk. As we turned right on South Avenue and approached the huge main library, he went to the heart of the discussion. "And what happens if we lose this confession that Graham gave?"

"We've got a problem," I conceded.

"Wrong, Mike! We have more than just a problem. We have no case. We've got nothing." He let the statement sink in before he drove home the point. "We don't have any witnesses to speak of. Oh sure, we have a few people who can say they saw a red car or a black van, but none of them can identify Graham. We have Capwell who can say he loaned his van and car to our defendant on certain days. Big deal! Put them both together and Longler will take them apart in a minute."

When he paused, I picked up the argument he was making. "And if we lose the confession, we lose everything we obtained as a result of the confession. We lose the search warrant, the compass off of the Bidwell kid, the Guardian Angel from Traci Taylor…both of those items go south. The information he provided about the donut shop and the motel he stayed at, those also go away. Parts of the search warrants came from what he told us. If we lose the warrants, we lose the whole ball of wax." My words were no more than spoken thoughts, thoughts that disturbed me.

As we approached a small restaurant that had been renovated out of an old train station, John pointed at the front door and asked, "Get some ribs?"

"Okay with me, but if you planning on ruining my lunch, you're buying!"

After placing our order, I put my arms on the table and asked, almost secretively, "So, what do you make out of Longler calling Jimmy and me as witnesses?"

"He must see you two as a way to compromise the confession."

"There's no way he can do that through us. The interrogation and the resulting confession that Graham signed are golden."

Niemeyer shrugged. "Mike, up until yesterday I figured he was asking for the Huntley Hearing as a matter of routine. Up until yesterday I thought he was going to try to pull an insanity defense, or try a plea to insanity." He paused to point a finger at me to emphasize, "But he hasn't even raised the insanity issue in any discussions, motions, or filings with the court."

When our order came, we ate and nodded our approval of the food. There was some conversation about bosses, rumors, and office politics, but we held the main topic at bay until we left the restaurant and headed back toward Exchange Street. Crossing the Court Street Bridge, Assistant District Attorney Niemeyer began to probe.

"How long have we known each other, Mike?"

'Twenty, twenty-two years, maybe longer. Our first case was that midget hooker I bagged over at the old Eastman Hotel." The memory earned a grin from both of us.

"And I would venture a guess that we've handled a hundred and fifty—maybe two hundred cases—together. And probably better than half of those were major felonies and murders. Is that fair to say?"

"Sure," I responded. "Maybe even more."

"Mike, I never asked you this question before. I never asked because...well because of a lot of things. But right now, on this case, I have to ask you something. I'm going to ask it, and I assure you, the answer stays with me. It will impact what I do with the case, but the answer stays here, with me. Okay?"

"Ask," I said flatly, suspecting what was going to be asked.

"Did you have to do anything, ah, anything improper in order to get him to confess?"

"You know, I should take you by your curly locks and toss you in the frigging river." The words were spoken without a smile. "I should tell you to kiss my dago ass, John, but I'm going to look you right in the eye and tell you, no! No, I did not do anything wrong, improper, illegal, immoral, unethical, or even not nice to Graham. The son-of-a-bitch wanted to confess. He couldn't wait to confess. Damn you, John! You piss me off!"

"Mike, I had to ask."

"Screw you!" My Sicilian temper was taking hold of me, and although I was not mad at the man who asked the question, I was mad at the question itself. It was something that was always hanging out there in every citizen's mind, every dumb juror's mind every time there was a confession. If we didn't get a confession, we were thought of as being too stupid to get the guy to admit. But, if we did get a confession, then it must be that we beat it out of him. That's what every juror, almost every citizen believed.

"I received word from one of the corrections officers at the jail that Longler has been arguing with his client lately."

"About?" I asked.

"The way I heard it is Longler wants to attack the confession, but Graham wants him to leave the confession alone. Graham wants him to try for an insanity plea instead."

"Well, regardless of what you heard," I insisted, "there's no problem with the confession."

"Then why is Longler calling you as a witness?"

"How the hell should I know?"

"What about Jimmy Paskell?" Niemeyer asked.

"What about him?"

"Did he do anything, maybe something careless, or something legally improper, maybe without knowing it, that's going to creep into this thing?"

"No way, John. All Jimmy did was stake out the house after Graham was settled in. When we got some help down to Jimmy, he went in and said we wanted to talk to him. Jimmy didn't even have to con the bastard. Graham said he was expecting us and made a big deal out of wanting to talk to me."

"Did the guys have to, you know, maybe, kind of *encourage* him along?"

"John, I'm telling you once and only once, we didn't play any games with Graham. The piece of shit almost raced Paskell to the car. He wanted to tell his story. That's the entire thing—he wanted to tell us why he was killing the kids. He wanted us to get the story out so he can make his old man look bad. It sounds stupid, but that's the fact!"

"Okay," he said as if conceding a point. "But I want to ask you something the defense is going to ask you." He paused and looked at me to see if I was calm enough to handle another insult. "Why didn't you guys get a warrant for Graham's arrest?"

"Off the record, John. Just between you and me out here on the street, we didn't get a warrant because if we did, according to the liberal, dumb shit, retarded State Appellate Court Justices that New York is stuck with, once we had the warrant, he would automatically be entitled to a lawyer even before we gave him the Miranda warnings. And, once he had a lawyer, we wouldn't be able to legally interview him until his lawyer waived his rights for him. Now then, I say that out here on the street to you. However, in the hallowed halls of court, my answer is that we saw the van drive up to his house and detectives went to his door to confirm it was him. Once they were there, I told them to see if Graham wanted to talk to us. Shortly thereafter, Detective Paskell advised me he was on the way in with the suspect. In other words, we never arrested him without a warrant! Graham came with us voluntarily when Jimmy Paskell told him we considered him a suspect in the Bidwell killing."

"Good enough," John Niemeyer said with a nod. "The defense is going to hit you two hard about whether or not Graham was handcuffed, led to the car, forced, threatened, or conjoled in anyway. You know that, right?"

"I've been through it before."

We were almost back at the Hall of Justice when Lethal John stopped me again by placing his left hand on my right forearm. "Mike I'm going to ask you a rhetorical question. I don't want to know the answer now. I just want you to think about something. Now don't get your Italian ass in an uproar. Okay?"

"So, ask already."

"Is there any conflict in your squad? Does anyone have a grievance with you? Could it be that one of your guys, maybe some other cop, maybe some cop that was in the hallway, is going to come in and say he saw Lieutenant Mike Amato slap Wayne Graham around? Is that possible?" Having asked the question, he took a deep breath and added, "I ask you this because that's the only other possibility here. If Longler can get another cop to say he saw you coerce a confession, or use duress to force the confession out of Graham, then we have a problem...a big problem!"

"There's no one that would say that because there's no one who *could* say it. Besides, the only other witness he's calling, according to you, is Jimmy."

Lethal John Niemeyer looked up at me and slowly nodded his head. "Well, if there's nothing to worry about, then fine. I feel better knowing that. However, here is something to worry about." He paused for effect. "I forgot to tell you who we drew as a judge."

"Don't tell me!"

"Oh yes, my friend. The one, the only! Judge John LaVacca."

"Oh shit!"

In silence, we rode the escalator up to the main level. Once we stepped off the conveyance, and took a few steps, I spoke.

175

"Why would Longler subpoena Jimmy and me? He knows that you're going to call us as witnesses, and after you get done with us he can take all day to cross examine us."

"True enough," Niemeyer said with a shrug. "However, he can only cross examine you on the issues I raise in my direct examination. If I don't open a door he wants to walk through, he's shit out of luck. Besides as his witness, he can ask the judge to declare you a hostile witness and then take some liberties with the questioning."

"Me? Hostile? Hostile toward a scumbag defense attorney?" I asked with feigned shock and hurt feelings.

Lethal John gave one of his patented baritone chuckles. "Yes, well as unbelievable as that may be, once he has you declared as a hostile...reluctant, at least...witness, he can ask all the leading questions he wants to. Astute jurist that our beloved Judge LaVacca is, once he hears the leading question, he will assume the question is a fact. Longler knows that and I'm sure he's banking on it."

Reaching the courtroom that was John's destination, we stopped to shake hands. In the middle of our good-byes I commented. "I think Longler is still going to try the mental angle. My bet is that he's going to try to get me and Paskell to testify to something that will substantiate Graham was not capable of giving an *intelligent* waiver of his rights."

"Good point, Mike," the ADA acknowledged with some thought etched on his face. "I don't see it that way, but that could be an angle. He may try to suck you guys into saying that Graham was so eager to talk, he had to be mentally incompetent and therefore he could not, in the legal sense, give you an intelligent waiver." After a few nods of his head and some more visible thinking, Niemeyer grimaced. "It's possible I guess. But, then again, if he were going that route, he would have some psychiatrist lined up as a witness, you know, to give the argument some weight."

"Maybe he can't find a shrink to agree with him, but, knowing how gullible LaVacca is, he's going to try to plant the seed with the Honorable Judge."

"It's something to think about," the prosecutor allowed as he pushed open the tall, heavy door leading to a courtroom where, supposedly, justice lived.

It was Wednesday of the following week before I was able to sit down and have a casual conversation with Jimmy Paskell. Gail Walz had taken a day off to handle some personal business and then see her daughter act in a school play. Frank Donovan, my usual partner, was scheduled to testify in an armed robbery case he had handled, so it was not out of the norm when I suggested that Investigator Paskell partner up with me.

"I'm going to be running down some loose ends on the Humboldt Street homicide, so it's not going to be anything special," Jimmy said. "But sure, if you want to come along, I welcome the company."

After talking to two supposed witnesses on the month-old case, we headed for lunch. As we discussed the two less-than-cooperative witnesses, Jimmy headed toward the Golden Diner on Thurston Road. As we stepped through the door of the little restaurant, the Lebanese grandmother, Margaret "*Sitto*" Tannous greeted us with a hug and a strong admonishment for having become strangers to her place of business.

"Well, well! Mister Big Shot Lieutenant and Mister Big Shot Detective! Come on in. You're letting all my air conditioning out. What do you think, I'm going to provide cooling for the whole Nineteenth Ward? Come on in and sit down."

The elderly woman gave us a quick rundown on the day's menu and then told us what we would want—the roast beef or the fresh-made lamb stew. Jimmy and I traded smiles over the loving lady and her mothering ways.

"I'll have a BLT, *Sitto*," Jimmy said.

"A BLT?" she inquired in more of an admonishment than a question. "The tomatoes are those hot house tomatoes, not the garden ones. And, bacon? Why do you want bacon with all that fat? You want the roast beef and mashed potatoes, not a BLT." Her decision was final.

"Right," Jimmy said with resignation. "That's what I want. The roast beef."

"And what do I want, *Sitto*?" I asked.

"Why are you asking me?" she asked with genuine curiosity. "How do I know what a big shot like you wants?"

I decided to have some fun. "I'll take the BLT that Jimmy doesn't want."

"What are you, a wise guy?" she asked as the fingertips of her left hand tapped me solidly on the top of the head. "I just told you that's not a meal. Your mother, God rest her soul, would never feed you that. Be serious, Lieutenant! What do you want?"

"I guess I'll go for the roast beef too."

"The roast beef? Why would you want the roast beef? Your friend is having the roast beef. Get something else. That way you can share and have a little of both."

"Okay, I guess I'll go for the..."

"You want the lamb stew," Margaret Tannous proclaimed as she wiped her hands on her ever-present apron. "I know it's warm outside, but it's a good, hearty meal you can use. The way you eat since you made that wonderful girl, Diane, leave you, the stew will be good for you."

"Iced tea?" Jimmy asked. "Is it okay if I have iced tea?"

"Of course you can have iced tea. What do I care what you drink?"

"Coffee for me," I said.

"Coffee? You drink too damn much coffee. But...what do I care?"

After the woman left, Jimmy and I guessed that each one of us must have gone through the same meal ordering routine with the woman at least a hundred times since we discovered the restaurant several years earlier while investigating a bank robbery in the area.

Carol Ann Tannous, Margaret's daughter, brought huge salads to the table.

"Carol Ann," I said. "We didn't order salads."

"Please, Lieutenant, don't start!" the robust young woman with crimson cheeks said with a big smile. "Ma says you're going to have salad, so you're having the salads! She said that if you gave me any trouble to tell you to eat the salads because the greens are good for your bowels!"

With that, all three of us broke out in loud, boisterous laughter that brought tears to our eyes...and earned a scowl from *Sitto*.

Completing the lunch with a swipe of bread around the remaining stew gravy, I asked Paskell, "So tell me, Jimmy, is everything all right between the two of us?"

"What do you mean, Lute?" the man questioned before he took a sip of iced tea.

"Well, during the Graham thing, I know you were kind of pissed off at me. There was that instance when I called in some other squad members, and, well, you let me know you felt like I was slighting you."

Detective Paskell set down his glass and wiped his mouth with the paper napkin. He obviously needed time to organize what he was about to say. "I was off base, Mike. I mean, you know how it is. We...I guess we kind of get attached to a case and feel like it's ours, ours alone. I just wanted the case. I wanted to be able to grab the son-of-a-bitch and put him away. And, ah, and I kind of got possessive about it."

"Do you understand why I did what I did?"

"Yeah, sure. I, I guess all of us, we kind of look at a case from our angle. But you, you have to look at, what do they call it? The 'big picture.' We want to go out and kick ass and take names, but you have to look at the case and keep the entire squad in mind. I know you've got the Major, the Deputy Chief, the Chief, and a whole bunch of other people breathing up your ass."

"It isn't all that bad," I offered with a grin.

"Well, maybe so. But like I said, I was off base, way off base. I was looking at it from my end. You were right to do what you did. I know that now. It doesn't cause me any heartburn. Really, Mike, it doesn't."

"What about being cut out of the interrogation? I know you, Jimmy. You really wanted a piece of that interrogation."

"Sure! Sure I wanted to be the one in the room. I wanted to get the confession. But, what the hell, Mike. Very simply, the guy wasn't going to talk to me! He wanted you because he wanted to feel important and demanded to see the main man. I could have stayed in there forever and he still wouldn't have told me diddly squat."

"But it bothered you, and I'm sorry about that. Really, Jimmy, I am."

"Mike, I'm serious. There's no hard feelings on my end. I appreciate you bringing it up and all, but it's not necessary."

"So, ah, so we're okay with each other?" I asked with some caution.

"No problems from me, Mike. You're about the best boss I ever worked for. I'm not blowing any smoke up your ass. Really, I mean that!"

"Well, it was a rough case for all of us."

"It sure was. It sure was a rough one," he confirmed as he looked out the window.

"I'm glad it's behind us…and I'm glad there's no hard feelings between us."

Jimmy swallowed the last of his iced tea and then looked out in space, over my left shoulder. He had more to say, but he needed to find the way to say it. He swirled the ice in his glass and looked into the container as he spoke. "It was a rough one. I don't know if I ever told you this, but that first victim, that little Becky Chilsom, well…she was the spitting image of my little Tamara. It kept me awake nights, you know, thinking about if it had been Tamara." Paskell looked down at his empty plate as he spoke once more after a long pause. "I even had nightmares about it. I probably shouldn't tell you that because you'll think I'm losing it, but I did. I actually had nightmares about that bastard grabbing Tamara, and me standing there, not being able to help in any way."

"Jimmy, we all have nightmares now and then about the crap we do, the stuff we see. Don't let anyone tell you otherwise."

He looked up at me and offered a weak smile. "Well, at least it's over."

After a round of hugs and cautions from *Sitto* about not being a stranger, Paskell and I returned to the car and headed out to locate another alleged witness to his open homicide case.

"From what Lethal John told me, the defense is going to go after the confession, Jimmy. Niemeyer feels like he can successfully protect the confession, but the defense is going to have to take a run at it." My comment hung in the air a moment before I cautioned, "We're going to have to be on the same page of music at the Huntley

Hearing. We have to make a strong case that Graham acted normal and gave us an intelligent waiver to his rights."

"Mike, you're worrying about nothing," the detective next to me said with a whisper of a laugh. "When I get on the stand, I'll open Graham's coffin and put him in it. All you have to do is nail it shut when you get up and testify to his confession." Giving me a big smile and a thumbs-up gesture, Paskell assured me, "It's in the bag!"

Margaret Tannous had been right. The good meal of the afternoon would have to hold me through the night. After going home and changing clothes, I skipped dinner and took the Corvette and Max out for a drive down by the lake. Once the car was parked, I walked over to get a chocolate ice cream cone at Abbott's Ice Cream Stand and a small dish of vanilla ice cream for my little buddy. Then, with both of us content, we strolled out to the end of the pier that jutted into Lake Ontario about an eighth of a mile. It's there that I do my best thinking.

Replaying the conversation with Jimmy Paskell, I felt fairly confident I could believe the man. If there was a monkey wrench being thrown into the court case on Wayne Graham, I couldn't believe Jimmy was the guy throwing it in.

It was summertime in Rochester and things were going good…but if that was so, why did I have the nagging worry that things were soon going to turn to crap.

CHAPTER FOURTEEN

POISON TREES AND SPOILED FRUIT

Monroe County Court Judge John Joseph LaVacca is an egotistical, self-centered, pompous, arrogant, egocentric, obnoxious man who, as you may have detected, I have not included on my very short Christmas card list. In all fairness, I have to admit he is also a tall, good-looking man, with salt and pepper hair that is always perfectly combed with every strand in a smooth flow toward the back of his head. Be that as it may, it contributes nothing to his abilities as a judge and his knowledge of the law, which by the way, is akin to Hitler's knowledge of human rights. Trite in his words, as he is in almost all of his dealings.

Judge LaVacca is quick to note for the uninformed, uncaring, citizenry, "The law *is* the law!" and "We either live by laws or die by anarchy!" Few of the masses have yet to grasp the meaningless insignificance of the words.

His slender, athletic built belies his 48 years, and it is that combination of looks, build, and his supposed silver tongue that make him attractive to voters who are too stupid or too lazy to understand issues. As a woman at a cocktail party once told me, she voted for LaVacca because, "He looks like a judge!"

Robert Nedderly, a long-time defense attorney who is a legend in his own right, once summed up Judge LaVacca with the observation, "If you could buy the man for what he's really worth, and sell him for what he thinks he's worth, you could make a hell of a lot of money!"

All that was floating around in my head as Detective Paskell and I waited outside Judge LaVacca's courtroom. The subpoenas we held ordered us to be at his court at 9:00 a.m. My wristwatch told me that the Honorable Judge LaVacca was now 70 minutes late in opening his courtroom for business. I knew it was more than the lack of punctuality that was kicking my nerves into overdrive.

The phrase, "Something is wrong with this picture," kept playing over and over in my mind. The defense attorney, Jeff Longler, had something up his sleeve, some special battle plan drawn up in his mind. Perhaps he would try to establish a reasonable doubt in the judge's mind—such as it is—that either Paskell, myself, or some other cop had coerced the confession out of Wayne, or that we had used some type of duress to force him to admit to the killings. Those allegations were easy to raise, but I felt I had the appropriate ammunition to easily shoot them down. Of course, the problem was what the hell was a "reasonable belief" in the mind of our unreasonable Honorable Judge John LaVacca?

After Detective Paskell was finally called into the sanctity of the courtroom to provide testimony on the matter, I stepped outside for a much needed cigarette. Over the course of the next two hours and fifteen minutes, I arranged to have a court attendant stand by the courtroom doors while I darted out for seven more butts. Finally, at 12:25 in the afternoon, Jimmy Paskell exited the courtroom. The look on his face frightened me.

"Call your next witness now, Mister Niemeyer," I heard LaVacca command from behind the doors that were swinging shut.

"What happened, Jimmy?" I asked with my eyes glued to the man.

"I screwed up, screwed up bad, Lieutenant," Paskell answered as he passed me.

"Lt. Amato, you're being called to the witness stand," the Bailiff said from the doorway leading to LaVacca's lair.

"What happened, Jimmy?" I repeated in an angry whisper.

"Longler got me to say that I arrested Graham at his house. It was stupid...I was stupid. I screwed up."

"Get that witness in here now, Bailiff!" LaVacca commanded loudly with a strike of his gavel on the wooden block that sat on his bench.

I looked back at Jimmy Paskell as I entered the courtroom. He walked like a zombie toward the elevators, shaking his head and running his hand through his hair.

"Mister Amato," LaVacca said as I walked down the aisle to the witness box. "I will not be kept waiting, and I will not tolerate your obstinate attitude toward the authority of this court!"

"Yes, sir," I said with a nod as I approached the witness chair.

"I am not one of your salute-happy, quasi-military bosses, *Mister* Amato. You address me as, 'Your Honor', and not as 'sir'."

"Yes, Your Honor," I replied politely as I turned to face the bailiff and raised my right hand for the oath.

Once I was sworn in and while still trying to wrestle with the information Paskell had dumped on me as he went to the elevators, LaVacca leaned back in his chair and announced, "We will now break for lunch, gentlemen. As has been requested by the Defense, Mister Amato will remain in the care and custody of a court attendant while we are at lunch."

I looked up at the judge's bench and then to Lethal John. I had never heard of this kind of crap being pulled. The only one who seemed to be more pissed than me was Wayne Graham, who sat at the defense table wearing a scowl on his angular face.

LaVacca continued. "You are free to go to lunch, *Mister* Amato, to go window shopping, or walk around town if you like. However, you are not permitted to have any contact with any police officers, detectives, any member of the District Attorney's staff, or any other employee of the City of Rochester or the County of Monroe. In other words, you are to be held *in communicado*, during our lunch recess. If you speak to, or in anyway communicate with any other police, I will find you in contempt of court and throw your carcass in jail." Without any pause to take any input, the judge, added, "By my watch it is now almost 12:30 p.m. We will re-convene at 2:00 p.m., sharp." Once again the gavel struck the wooden block loudly, and LaVacca vacated the bench.

Wayne Graham, seated next to his attorney, continued to look at me with a screwy sort of pathos on his face. When I gave him a quizzed look, he shrugged his shoulders and mouthed the words, "I'm sorry."

I left the building in the company of a court security officer. The kid apologized to me repeatedly for having to escort me everywhere. The fact of the matter was that he had no better idea of why he was with me than I did, so I told him not worry about it.

As we walked through downtown, I tired to keep my mind focused on figuring out what the hell was happening...and how I could get us out of the jam in which we had landed. Part of my mind was wondering why Wayne Graham was sorry. Sorry about what? However, foremost in my head was the significance of what Paskell had said. His message was that the defense attorney had gotten him to admit that he had arrested Graham at the house on Silver Street. If that was accurate, there were serious problems attached to this hearing.

New York State is rather particular about how cops go about getting a person out of the sanctity of their home. Basically, it recognized only three ways to accomplish the task. One, the cops could arrest the person on a warrant. Two, a person could be taken from his home without a warrant only if probable cause existed as a basis for that arrest. And, the third legally accepted way was if the person voluntarily agreed to accompany the cops away from his home.

Well, my brain summarized, we sure as hell didn't have an arrest warrant for Graham, and there wasn't anything close to what the court would accept as probable cause in order to effect his arrest without a warrant. Therefore, the only legal way in which we could have had Graham come down to the cop shop was if he accompanied the cops voluntarily...and, damn it, he did! What the hell was the problem? Jimmy Paskell and I had gone over that testimony more than once. He knew it was important for him to emphasize the fact that Graham came along willingly, eagerly.

Wayne Graham had not verbally or physically—as far as I knew—resisted Jimmy's request that he come down to the Public Safety Building. In fact, Graham had been more than happy to be identified as the killer. His coming to headquarters was actually, factually, legally, and really a voluntary act. So what the hell was Jimmy talking about when he said the defense attorney had gotten him to admit he "arrested" Graham?

What had Paskell said in court that would have indicated anything other than the suspect's voluntarily coming to the cop shop? Did Jimmy use the word "arrest" when he should have said that he "accompanied" the suspect to the detective bureau? Paskell and I had also covered that very issue as we prepared to testify. If Jimmy had accidentally used the word "arrest" in his testimony, he was right, it was a stupid mistake. However, if it were a simple slip of the tongue, either Niemeyer or me should be able to get that across to the deficient legal mind of John LaVacca. It was obvious that my testimony would have to be ripe with references to Graham's free choice to go with Paskell and his eagerness to tell us what he had done.

At 1:55 p.m., my shadow and I returned to the courtroom. Within a matter of minutes, John Niemeyer, Jefferson Longler, and the defendant joined us. Twenty-two minutes later, the Honorable Judge made his garish entrance. Evidently his three Martinis, or three Manhattans—whatever the hell it is that judges drink for lunch—kept him from arriving on the mandated schedule he had set for everyone else. It was his reputation for starting afternoon court session late after his well-known liquid lunches that had earned him the nickname, Vodka LaVacca.

"Call your witness, Mister Prosecutor," LaVacca decreed without a word of apology about his tardiness.

"People call Lieutenant Michael Amato," Lethal John said officiously.

I walked up to the witness chair, greeted a good afternoon to the Judge, and was reminded by him that I was still under oath. With that done, I sat down, crossed my legs and rested my hands on my lap. My mind was now set in its testimony mode.

LaVacca again, for the second time in less than a minute, reminded me I was under oath from having been sworn in prior to the lunch break. He then asked if I had had any conversations or communication with any member of the Rochester Police Department, City or County legal staff, or any other person associated with the administration of justice in our neck of the woods. I assured him I was as pure as the driven snow.

Assistant District Attorney Niemeyer stood up behind the prosecution table and asked the mechanical questions related to my occupation, place of employment, assignment, and duties. He then asked where and when I had first talked to Graham. Once that was out of the way, he stepped to the side of the table and continued.

"And, Lieutenant, how did it come to be that you and Graham met?" Niemeyer asked with a genuine look of interest on his usually placid face.

"He insisted on talking to me."

"He *insisted* on talking to you?" The ADA looked puzzled as he flipped my statement to a question. I had to allow myself a secretive, inner smile. Lethal John was playing his role nicely. "Would you elaborate that point for us, Lieutenant."

"I was in my office doing some work. Detective James Paskell came to me and said he was talking to Mister Graham and that he, Mister Graham that is, wanted to speak to me. I at first told the detective I was too busy to speak to Mister Graham. However, the detective came to me twice more within a half-hour or so and told me that Mister Graham was very emphatic about his desire to speak to me. Fearing that I might receive a citizen's complaint if I still did not talk to Mister Graham, I went to speak with him."

Niemeyer nodded. "Where was the defendant when you spoke with him?"

"In Interview Room Two, sir."

"Was he under arrest?"

"No, sir, he was not."

"Was he in...well, was he in custody?"

"No, sir."

"Come now, Lieutenant, let's be frank here," Niemeyer said as he took a step in the direction of the witness chair. "The defendant was in the police building, up on the fourth floor, in the Detective Bureau, in an interview room. Is that not true?"

"That is correct, sir."

ADA Niemeyer gave me a quizzed look. "I need to press you on this point, Lieutenant," he said with a serious tone.

Having been through many, many trials with Lethal John, I knew the comment about pressing me on a point meant that he was going to ask a question that would surely be asked by the Defense, but Niemeyer wanted to steal the defense's thunder by asking the question himself.

"Sir?" I questioned as if his last comment concerned me.

"How could you possibly ask this court to believe the defendant was not in custody if, in fact, he was in an interview room on one of the upper floors of the Public Safety Building?"

"Sir, the defendant was not locked in the room. He had come into the building voluntarily and was free to leave whenever he wanted to do so. There was no guard posted on the room and the room was not locked."

The ADA nodded, signaling that the response made sense to him and that it should make sense to the court. "So then, Lieutenant, did you actually go to speak to the defendant?"

"Yes, sir I did."

"What, if anything, took place at that time?"

"I introduced myself to Mister Graham, and he began to speak to me. I stopped him and asked him if he had been advised on his rights and if he had waived those rights. He said that he had been told his rights and that he didn't care about them, that he had things to tell me. He began to say some things to me, but I stopped him and gave his rights to him in their entirety. He said he knew his rights and that he still wanted to talk to me."

"Well now, Lieutenant," Niemeyer said in huff. "Let me press you on that point right there. If the defendant was not under arrest, and, as you testified, he was not in custody, why would you be so concerned about his rights? I mean, after all, you only have to advise a person if he is under arrest, or at least in police custody, or if he's a suspect and you plan on questioning them. Isn't that right?"

By "pressing" me on this point, Niemeyer once again let me know that this was an area that was going to be brought up by the defense counsel when he had his turn at bat.

I drew a breath and answered the question. "Although Mister Graham was not under arrest or what I would consider to be as 'in custody,' I did feel he was a suspect in a string of murders we were investigating, and I did feel he was in—what the court may consider—a 'police dominated atmosphere.' Therefore, I felt duty-bound to insure he had been advised of his rights and that he understood they still applied with me in the room."

Once again Niemeyer nodded before continuing. "Now, before we get into what, if anything the defendant may have said to you, I need to ask you one important point." He paused and then asked, "How did it come to be that the defendant was in this interview room in the Detective Bureau? I mean, did he simply walk in off of the streets and ask to see you?"

"No, sir," I responded with a little smile to suggest that was a stupid question…and that I was glad to clarify it. "Mister Graham had become a suspect in several murders we had been investigating for a couple of months. He had access to two vehicles that we had connected with three of the murders, and he fit the description we had received from a couple of witnesses. He was also described to us as the person who abducted the third victim. In fact, at the third abduction, he was seen to be driving a vehicle that he was subsequently seen driving when he arrived at his house shortly before Detective Paskell approached him."

"So then, with all of that, are you telling this court that you had him arrested by Detective Paskell?"

"No, sir. I don't mean to imply that at all. What I mean to say is when Detective Paskell saw the vehicle, one just like the van that had been seen at the most recent abduction, I requested that Paskell approach the defendant and verify who was driving the van. Based on what Paskell has told me, *and* what Mr. Graham himself told me, and also based on what Investigator Paskell put in his official police report regarding the matter, that the defendant came with him willingly to the Detective Bureau."

"So, you are relying on Detective Paskell's account of the matter, based on what he saw, said, and heard?"

"To a certain point. But, sir, I also confirmed Detective Paskell's assessment by personally seeing and hearing, from the defendant himself, how willing, even anxious he was to talk to me."

"You tell them, Mike!" Graham shouted from his chair. "Tell the bastards I was anxious to tell you about my loving daddy!"

LaVacca looked like he had been shot. The surprise on his face blended with the expression of indignity that one had dared to speak in *his* courtroom without his expressed blessing. "Counselor!" the judge shouted in his own right to Jeff Longler. "Restrain your client! Restrain him!"

When calm had returned to the room, ADA John Niemeyer turned his back to me, faced the defense attorney, and asked, "What did you see or hear that made you think the defendant was, as you put it, 'willing, even anxious' to talk to you?"

"Well, Mister Niemeyer, the defendant asked, even insisted on talking to me three times. When I went into the room, he said he was glad to meet me and wanted to tell me what he had done. It was even necessary for me to stop him from talking so that I could give him his rights! I actually had to ask very few questions because the defendant just kept on talking, describing what he had done."

"So, are you saying that based on what you saw, what you heard, what you gathered through your senses, led you to believe the defendant was giving you a confession that was totally voluntary on his part?"

"Yes, sir. That's exactly what I'm saying…and that he was there, in the Detective Bureau, voluntarily."

Niemeyer turned to face me again and began asking questions about my conversation with Wayne Graham. Over the next 15 minutes or so, I went over the broader points of the man's confession. Finally, the ADA asked if I later reduced my conversation with Graham to any form of document. When I stated I did, he introduced the 14-page confession into evidence.

"I object, Your Honor!" Jeff Longler almost shouted as he jumped to his feet. "It is the admissibility of that alleged confession that we are here to address. I object to it being offered into evidence when we are here, in fact, to determine if it should be placed into evidence."

Even I knew that was a stupid objection, and assumed it was being made merely for show-and-tell so the defendant would believe his lawyer was working hard for him. Obviously, Graham also thought it was a stupid objection.

"Will you shut the hell up, you stupid asshole," Wayne said loudly to his attorney as he stood up and slammed his palms on the table. "This is the good part. Let Mike tell it like it is!"

Again Vodka LaVacca looked like he was bound for a heart attack as he demanded the defense counsel to control his client. "You silence his outbreaks, or I will have him removed from *my* courtroom!"

When Graham was finally seated once again with a look of great satisfaction on his face, Judge LaVacca asked Niemeyer if he wished to respond to the objection raised by the defense.

"Your Honor," Lethal John said with obvious disdain in his voice. "As you and I fully know, we are here to determine if this confession shall be admitted *into trial*. For purposes of this *hearing,* it is being admitted simply for your review. Also, I submit to Your Honor that the document itself contains elements which go to the heart of the matter, and that is, voluntariness of the statements made by the defendant."

LaVacca looked bored as he said, "Overruled. Proceed."

"Lieutenant," Niemeyer asked with a similar bored tone, "I show you this document marked as 'People's One' and ask you if you can identify it."

I took a few seconds to look at the front sheet, thumb through the pages, and then responded, "Yes, sir, I can. It's the confession that I took from Mister Graham on the day in question."

Niemeyer stated for the record that the defense attorney, Jefferson Longler, had already been given a copy of the confession. He then asked, "Is this document a verbatim account of your conversation with the defendant?"

"No, it is not," I answered. "It is a narrative re-counting of our conversation, which I reduced to writing, and later had the defendant read to insure that I had accurately represented our conversation. He read it thoroughly and confirmed that it did accurately reflect what he had said to me, and he then signed it."

The ADA moved next to me and pointed to the pages as he flipped them. With an apparent look of real interest on his face, he asked, "Lieutenant, what are these little squiggles and markings that I see on virtually every page of this 14-page document?"

"Those are corrections the defendant made as he reviewed the document. Each correction he made has his initials over it or next to it."

"And, who put his initials on this document?"

"He did, sir."

"So, Lieutenant, is it then your testimony that the defendant read this long, detailed confession, and that he was permitted to change anything he wanted to change, and that…"

"Objection, Your Honor," Longler again shouted as he once more jumped to his feet and kept his left hand on Graham's right forearm. "The question is leading."

"I'll rephrase that last question, Your Honor," Niemeyer volunteered.

LaVacca said, "You'll rephrase it carefully by not repeating anything close to what you just led the witness to answer."

"Yes, Your Honor," Niemeyer acknowledged the judiciary ass chewing. "My apologies to the Court if I was out of bounds."

"Ask the question and quit sucking up, Mister Niemeyer. It won't earn you any points with me."

"Yes, Your Honor," John said and nodded to the judge. Then turning his attention to me, he asked, "How did it come to be that the defendant wrote on this document."

"Well, after I put it all down in the computer, I printed the document. I then gave it to the defendant to read. I advised him it was okay to cross out the word or words he didn't like, write in any correction, and then initial the change to show that I didn't make any changes to what was his accounting of things."

"And, Lieutenant, how many changes did the defendant make?"

"Well, let's see. I guess I'll have to count them up."

"Please do, Lieutenant," Niemeyer said. He then added, "Take your time."

I began to count the corrections out loud. When I was done, I announced, "Forty-six, Mister Niemeyer. The defendant made 46 corrections or changes."

"Forty-six? Forty-six, you say? Let's see, that's about, ah, if my math is correct, that's, ah, about 3 corrections or changes per page, isn't that right, Lieutenant?"

Taking a few seconds to multiply the 14 pages by three marks per page, I responded, "Yes, sir, I guess it is. Three corrections to a page would be 42 corrections, so I guess it would be more than three to a page."

"Please read the confession for the benefit of the court record," Niemeyer said as he returned to the prosecution table.

"I can read it for myself, Counselor," LaVacca decreed from his lofty roost. "There's no need to take up courtroom time with a lengthy reading that I will accomplish much quicker in the privacy of my chambers."

"Let him read the fucking thing!" Graham yelled from his chair.

"Silence that man! Silence him! Silence him!" LaVacca shouted as he pointed the handle of his gavel in the direction of Jeff Longler.

Assistant District Attorney John Niemeyer ignored the outburst as if it had not occurred. "There is one more thing, Lieutenant. In all the time of your lengthy conversation, your typing, and your review of the confession by the defendant, did he ever say he didn't want to come to the Public Safety Building with Detective Paskell?"

"No, sir. He did not."

"Did he ever say or insinuate that he had planned on running from Investigator Paskell?"

"No sir. Not at all."

"Nothing more," Lethal John said casually, almost flippantly.

Jefferson Longler, Attorney for the Defense, pushed himself up from his chair, messed with some papers on the table, and moved absent-mindedly in my direction.

Although I am not what one would consider to be a fashion plate, Longler's mismatched, wrinkled ensemble of brown sport coat, blue slacks, gray shirt, and sort of yellow-ish tie would have made any respectable clothier gag. It would be fair to say the sport coat and pants had not felt the warmth of an iron in well over a year, and there was more than a reasonable doubt they had ever seen the inside of a dry cleaning establishment. His unkempt mop of black hair appeared to be the result of several nights of fitful sleep and the subsequent absence of a comb. The man's pear-shaped obesity added nothing to his overall sloppy appearance.

"Good afternoon, Lieutenant," the hairball of an attorney said with a pleasant smile that was obviously meant to disarm my defenses. His fat, protruding lower lip was covered with a glistening of saliva.

"Good afternoon to you, sir," I replied with a disarming smile and nod of my own.

"I'm going to ask you to indulge me for a moment, Lieutenant Amato." He paused so I could jump in with something snappy, but I simply raised my eyebrows and smiled more disarmingly. "Please help me understand the rank structure of your police department."

"I'll help in anyway I can, sir."

"I'm confident you must outrank the detectives who work under your supervision. Is that a correct assumption?"

"It is, sir."

"Now, clarify for me, how many ranks are there between you and a detective?"

"Well, sir, there is investigator or what the public refers to as 'detective,' the rank of sergeant, and then lieutenant."

"So then, is it fair to say you outrank a detective or investigator, any detective, by two grades of rank?"

"That would be a fair statement, Mister Longler," I agreed with a generous nod.

"So, if you were to give an order to a detective, say a detective such as Detective Paskell, he would be duty-bound to obey it, would he not?"

"Yes, sir, he would," I acknowledged, and at the same time noted to myself, so this is the scam! He's going to try to get me to say that I ordered Jimmy Paskell to arrest Wayne Graham. I then added quickly, "That is, if it were a legal order."

The stout defense attorney ignored the latter part of my response. "Now then, if a detective refused to obey an order from you, he would be in serious trouble, wouldn't he?"

"Well, sir, I don't know what 'serious trouble' means, but yes, he might face some form of departmental discipline."

"He '*might*' face departmental charges?"

"As I said, the order would have to be a legal one, and it would need to be one that was in the line of duty."

The unkempt attorney appeared to muddle over a thought about pursuing that line a little farther, but then seemed to decide against it. He then asked, "So if a detective received some instruction from you and he perceived it as an order, a legal, duty-related order, he would have to obey, would he not?" Longler asked casually, even though he had slipped in a new factor, i.e., what the detective would *perceive* to be an order.

"I'm not clear on the concept you are hypothesizing, Mister Longler," I said with a furrowed forehead.

"Very simply what I am saying is this, if you told a detective to, ah, let's see, what analogy could I use? Hmmm? Let's say that you mention to a detective that his shoes are very dirty, and he takes that to be an order to polish his shoes, he would then have a duty to shine his shoes, would he not?"

"I don't think so," I answered with a shrug.

"Why not?" Longler asked with a serious look of interest on his face.

Niemeyer came to his feet. "I object, Your Honor! Mister Longler is way afield here with this hypothetical discussion. I object based on relevance and also that the line of cross-examination is far removed from the limited scope of my direct examination of the witness."

Vodka LaVacca seemed bored by the objection having been raised. Without any hint of interest he inquired, "Do you wish to respond, Mister Longler?"

"Your Honor, I submit that my questioning is very relevant to the issue at hand. We had a witness in here earlier today who stated he felt it was his duty to do as his boss instructed. We now have his boss on the stand and I want to clarify that position before I proceed. Also, Your Honor, in the direct examination of the witness, the Assistant District Attorney did question the witness regarding his rank and duties, and therefore, clarification of that position is subject for cross-examination. Additionally, if it please the court, I have also subpoenaed Lt. Amato. I can dismiss him as a prosecution witness and then call him as my own witness."

"I wanted a response, Mister Longler, not a lecture suited for idiots in a pre-law class." Having made his crass observation LaVacca summed up, "The objection is overruled. However, defense will get to the point quickly so we don't spend the rest of this wasted afternoon on a tirade."

"Yes, Your Honor. Of course, Your Honor," Longler bowed and scraped. Then turning his attention to me, he fired, "If the Detective perceived your remark to be an order to shine his shoes, would he not be duty bound to shine them?"

"No, sir!" I responded emphatically.

"Why not?"

"Because there was no order to do so."

"But if he perceived it as an order, he would have to."

"He would not *have to*," I answered again.

"Your Honor," the ADA Niemeyer said in a plea. "Defense is being argumentative and I object to him repeating the same question, getting the same answer, and then asking it again."

"I agree, Mr. Prosecutor," LaVacca said eagerly. "The objection is sustained and Defense will move on!"

"Nana, nana, na-na," Graham sang to his lawyer from his chair. "You got hollered at."

Without waiting for Vodka LaVacca to chew his ass again for his client's conduct, Jefferson Longler fired a question in my direction. "Lieutenant Amato, is it not a fact that you ordered Detective Paskell to arrest my client?"

"It is not a fact," I responded calmly.

"Lieutenant, did you not tell Detective Paskell, over the police radio, to bring my client to your office?"

"There was some communication over the radio between myself and Detective Paskell when the detective saw Mister Graham arrive home. I don't recall specifically what words were used."

Longler went back to the defense table, dug through an accordion file folder and brought out a sheaf of papers. Flipping through them as he returned to the witness stand, he said, "Lieutenant, I have here a transcript of the radio communications between you and Detective Paskell on the day my client was arrested, and in here it quotes you as saying…"

"Objection!" Niemeyer damn near shouted as he jumped to his feet.

"Basis?" the bored jurist, Vodka LaVacca asked.

"Based on the fact, Your Honor, that there has been no foundation laid for that document. Based on the assumption that if the document

196

is indeed a transcript, then the best evidence would be the actual tapes and the Best Evidence Rule mandates that we hear the tapes and not what some typist thinks she heard on the tapes. Based also, Your Honor, on the fact that I was not notified in any discovery proceeding or filing of the existence of such a document or the tapes. Based on…"

"Enough! Enough, Mister Niemeyer," the judge interrupted with some noted anger in his voice. "I get the idea of your objection."

"Your Honor," Jeff Longler pleaded. "I just learned of the existence of the tapes yesterday afternoon, and only had them transcribed this morning. They were delivered to me during the lunch recess. I had no time to offer them for discovery."

"That doesn't play, Judge," Lethal John said with disgust. "Defense had an obligation to let me know he planned on using this alleged piece of evidence, even if he only received them five minutes ago. Besides, they are not the best evidence we have available and the use of…"

"Shut up!" LaVacca said firmly. "Both of you shut up and get in my chambers. Now! I want you in there now!" Then, turning to me after he stood, the judge ordered, "The witness and defendant will remain in the courtroom until our return. Both are under the guard of the bailiff, and neither will communicate with anyone in any manner during my absence from the court."

When the room was void of the legal lips, I stood and stretched. My gut told me that a cigarette was needed, but my mind said I better stay put. I walked to the back of the room so I wouldn't have to see or deal with Wayne. After having reached the large, brass doors, I turned around and my eyes caught sight of the letters over the judge's bench. "In God We Trust" was the message. Seeing the phrase made me laugh. How could we trust in God while we were standing in an American courtroom? God was concerned with justice, right and wrong, honor, and what was righteous. In this room all that was of concern was a matter of procedure. This room, this building was devoted to procedure…not facts, not honor, not righteousness, not justice.

In what we laughingly refer to as a *system* of justice, we are not interested in fact. Fact has nothing to do with American justice. The court, the judge, the *system* doesn't care, doesn't give a fat rat's ass about the question, "Did A kill B?" All our supposed system cares about is, "How did you *find out* that A killed B?"

And that's why we were going through this charade today! Our bogus, bastardized concept of justice didn't care that Wayne Graham choked three kids to death. It didn't give a crap that he tormented the parents of those three children with his disgusting details about how their children suffered at his hands. Our trust in God wasn't interested in the *fact* that he confessed to what he had done. Justice didn't want to hear the *fact* that he took great pride in telling me, bragging to me, about what he had done. Our faulted so-called *system* wasn't about to be bothered with the knowledge that Graham's confession was free and voluntary, factual and filled with evidence regarding what he had taken off the bodies of those three babies.

No! Fact was not the issue here. Fact was not on today's menu. What was being served up today was bullshit - pure, unadulterated bullshit! Today's fare was procedure. The main course was called "Thought." What were the police *thinking*? Were they thinking the arrest word? Were they *thinking* about simply giving a murdering maniac a ride or were they *thinking* they had a suspect in custody? Facts and truths are not on the menu of justice. Only thoughts and procedure matter in this restaurant.

My angry internalized screaming was interrupted when the door behind the judge's bench swung open and the three learned minds re-entered the room.

"Be seated," LaVacca instructed, believing we were all standing with our thumbs up our asses just to honor his presence.

"Mister Amato," the Honorable Lush said in my direction. "There are some facts in dispute which will become resolved with additional facts at a later portion of the hearing. However, for the time being you may be asked certain points of fact that are not, in essence, established legal fact, but may be presented as fact for your response to the factual context thereof. Are you clear on that?"

Even though I didn't have the slightest idea what the hell he was talking about, I nodded and said, "As a matter of fact, yes, I factually am clear on that fact, Your Honor." I instantly realized I had wasted a great one-liner on a man who was too stupid or drunk to appreciate it.

Actually, the way I understood it, I was going to be asked some questions which I was supposed to believe were factual, but were really just more bullshit.

"Proceed," the Great Robed One said.

"Lieutenant Amato," Longler said from his table. "Is it not a fact that you instructed Detective Paskell, in reference to my client, to 'Bring him in' when Paskell advised you that Mister Graham had arrived home?"

"I don't remember my exact words," I answered somewhat truthfully.

"Could you have said, 'Bring him in'?"

"I may have, but I don't remember using that phrase."

"Well, Lieutenant, when you hear your very own voice on recorded audio tape using that phrase, would you then remember using the phrase?"

"I don't know if that would make me remember," I responded.

"Okay, Lieutenant," Longler conceded, tiring of the game. "If you were to have used the words, 'Bring him in', would that not mean that you wanted my client arrested?"

"Not really," I said with a shrug.

Longler then made the mistake of asking a question that left me an open field on which to run. "Well, what else could the phrase mean?"

"It could mean, 'See if he's willing to come in'. It could mean, 'Use your discretion,' and if appropriate, bring him in if he volunteers to do so'."

"I really doubt that," Longler said with a forced laugh, trying to minimize his loss.

"Objection!" Niemeyer intoned from a seated position. "Argumentative."

"Sustained," LaVacca said with little enthusiasm.

Longler didn't miss a beat. "Lieutenant Amato, please explain to me how 'Bring him in' could mean anything less than you ordering my client to be arrested."

I leaned my head back and looked at the ceiling to let the court know I was giving some serious thought to the question. Finally I offered, "If one of the detectives, Paskell, whomever, was to stop for lunch and call me to say he was out for lunch, I might say to him,

'Bring in a ham sandwich when you come back to the office'. Now then, that would not be an order to seize the ham sandwich."

"Be careful, Mister Amato," LaVacca warned, and then shot a threatening look at the smiling bailiff.

I nodded in the direction of His Excellency as Longler pushed forward. "Maybe not, but it would be an order, would it not?"

"No, sir. Not at all."

"It wouldn't?" Longler asked with a smile.

"It would not," I answered without a smile.

"But you would be angry if the detective returned and did not bring you this ham sandwich, would you not?"

"No, sir."

"You're under oath, Lieutenant."

"I know that, Mister Longler. I am under oath and I'm telling you that I would not be mad if the detective came back to the office without a ham sandwich." I made the comment fully believing that someone other than me could see how utterly stupid this was becoming. That belief was ill-placed.

"You're in the office," Longler proposed. "You're hungry. You want some lunch badly. A detective calls you. He says he's out at a wonderful café, in fact, your favorite café. You tell him to bring in a ham sandwich for you. You can almost see the sandwich, smell it, can almost taste it. Then, as the detective walks in the office an hour later, you see he has no ham sandwich. You wouldn't be angry with the detective?"

"Where was he?" I asked.

"Who?" Longler asked of me.

"The detective!" I answered.

"What difference does that make?" the defense attorney asked with an apparent loss of patience.

John LaVacca came to life. "I'm getting tired of the both of you. If you think you're going to use my courtroom for some Abbott and Costello act, you're seriously mistaken. Move on to something else, or call it a day, Mister Longler. Personally, I am getting sick and tired of your parables of shoe shinning and ham sandwiches." Then turning to face me, the judge intoned, "And as for you, Mister Amato, I don't think, not for one damn minute, you're amusing."

"Your Honor," I said with my best look of sincerity. "I wasn't trying to be amusing. My point is that I expect my detectives to use common sense. If the detective has a reason for not doing as I requested, I would not get mad at him for not bringing in the ham sandwich or Mister Graham."

Jefferson Longler tried to get back on the offensive, but his steam was gone. After three or four more questions, he relinquished the floor.

"Re-direct, Your Honor?" John Niemeyer asked immediately.

"Make it brief and to the point," LaVacca said. "And I will not have more discussion about ham sandwiches, or any nonsense like that."

"Of course, Judge. The Prosecution will not go there." Niemeyer conceded. Then, turning his attention to me, he asked, "Lieutenant, how long has Detective Paskell worked for you?"

"About four years, sir."

"And do you know him to be a man of good judgment?"

"Yes, sir, I do."

"Have you ever told him to do something, and he failed to do it or refused to do it?"

I had to think about that one. Jimmy Paskell is about as loyal as they come, but yet, from time to time we did have our disagreements on how best to attack a case. "Well, sir, there was a time when I instructed him to locate a witness we were looking for. We received a lead about where the guy might be staying. Paskell went out to find the guy, but instead of going to the location, he went onto something else. He was on his way to get the witness and he got sidetracked with two guys he saw near a corner grocery store. He never got to the witness but he did manage to bag two guys who were about to do an armed robbery."

"Did you discipline him for that? Did you yell at him? Punish him?"

"No, sir. The man used good discretion. I couldn't fault him for that."

"Therefore, Lieutenant Amato," Niemeyer said strongly. "Is it your testimony here today, while under oath, that you want, that you expect your personnel to use, to exercise their own discretion?"

201

"That is absolutely correct, Mister Niemeyer."

"No further questions, Your Honor."

"Re-cross, Your Honor?" Jeff Longler requested almost before John Niemeyer completed his statement.

"This is not going to go on all day, gentlemen," Vodka LaVacca bellowed from his elevated position. "Each of you need to get your case together, ask your questions, and move on to the next witness. It's almost four in the afternoon, and I do not plan on being here all night. Mr. Longler, you will re-cross, and then I will allow the prosecution one last round of direct examination. You will then have a final, and I do mean final, cross-examination."

I could understand the judge's exasperation. After all, the man had put in more than a full hour in the morning before taking a two-and-a-half hour lunch. And now, during the afternoon, he had been forced to sit on his ass for almost another hour-and-a-half. That was hard work for an elected official who was pulling down well over a hundred grand a year.

Pulling my mind back from its journey to cynic-land, I became aware of Jeff Longler asking, "So, as you've testified, Lieutenant, you do allow and expect your detectives to use discretion?"

"Yes, sir." I responded.

"So, when you instructed Detective Paskell, in reference to my client, to 'bring him in' what you were saying was, 'Use your best discretion'."

"Mister Longler," I said with some exasperation in my voice. "I don't recall using the words 'Bring him in,' but if I did, I was expressing my desire to have the man interviewed, preferably in our offices, if that fit the circumstances."

"Lieutenant, that is enough of a run-around for me," the shabby defense attorney said with exaggerated disgust. "I just have one more question for you. Whatever you said to Detective Paskell, it was not in any way, shape or form, an order for him *not* to bring in, *not* to take into custody, and *not* to arrest my client. Is that correct?"

"That may be somewhat correct."

"Somewhat correct? Somewhat correct? What is that supposed to mean?" Longler asked loudly.

"It means whatever I said to the detective was meant for him to use his best judgment in dealing with the defendant."

"Nothing more, Your Honor," Longler said with notable exasperation as he tossed his notes on the defense table.

"Mister Niemeyer?" LaVacca asked in a threatening tone.

"I have nothing further, Your Honor."

"Mister Amato, you are excused," the judge said. Without a breath he continued, "It is now four-oh-five, gentlemen. If you have another witness to call, then call him. However, in any event, we will finish by 4:30 p.m. If you can do it by then, call the witness.

Jeff Longler spoke up. "If the prosecution is finished, Your Honor, I have only one witness to call. It is my understanding that she is here and ready. Her testimony should only take ten minutes."

As I picked up my notes and case file from the prosecution's desk, I found a note on top of the folder. It read, "R&G >work!!" Cupping the note in my palm, I nodded at the ADA. With the silent conversation finished, I turned to leave the courtroom.

"Defense calls Shirley Hillyard," Jeff Longler announced to the judge.

Pushing my way out of the unnecessarily large courtroom doors, I saw the next witness standing in the hallway. An audio tape was clutched in her right hand. Being that Shirley is the Senior Supervisor of the Emergency Communications Center, it was obvious she had been called as the one to fetch and play my recorded words. The words I spoke over the police radio on the day Jimmy Paskell saw Wayne Graham return from killing Timmy Bidwell—"Bring him in"—were the words that were going to possibly ring the death knoll to our case.

Shirley gave me one of her beautiful smiles and then pulled it back to grimace as she passed me and said, "I'm sorry, Mike."

"It's not your fault," I answered as I held the door open for her. "Do the right thing."

In response to Niemeyer's cryptic note, it was almost five o'clock in the afternoon when I entered the bar. At that time of the day, the Robe and Gavel held a moderate crowd of attorneys, cops, court stenographers, clerks, and a couple of *Democrat and Chronicle* newspaper reporters. Not seeing Lethal John in the place, I ordered a double Scotch and eased myself into a corner. The main reason I came to the joint was that I had to know what Jimmy had said in court before I got on the stand.

It was a question I dearly wanted to ask Paskell myself, but by the time I made it back to the office after court, he had already left. Donovan asked me what the hell was going on, but rather than get into details, I simply told him the Huntley Hearing wasn't going well.

If Jimmy had really testified that he intended to arrest Graham, then Longler was going to be able to make a lot of legal hay when he summed up his position to LaVacca. My testimony had, in all reality, done little to help the case.

"Let's find a table," John Niemeyer said as he walked up on my left side.

A minute later, we were in a corner of the room, seated at a small, round cocktail table.

"So, what the hell happened with Paskell today?" was my opening question.

"Longler led him down the primrose path," Niemeyer said with a shrug. "He asked him all the preliminary questions like did he arrest Graham, did he handcuff him, did he control his movements in anyway, did he escort him to the car by guiding him by the arm, all the routine stuff."

"How did Jimmy handle it?"

"He did fine with all of that, Mike. He kept answering 'No'. Then Longler switched tactics and started attacking Paskell, accusing him of being disloyal to you, asking him if he was a renegade cop, if he was in the habit of being insubordinate. I hate to admit it but Jeff Longler was smooth. It was a beautiful approach. He knows Jimmy is as loyal as a basset hound, but he kept attacking his loyalty, his integrity, his respect for his superiors."

"So?" I asked, somewhat confused by what I was being told.

"So, when he told Paskell that you had twice ordered him to pick up Graham and ordered him to bring in Graham, he then popped the magic question. I saw it coming, but there was nothing I could do to prevent it. I had been objecting all over the place. LaVacca was overruling every single one of my objections. Finally, after having

Jimmy defend his honesty, loyalty, integrity, obedience, and the rest of the Boy Scout oath, Longler asked him, 'So when the Lieutenant orders you to bring a guy in, and that guy tells you he isn't going with you, and he breaks to run from you, do you just let him go?' Paskell fell for it hook, line, and sinker. He sat up straight and said, 'When the Lieutenant says to bring them in, I bring them in one way or another!' Bingo! That was it. Longler just smiled and said he had no more questions of the witness."

"Okay," I conceded. "That was stupid, but why the big deal? It was an off-hand remark, a wise crack in response to a hypothetical question!"

"It shows his intent, Mike. It shows that Paskell's intent was to arrest, physically, forcefully, do whatever he had to do in order to get Graham into the Public Safety Building. If that was his intent, without having sufficient probable cause and without a warrant, the arrest is illegal, and the poison tree bullshit kicks in."

We sat silent for a minute, maybe two. My mind was having a difficult time understanding that even though we did everything correct and legal, what was really important was what a guy was *thinking*! Paskell and I acted right, did the right things, but Jimmy's private thoughts could set a killer, a child killer, a repeated child killer free. It was stupid, idiotic. It was nonsense.

"So, did we lose it?" I asked.

"Not yet," was his direct reply that offered no solace.

"Did I say 'bring him in' on the tape?"

"Not once, but twice!"

"Shit!"

"Actually, the first time you said 'Pick him up' and the second time you said, 'Bring him in'."

"Brilliant. That was absolutely brilliant of me!" I said in disgust.

Lethal John gave me a tiny smile and said, "Shirley Hillyard did a nice job of playing down the quality of the tape, saying the tapes are re-used many times, and that the quality suffers from all the overuse. Still in all, it was there, pretty much plain as day."

"She's a nice kid," I commented while swirling the Scotch. "She was a hell of a dispatcher, and is one of the best supervisors they have over there." After downing a healthy swig I suggested, "We can still go forward even if we lose the confession…can't we?"

"On what, Mike? Without the confession we're holding an empty bag."

"We have the note he wrote to the Taylors. There's the audio tape he sent to the Bidwells. The crime lab people already confirmed it's Graham's voice on the tape, as well as his handwriting on the note. Both of those items tie him to the killings. We also have the two vehicles used in all three killings. We can put him in the red Honda and the black van. All of that should be good enough to get us into a trial."

"Sure," Lethal John nodded without looking at me. "It will get us *into* a trial, but there's no way on God's green earth it will get us *through a trial.*" He then looked up to me. His face was expressionless. "We can prove he wrote the letter and made the tape, but all that shows is that he's a sick opportunist who was terrorizing the parents. There's nothing on the tape or in the letter that tells us anything more than the kids were strangled…and that little item was in the paper almost every day."

"And the vehicles?"

"Mike, how many red Hondas did you guys have to run down? Two hundred? Three hundred? The defense will make a hell of a point of that number and the limitless possibilities of the number of people who have access to those cars, *and* all the ones of those who own, borrow, or have access to black vans."

I had to swallow that one. My only retort was, "Yeah, but…"

"But nothing, Mike. Sure, we can push this thing to trial, but if we lose, that's the end of it. There are no second chances."

"So what is there to do if LaVacca throws out the confession?"

"You hope for a break, for a new witness, for Graham to brag to someone. Then when…if that happens, we take the tape, the note, the cars, *and* the new information and we try to run it past a jury. Up until then, we're up the creek without a paddle…and in a very leaky canoe!"

We downed our drinks and stood. Walking to the door, I asked, "What are the odds that LaVacca will let the confession stand?"

Lethal John looked up at me, smiled, and asked, "What are the chances we won't have any snow next winter?"

"You know if Graham gets out, he's going to hit again. This boy likes what he's doing. If he walks, we're going to hear from him again...and maybe more than once."

"Do you really think so?" John asked. "Maybe this scrape with us will scare him into stopping."

"I *know* so, John. Just as sure as we're standing here, Graham will kill again! He enjoys it too much to stop now. We haven't scared him one little bit; all we've done is enriched his appetite for notoriety!"

Outside the tavern the ADA took a couple of steps and stopped. Turning to me with a solemn look he said, "Mike, you need to know that if LaVacca tosses out the confession, the DA is not going to take any chances with a trial."

"What are you telling me?" I asked Niemeyer.

"We'll try to get LaVacca to delay the trial date to say, maybe September, October, in the hopes that something new will pop up by then. But more realistically, my boss will probably want me to move for a dismissal on the Graham case."

"Dismissal? Are you nuts, John? The public will go ape shit! They'll be up in arms over Graham being back out there."

"You're right, Mike. There will be political hell to pay. But, if we ask for a dismissal *without prejudice,* and if we can get LaVacca to go for it, at least we will be able to push for a new trial at a later date. If we go to trial, the instant we swear in the first witness we, can't back out without attaching double jeopardy to the case."

As I returned to my car, it dawned on me that I was living a very sick good news-bad news joke. The good news was that if Wayne hit the streets again, we would get a fresh crack at him. The bad news was, in order to get that shot at him, another child would, in all likelihood, have to be sacrificed.

CHAPTER FIFTEEN

A DUTCH ACT

We waited five days for Vodka LaVacca to announce his ruling. Finally, like the anticipated second shoe, it hit! Rochester's daily newspaper, the *Democrat and Chronicle*, carried the not-too-flattering story on the front page.

Police Error Puts Graham Trial at Risk

> *In a decision announced yesterday, Monroe County Court Judge John LaVacca ruled any statements which may have been made by Wayne Graham, the person charged with three recent killings of local children, would not be admissible in the upcoming criminal trial. LaVacca cited serious errors made by police as the basis for his decision.*
>
> *In announcing his decision, Judge LaVacca declared, "The police will not make an illegal arrest, interrogate the person, and then hope to come into my courtroom touting a confession. The law is clear on this matter. If the arrest is improper, then everything after the arrest is improper. I find sufficient evidence of the arrest being not only morally improper but also illegal. Therefore, with the interrogation being tainted, any alleged confession is tainted, and everything that comes from the alleged confession is*

tainted. It (suppressing the alleged confession) is the penalty overzealous police pay for making the error of disregarding the laws of this land."

The judge stated Rochester Police Detective James Paskell admitted in court that it was his intent to arrest Wayne Graham when he went to the defendant's home shortly after the body of Timothy Bidwell was discovered. The detective also acknowledged he lacked sufficient probable cause to make the arrest, but that he had been ordered to do so by his supervisor, Lt. Mike Amato of the Violent Crimes Unit.

Assistant District Attorney John Niemeyer stated he respects the court's opinion, but believes, "The judge may have failed to consider the totality of the situation when he made his ruling." He stated he does not know if the District Attorney's office will appeal LaVacca's decision.

Jefferson Longler, the attorney representing Wayne Graham, stated he doubted any appeal was possible. Speaking from the steps of the Hall of Justice he said, "When the police go into the sanctity of man's home, drag him out of there, bring him to a police interrogation room and bully him, they cannot expect to have any contrived statements admitted into a United States court of law." Asked if he thought there were police abuses in this case, Longler said he complimented Detective Paskell for having the courage to tell the truth on the stand. He did, however, condemn the acts of Lt. Amato who pressured Paskell to make the arrest. Graham's attorney said it was his intent to file for his client's immediate release from custody and that he may file a civil suit on behalf of his client against the police for the civil rights' violations allegedly suffered by Graham.

Highly placed sources in the Rochester Police Department thought it likely that Detective Paskell's immediate supervisor, Lt. Amato, may be disciplined

> *for his role in the arrest of Graham. According to*
> *court records, it was Amato who ordered Graham's*
> *arrest."*

My obscene litany caused Max to retreat to a far corner of the kitchen. Taking my morning cup of coffee over to the intimidated pooch, I scratched him behind the ears and assured him he was not the target of my anger.

When I arrived at work, a dark cloud of doom and gloom hung over the squad room. Copies of the morning paper sat crumpled on three desks. Bobby St. John and Tommy Romano were hunched over their computer keyboards, punching out reports concerning a string of recent rapes they had been assigned to investigate. Frank Donovan simply looked at me and shook his head. Gail Walz gave me one of those half-smiles that one offers when they don't know what to say. Only Jimmy Paskell was on his feet and obviously in the midst of an animated oratory.

"Did you see this morning's *Demagogue and Comical*?" Jimmy asked as he extended a copy of the paper to my face.

"I saw it, Jimmy."

"What are we going to do about it, Boss?"

"Do? What can we do? They're the media, they can say whatever the hell they want to say," I said in disgust.

Following me into my office, Paskell pushed the issue. "You have to do something, Lute! This is bullshit! They're making it look like I sold you down the river. I didn't do that. I was just telling the squad what really happened. I didn't sell you out."

"Jimmy, I know you didn't sell me out. I know you, and I know you're not the type of guy to sell me out. It's not an issue with me." Facing the man, I put my right hand on his left elbow. "Just let it be. It'll blow over in a few days and everyone will forget it ever happened. The public has a short memory."

"But you have to do something, Boss. No one dragged Graham out of the house. You have to call a press conference and set the news people straight. We didn't do anything wrong. You, the chief, somebody has to tell them that Graham came with me willingly, eagerly."

"Screw the bastards," Romano contributed from his desk. "Shut the sons-of-bitches off for a few weeks. Don't give them any news on anything."

"Put a lid on it, Tommy," St. John said to his partner.

"No. He's right, Bobby," Paskell said as if he had just been hit with a revelation. "We shut them off completely. We don't tell them anything. Tommy's right. The media has to come for us for their information. If we don't give them anything, then they'll have to back off."

"Jimmy," I said in a way that I hoped would calm him. "You don't do battle with an organization that buys paper by the ton and gets their ink in 50-gallon barrels."

"What's that mean?" the agitated detective asked.

"We can go to war with them, but there's no way we're going to win. We might get our side of the story in the paper once…and even if we do, they'll bury it. They go to press every day. They can run their side over and over again, put it in their editorials, make it part of future stories. We might win a battle or two, but they'll beat us to death during the war." I took a deep breath and consoled, "Let it go. Let the thing die its own slow death. We've got other cases pending, other things to do. Let's keep our focus on that. It'll work out. Really, it will."

"But I'm being made to look like an idiot or something. My wife's calling me, asking if I'm in trouble. My damn father-in-law wants to know why I would do something like arresting a man when there was no proof. Everybody thinks I'm a jerk."

"Look, Jimmy, you have nothing to hide." My voice was louder and angrier than I intended it to be. "You did exactly what I told you to do. That's all there is to it! What you said in court was the honest-to-God truth. If I tell you to bring in someone and you don't, I'm going to climb all over your ass. You have nothing to hide or be ashamed of. You tell your relatives that you work for an idiot and that it was me who messed the whole thing up."

"Well, that isn't…"

It was some relief that my phone rang and Major Skip Winston asked me to come to his office post haste.

The relief quickly dissipated when I entered the Major's hideout and saw Deputy Chief Ernie Cooper seated there. It was obvious the bad day was going to take a turn for the worse.

"Lieutenant," Skip Winston said as I entered the room. "Based on the information you've been giving me, I've been keeping the Deputy Chief updated on the developments of this Graham matter." Then gesturing with his right hand to the sawed-off excuse for a cop, he added, "However, the Deputy would like to have you address some specific concerns he has."

"What concerns are those?" I asked both men with a hint of belligerence.

"Concerns such as how we got ourselves into this pickle with the Graham case being tossed out by Judge LaVacca?" Edgy Ernie Cooper asked.

"You would have to ask the judge, Deputy," I said matter-of-factly. "I don't understand it, and I sure as hell don't agree with his ruling."

"The papers say you ordered Paskell to make the arrest," Cooper said in an accusatory tone I didn't like.

"The papers say whatever the hell they feel will sell newspapers," was my response. "I told Paskell to pick up Graham. I didn't mean it literally, but that's the line of crap the defense pushed on to LaVacca, and, as it turns out, LaVacca was drunk enough to buy it."

"What about you?" Cooper asked as he stood up so that he could almost tower over my seated frame. "Were you so drunk, you don't know what you said?"

"If you want to back that statement up with some charges, Deputy, then say it again. If you can't, then, if I were you, I wouldn't go there a second time."

"Is that a threat, Lieutenant?"

"No, sir, it is not. It's simply advice." I stared at him as I said the words, and then for a full ten or fifteen seconds longer before I added, "Look, Deputy, with all due respect, if you want to rip me out for using a bad choice of words with Paskell, then do it. I was wrong and I have an ass-chewing coming. But don't take cheap shots at me for mistakes that were made in the heat of an investigation. You wouldn't like someone going into your history of mistakes, or referring to instances that gained you the nickname of 'Quick Draw', and I sure as hell don't like having you bringing up my old ways."

Cooper took a minute to draw a deep breath and then narrowed his eyes as he blew the air out of his lungs in a manner that I guess was supposed to send shivers through me. Noting that I wasn't shaken by his fire-breathing-dragon routine, he finally spoke.

"Lieutenant, I expect you to file charges against Detective James Paskell."

"For what?" I asked with ire in my voice and eyes.

"For making an illegal arrest," Cooper noted calmly.

"You guys don't get it, do you?" I asked of Skip Winston and Cooper. "There was no arrest! Paskell did not arrest the man! He went to the home of Graham, a suspected serial killer, told him he was a suspect, and asked him to come in to talk to us. Graham came freely and willingly. That's it. End of story. Period!"

"I have reviewed the matter with Judge LaVacca and the District Attorney," Edgy Ernie said with an air of superiority. "Both confirm that Paskell contradicts that little cover story of yours, and both confirm that he admitted in open court that it was his very intent to arrest Graham."

"He got set up by the defense attorney. Longler threw out a hypothetical question, asking Paskell what he would do if Graham tried to run. Paskell answered, somewhat flippantly, something to the effect that he would have brought him in." I looked at both men, and although Winston seemed to understand, he also seemed unwilling to jump into the discussion. Cooper, on the other hand, wore a thin smile that said he was not giving in to rational thinking.

"I want him charged," the pint-sized Deputy Chief repeated as he began to move toward the office door.

"And what good will that do?"

"It will help preserve the integrity of this department, Lieutenant, That's what it will do!" Cooper stopped and said as his hand reached for the door. "By six o'clock tonight, every evening news program, every damn talk show in the area, all of them will be raking the department over the coals about the way *you*, handled this case. I'm not going to have that happen while I'm running…ah, involved in running this department, Lieutenant. Paskell will be somewhat inconvenienced but the department will be spared more mud slinging by the damn media."

"Really, Deputy? Do you really believe that bringing a good, hard working, decent cop up on some bullshit charges will redeem the department against some courthouse crap slung by an erratic, sloppy attorney and a pompous, drunken judge?"

"You just do your job, Lieutenant Amato."

"And you get in touch with reality, Deputy!" I spit back. When the deputy chief froze at the door, I demanded, "I want to see Chief Murphy on this matter."

Without turning around, Cooper said, "If you read your e-mail now and then, you would know the Chief is out of town for the remainder of the week. He left me in charge, Lieutenant. And, contrary to you, I will live up to my responsibilities and take charge. When the Chief comes back from his vacation, he will find that I have been running things very well...and he will find the department intact."

When the door closed behind the Napoleonic ass of Ernie Cooper, I turned to Major Winston. "You do know he's wrong, don't you, Major?"

"Sure he's wrong, but what can we do about it? He has the rank and we don't."

"So we just go ahead and ruin a guy's career because that asshole wants a pound of flesh for his trophy case?" I questioned mockingly.

"Mike, just do as he says, and when the Chief comes back, the investigation into the allegations will still be bogged down in Internal Affairs. The entire thing will end up being buried after Murphy sees what's gong on. I'm betting the charges will never see the light of day."

"Yeah. Right, Major. I'll screw up a guy's career and life just to take the easy way out."

"There's no other way, Mike," Winston cautioned. "If you don't bring Paskell up on charges, Cooper will end up bringing you up on charges for insubordination."

"I'll take my chances with that, Major," I said over my shoulder as I left the room and didn't bother to close the door behind me.

Back in my office, Jimmy Paskell again hit me with a plea to deal with the press. I wasn't in the mood to deal with it.

"Look, Jimmy, just go out and do your damn job the way you've always done it. I'm telling you, in a couple of days all this will be behind us. It'll be forgotten and some other poor son-of-a-bitch will be the target for the media animals."

"But in the meantime, Lieutenant…"

"In the meantime, you do your frigging job!"

Paskell stepped toward me quickly, in a manner I didn't like. Sticking his finger in my face, he yelled, "Why don't you have the balls to stick up for me?"

Grabbing his finger and pulling it down, I asked him through clenched teeth, "Do you want to see balls, Mister? I'll show you balls! I'll rip this finger off your hand and shove it up your ass!"

When I let go of my detective's finger, Gail Walz took her partner by the arm and told him, "Come on, Jimmy. Let's go. This thing's getting out of hand."

Paskell backed away as he and I continued to glare at each other. Finally he turned away from me, slipped on his sport coat and left the office. At the door he stopped to throw one last punch. "If it was one of your prima donnas, if it was Bobby or your *paisano* Tommy Romano, you'd go to bat for them!"

"Hey, fuck you, Jimmy!" Romano said as he got up from his desk and took a giant step toward his brother cop. Walz, sensing the explosion that was about to happen, took her partner by the arm to lead him down the hall to the elevators.

The incidents with Cooper and then Paskell seethed in me all morning. Although I poured through a ton of paperwork, signed reports, approved requests and budget items, opened mail and sent other mail out in yellow departmental envelopes, my mind never focused on the tasks at hand.

Jimmy was right. I lacked the balls to fight for him. I was getting as bad as Skip Winston and Edgy Ernie. With me asking him to ride out the storm, I had sunk to the level of the bosses above me. Cooper wanted Paskell as a sacrificial lamb. I simply wanted him silenced. I owed the man more than that.

215

I left the building for a short walk around the Civic Center Plaza. Besides needing the air, my nerves were begging for nicotine. Sitting on the plaza on the east side of the Public Safety Building, the solution to my problem walked up to me and smiled.

"You're making a lot of work for me, Mike Amato," Monica Sheldon said.

Squinting the sunlight out of my eyes, I looked up at the attractive woman. "Hi, Monica," was my lame greeting.

"Be careful, Mike! Don't be too nice! You might ruin your reputation." Her tone told me she was offended by my opening.

"Sorry. I…I'm just mulling some things over in my head and you kind of caught me with my somewhat limited mind engaged in a couple of different thoughts."

"Well, if that's the case, I have more worries for you to consider," she said as she sat down next to me and pulled a cigarette from her purse. Without waiting for an inquiry from me, she continued. "The entire media establishment has been all over me since I stepped into the office this morning. The paper, the television and radio people, everybody's been calling and wanting some release from the department regarding the court ruling on Graham. I went down to see Cooper and he told me he would have a release for me later today. I'm on my way back from lunch, so I was going to stop up to see him now."

It was an impetuous thought, one that was not well thought out—a thought that didn't consider all the angles. It hit my head and without editing my mind, my lips volunteered, "Yeah, well, I was supposed to get in contact with you and give you a statement. That's what Cooper wants. I was just sitting out here trying to lay it out in my mind so I could write it up for you as a press release."

"There's no need for that, Mike. Give it to me right here. It's my job to write it up, polish it, put the right spin on it, and all that." After she took out her narrow reporter's pad, Monica asked, "So what is it?"

"The official position of the Department is that I improperly ordered the arrest of Graham and that Paskell simply followed my instructions. I received my reprimand this morning from Cooper and Winston. I don't know how you want to put that out, but the bottom line is that I was the one that screwed up and Paskell ended up taking the heat for it in court."

Monica jotted down some notes, paused for a half-minute, and then added more scribbling to her pad. Folding the spiral pad closed, she said, "I'll handle it, Mike. It's going to be difficult to sugarcoat it. I'll try to make it come out that your name isn't in the release, but I want you to know the media guys will speculate it was you who got the reprimand."

"Don't sweat it. Put my name in the release and take all the mystery out of it," I said as I stood up and made some excuse about having to go check on something. It was a given that Cooper would go through the roof when he saw the story, and that Monica would be royally pissed at me for feeding her the bum information, but hey, what the hell, I've kind of made a career out of pissing off people.

The next day was Saturday and over the weekend, after the splash about my reprimand, the story sort of faded away. Paskell called me Saturday morning to apologize for ripping into me. He added he was sorry that I was taking all the heat. After that, things stayed quiet…until Wednesday.

Without Graham's confession in the game, the case was going to go nowhere. If we tried to go to trial and then lost the case, we would never be able to re-open it. The best legal course of action was for the District Attorney to move for a dismissal of the case and wait to see if something new developed.

Although he could have ordered Graham's release, Judge LaVacca was not about to handle that political bomb. When he came up for re-election the next year, he would have no trouble justifying his decision to throw out Graham's confession. After all, it was the big, bad policemen who abused the defendant, and what else could an honorable Constitution-protecting judge do, but set the confession aside? However, it was quite another thing for him to order the release of a serial child-killer. His political opponent would make too much hay out of putting that headline into play when it came close to the election.

Therefore, the heat ended up in the lap of Rudy Cantor, Monroe County's District Attorney. He was the one left holding the political football. Unfortunately, it was he who had told the media that he personally would seek the death penalty. However, that was before Vodka LaVacca tossed out the confession. If the DA's office tried to prosecute the case now, without the confession, Cantor would end up looking incompetent when Graham was found not guilty. On the other hand, if he admitted the case was not prosecutable, he would ethically have to seek the release of Graham. And, the most unfortunate circumstance for the prosecutor was that he was also up for re-election in the coming year.

It was Wednesday when Cantor released the news that his office would not prosecute Wayne Graham…and in order to get the stench off him, Mister District Attorney spread the stink all over the police department. Personally, I don't hold that against the man. It wasn't his screw up that got the confession thrown out.

One indisputable fact of nature is that shit does flow downhill! In fact, recent scientific studies have shown that it not only flows, it also picks up speed and mass as it travels. That's where I was Wednesday morning…right at the bottom of the hill. When Cantor blamed the PD, it became necessary for the Chief—who has a partial responsibility for getting the mayor re-elected—to jump all over me. It was a bad scene all the way around.

Chief Matthew Murphy had returned from his vacation and eagerly devoured my ass for breakfast Thursday morning. Later, Deputy Chief Cooper reminded me, somewhat smugly, that if I had listened to him about Paskell, the matter would have been settled.

Later in the day, Investigator Paskell, upon hearing about my official, written reprimand at the hands of the chief, took the opportunity to beat up on himself once again.

Things were bad, but as bad as they appeared, they were about to get worse. Friday morning was going to reveal just how badly the entire case had impacted the squad…and especially, Detective James Paskell.

The office is sometimes a prison, and other times it becomes a refuge. This particular Friday morning it was both…and neither.

I had arrived at 7:30 a.m. and was getting reports together for the morning briefing with the teams. It was obvious the squad was coming apart. The teams had organized into sub-cliques, one barely acknowledging the existence of the other. It was my job, as their supposed leader, to keep the detectives' morale up so that they would continue to do their job as it related to four open homicides, a string of rapes, and a series of violent armed robberies at neighborhood grocery stores...all of which were still on our respective plates.

When the phone rang, I picked it up with one hand and lifted the ever-present cup of coffee with the other. Before I could announce it was I who was answering the call, Gail Walz's excited voice cut in.

"Lieutenant, this is Gail. Get over to Rochester General Hospital right away. They're bringing in Jimmy. He hanged himself, and it doesn't look good."

"When? What...?"

"I came by his house to pick him up and he wasn't waiting out front like he usually does. I went in to see his wife and she said she saw him going into the garage. When I went to the garage, I found him hanging. He used his belt. I lifted him up and yelled for his wife. She had to get the belt off the beam. She's a basket case right now."

"Is he...?"

"The ambulance is leaving now. He's alive but it doesn't look good. I've got to go. I'll see you at General, okay?"

"Okay. Right. Go ahead. I'll see you at the hospital."

I made the announcement to the squad, told St. John to make sure Major Winston was briefed, and then left the building. On the way through the city's morning traffic, I mentally kicked my ass for seeing the warning signs and ignoring them; for not ordering Paskell into the city's Employee Assistance Program so he could get the counseling help he so obviously needed.

Somewhere around St. Paul Street, about halfway to the hospital, my mind shifted gears and I tried to make sense of Jimmy Paskell's attempted suicide. I understood the desire to commit suicide— understood it all too well. In my days of heavy drinking I had looked down the barrel of my duty weapon more than once and thought— longed for—the peace the bullet would bring as it entered my brain. For me—divorced, alone, and alcoholic—suicide was a viable option. But for Jimmy...? He had a wife, family, kids, outside interests that went far beyond the cop job.

As I neared the hospital, my mind switched gears and went to thoughts of nonsense, thoughts that had little to do with Paskell's act of desperation. I guess the brain sometimes does that—it switches to safer subjects to save the thinker from the pain brought up by existing thoughts.

A Dutch Act. That's what the old-time cops called suicide. I don't know why they gave the act that name. I had never heard that suicide was all that prevalent among the Dutch people. In fact, I'm willing to lay odds on the fact that Holland is the type of place where one would be willing to spend an extended life. Why then was this act of stupidity, this act of self-indulgence given such a name? Who knows, my mind conceded as it shrugged off the thought.

The doors of the hospital's emergency ward glided open as soon as my foot stepped on the pressure-sensitive mat. Inside I was confronted by the tormented face of Detective Gail Walz.

"How does it look?" I asked as I approached her.

"They have a pulse and he's breathing on his own. They just don't know how long he was out or if there's any brain damage."

"Is his wife here?"

"She's over at the Administration Desk, giving them information."

"What's...what's her name?" I asked and flushed in embarrassment at my ignorance.

"Jane. Her name is Jane. The kids are John, Julie, and Tamara," Walz briefed me without hinting her disappointment that I didn't even know the names of my detectives' significant others.

Over the next half-hour, Gail and I sat together in the waiting room and made small talk. After a few minutes, I excused myself to call Skip Winston and give him an update. In a second call, the squad was also advised of the situation.

Gail found the coffee station reserved for nurses and doctors and retrieved two welcomed cups of coffee for us. With the comfort of coffee in our hands, Walz introduced me to an attractive, middle-aged nurse with a blue nametag that identified her as Ann Edenfield. The information she shared with us spoke volumes of the bond between cops and ER nurses—an affinity based on the similarity of our jobs in which we saw the very worst of what man does to his fellow man.

Nurse Edenfield told us that Jimmy was doing well and that the doctors believed there may not be any permanent effects from his aborted suicide attempt.

As the nurse stood to leave, Gail whispered to me, "Here comes Jane Paskell."

I stood as the two women embraced, and then, after they broke, I reached my arms out to Jimmy's wife. The slap she delivered to my face was instantaneous, sharp, and unexpected.

"You have a lot of nerve coming here, Amato," the woman said vehemently. "You did this. I told you! I told you this was going to happen. You drove Jimmy to this, you bastard! You did this and now you come here like some...like you have sympathy. It's too late for your sympathy."

Gail took Jane Paskell into her arms to comfort her...and perhaps to protect me from her hatred. Regardless of the motivation, I knew I couldn't remain there, so I stepped outside. With a fresh drag of nicotine in my lungs, I thought thoughts about me...and cops...and homicides...and spouses.

Five days later Jimmy Paskell was released from the hospital's care and was sent to the psychiatric ward at Strong Memorial Hospital. The doctors said he had suffered—in layman's terms—a nervous breakdown brought on by the stress of his job.

That night, for the first time in seven months, I went off the wagon, and went off hard. Sitting in the Robe and Gavel, about halfway to mind-numbing drunk, I saw a face in the mirror and scowled at the appearance. I hated the face. My first impulse was to throw the shot glass in my right hand at the figure, but instead, I got up from the bar and the mirror, and moved to a small table in the corner of the bar...a table far away from the mirror and my reflection.

CHAPTER SIXTEEN

DEJA VU

Summer turned to fall and life went on. The murders slowed their pace slightly, but the rapes and the violent robberies kept rolling in at their usual daily rate. With Paskell on a medical leave of absence, Frankie Donovan began to partner with Gail Walz and the squad continued to do their work, but the life had gone out of all of them.

Jimmy spent almost four weeks in R-Wing, the psychiatric ward at Strong Memorial Hospital, before he was finally released. He spent another six weeks in counseling and therapy before he returned to duty. He and I talked a couple of times while he was still out on leave. In response to his asking, I assured him his spot in the Violent Crimes Squad was still being held for him, but the truth was I feared the day he would return to work and there would be a new body, a kid's body, for him to see. Zack McGill, the department's psychiatrist, advised against Paskell's return to the job that had cost him his sanity. Both the Union and McGill tried to persuade Jimmy to avail himself of a psychiatric retirement, but he wouldn't hear of it. Finally, Jane Paskell stepped in and absolutely insisted that her husband not return to his former assignment. The department, in one of its finer moments, welcomed Detective Paskell back to the fold and offered him his choice of assignments in Crime Analysis, Forgery and Frauds, Research and Planning, or Internal Affairs. Jimmy opted for the Forgery and Frauds assignment and returned to work on a cool, clear October morning.

It had been slightly more than a year since the Becky Chilsom homicide, and somewhere along the way Wayne Graham had disappeared. Each member of the squad had taken on the unassigned responsibility to check Silver Street every so often just to see what Graham was up to. On two or three occasions, Bobby St. John had even engaged the killer in casual conversation. Bobby let Graham know we held a certain interest in him, and Graham let St. John know he didn't really care.

On one of those visits, Graham—in an intentional less-than-coy move—let Bobby know the insanity bit he had played in front of Judge John LaVacca was a well-rehearsed act. "I beat you guys," Wayne told St. John as he wore a big, goofy grin on his mug. "I didn't want my lawyer to get the confession tossed out, but still I beat you…beat you fair and square. Damn, how I wanted that confession to get out to the news reporters," Graham had said. "It wasn't supposed to go that way. I wanted everyone to know about that confession and then I was going to get off as being criminally insane. But, hey now, my old man is still hiding his face in shame, and I still got off scott free!"

"That really pissed me off," Investigator St. John said in an uncharacteristic choice of near-vulgar words. "But what really chilled me is when he told me, just as I was walking away, 'And I'll beat you the next time too!'"

Then, somewhere around the middle of September, Graham was gone. The house next to the railroad tracks was suddenly empty and the landlord confirmed that Wayne Graham had moved and left no forwarding address.

We let other departments know if they suddenly came up with a child killed and the parents tormented by the killer, they needed to contact us and we would name their killer for them. Our quiet investigation to find out where Wayne Graham had gone was fruitless. It was as if the man had resigned from the world and had ceased to exist…or had crawled back under the rock from whence he had appeared.

Before his disappearance, the perverted son-of-a-bitch brought suit against the department for our, "…gross disregard for his civil rights which resulted in the loss of Mr. Graham's standing in the community." The suit was filed for two point five million dollars, but he and his lawyer were happy to take the twenty thousand bucks the city offered them to put the suit to bed. I argued against the city settling the bogus lawsuit, but the city's lack of guts and their eagerness to resolve the matter resulted in the settlement being made and again Lady Justice took it in the shorts. It was just one more stake into the heart of the squad.

Then, in January, on a bitterly cold afternoon, six year-old Sandra Montgomery failed to come home from school.

I got the call at 9:15 on a Friday night.

"Lieutenant? This is Tommy Romano. I think Graham's back."

"What?" I asked, seeking clarification. "What's going on?"

"I just got a call from an investigator over in Maple Section. They're working on a missing person, a female, eight years old, by the name of Sandra Montgomery. She never made it home from school."

"Give me the address and then get a hold of Bobby. I'll meet you guys there."

Thirty minutes later, I was being briefed from Sgt. Curt Steplowski, one of the new breed who thought he was an old-timer.

"I don't know why you would want to jump the gun on this, Lieutenant," Steplowski said. "It's a routine missing person. The kid's probably at some friend's house."

"Yeah, well all that aside, Sergeant, it's about 15 degrees outside and the wind-chill factor puts it down to about minus 20 degrees. The kid was due home over six hours ago, and you just told me you called all her friends. In my way of thinking, all of that pushes it up out of the routine and into the unusual." With that out of the way, I asked to be introduced to the parents of the girl.

Ian and Bonnie Montgomery were in their mid-thirties. She was an office administrator for a group of doctors and he was a factory worker. Their other child, a son about 12 years of age, sat between them on the worn couch. The long and short of the story was that Sandra attended Number 2 School on the city's west side. The child was considered gifted in some areas, so she was sent to one of the "Magnet Schools" that centralized special programs for students who demonstrated an advanced ability in subjects such as math, science, and music.

Sandra's bus picked her up at about 7:20 every morning, took forty minutes to drop her off, and then returned her home at 3:40 every afternoon. Upon her arrival home, Sandra was instructed to go directly into the house, and remain inside with her older brother until one of the parents came home from work. If arrangements were made with a relative or trusted neighbor, both Sandra and her brother were allowed to go in the company of that adult. No such arrangements had been made this day.

From what the Maple Section cops had put together, it looked like the Montgomery girl had not made it to the bus after school. None of her friends saw her on the bus, and the bus driver specifically recalled she had not made the stop at the Montgomery home because Sandra was not on board. On the other hand, the victim's teacher swore up and down she had personally seen Sandra file out of school with the other third-graders and walk to the area where the buses were lined up for transportation to the children's homes. She estimated there was about a 45-second to one-minute gap of time when the children would have been out of her sight before they boarded the bus.

The plan for the investigation was simple. St. John and Romano would begin to interview every one of the victim's school friends; the Maple Section investigators would run down Sandra's relatives and neighbors who shared in her after school care. I would go out and talk to George Capwell, Wayne Graham's friend and former co-worker.

Heading over to the east side of the city, I felt my gut tightened into knots as my teeth chewed into a chunk of my lower lip. Putting murderous thoughts aside for the moment, I lifted the cell phone and called Major Winston to brief him on what was happening.

"Don't go off half-cocked on this thing, Mike," he cautioned when I mentioned it looked like we were once again dealing with Wayne Graham.

"Don't worry about it, Boss. I'm going full-cocked. I'm going to get this bastard and there won't be any reason, no goddamned reason in the frigging world, for the courts to play games with the case this time."

By 11:30 that night everyone was striking out. Capwell hadn't seen Graham since we busted him almost a year earlier. None of the relatives, neighbors, or school kids was able to provide any information that was of use.

Then Romano and St. John called. They had just woken up Candice Walker and her entire family. The parents protested—as did the other parents who had been awakened out of a sound sleep—about their child being disturbed for the investigators...that is until they found out it had to do with a missing child.

Candice Walker considered herself to be Sandra's "best-ever friend" and as such she was privy to our victim's secrets. Two of the secrets Candice had shared with her friend were that she had a classmate boyfriend...and also a special grownup friend. The boyfriend was Austin Dentori, another third-grader. The special friend was a man named Wayne.

Finding Wayne Graham became the focus of the entire investigation over the weekend. We were either going to have to find him or we were going to be finding another body. It was that simple.

By Saturday morning the entire squad was working. Romano, with all his connections throughout the city, was on the phone calling relatives, friends, and anyone who may have owed him the smallest favor. As the snow swirled in a nasty wind, he had people going into their places of work to operate their computers and thumb through company records looking for a hint of Graham being anywhere in or near Rochester. Gail Walz sent out faxes and called all the neighboring police departments asking that they quietly search their records for any sign of our man. The news people had heard about the missing person, but with the nasty weather capturing their attention, they never latched onto the story. We hoped to keep it that way.

By noon, the squad room was littered with grease-stained brown paper bags from Nick Tahou's "Home of the Garbage Plate" Restaurant. Each of us had inhaled at least two of the white pork hot dogs and an ample amount of grilled potatoes and macaroni salad. The office—and our breaths—now carried the aroma of the Greek sauce and onions...Nick's signature to each of his meals.

Gail Walz neatly rolled up her food wrapper, placed it in the empty bag and deposited it into the trash can next to her as she asked, "Now what?"

It was a good question. I only wished I had a good answer. My brain had no idea of where to go or what to do. It was a waste of money to keep the teams on overtime, but yet, I didn't want to admit defeat and send them home. We could go out and begin to look for the body, but then again, where would we look? In each of his three previous homicides Graham liked placing the body on the opposite side of the city from where he abducted the child. Sandra was most likely abducted right there at the school on the city's west side, and the fact the Number 2 school was less than 200 yards from the Cornhill Gazebo—the spot where we found Traci Taylor's body— was not wasted on us.

Bobby St. John was the first to raise the link. "If he abducted the Taylor child from the Charlotte neighborhood and dumped her in the Cornhill neighborhood, doesn't it follow that the creep would reverse himself on this one? I mean, just having talked to the guy a couple of times, I think he would get a kick out of messing with us and simply reversing what he did with Taylor."

"It's a good thought," Donovan acknowledged.

"Take it another step," St. John said as he got up from his desk and moved across the room. "After he grabbed the Bidwell kid, Graham went to a motel to do the killing. If he thinks we're on to him now, and if he believes we know where he lives, he may do the same thing."

"Shit!" Romano exclaimed. "We don't have enough cops in the state to check all the motels there must be in this county."

"You're right, but it's something that has to be done," Donovan noted in his pragmatic way.

In a matter of two minutes Walz, Donovan, Romano, and St. John had bundled themselves up under sweaters, overcoats, gloves and scarves, and were making their way out of the office. Rank having its privileges, I remained in the office to man the phones and wait for responses from any one or more of Romano's relatives and associates. It was also my task to call the on-duty supervisor in Lake Section and have him meet my crew at their section office. Next, I began calling each and every police department in the county, along with the New York State Police, and ask them to begin quietly checking all of their motels in an attempt to see if anyone fitting Graham's description had checked in during the past 24 hours.

I suspected it was an act of futility, but it was something that had to be done. We were relying on cops in other jurisdictions—cops who had their own cases to solve and their own families deal with—to take on an arduous task. Some would jump into the work eagerly and others would take it on begrudgingly, but all of them would do it because it was about a kid, a child, a little girl.

I was just about to make the third to the last call on the list of 21 police departments in the area when the phone rang.

"Is there a Detective Walz there?" the voice asked.

"She's out in the field," I responded somewhat impatiently. "This is her Lieutenant. Can I help you?"

"How you doing, Lieutenant?" the voice asked. Not waiting for an answer, it continued, "This is Sergeant Richie Alifano from the Batavia Police Department. We got a hit on your guy Graham."

"A hit? What kind of a hit?"

"It's nothing much, but one of our guys wrote him up for driving without a license and driving without insurance."

"When? What kind of car? Was it his car?" I asked in rapid-fire succession.

"Look, Lieutenant, before we go any farther, I have to get your word that all of this is on the QT for now. Understand? I'm not supposed to release any information from the department without the permission of the Chief."

"What?"

"We got sued about a year ago over releasing information. It cost the city about a quarter of a million dollars. Ever since then the Chief has been under the gun and we don't release information without his say-so. But, from what your Detective Walz said, this has to do with an abduction of a kid, so I'm passing this along for now, but it won't be official until the Chief signs off on it Monday. Okay? You understand?"

"Sure, sure, Sergeant. I understand," I acknowledged as the thought struck me that things were getting so screwed up that it was the cops that feared the law and it was the criminals who embraced it.

"One of our coppers, a young kid named Bob Wiesner, stopped your Wayne Graham back on November 29th. Graham was without a license and without insurance. Our guy wrote him and towed the car."

"What kind of car? Who owned it?" I asked without patience.

"It was a 1991 Chevy pickup, color blue, New York Plates 2WGR34. We towed it to a local shop. Two days later the owner, a Roger Kinkaid of 426 Alexander Street, your town, came and retrieved it."

"What kind of address do you have for Graham?"

"The same as Kinkaid. It's on Alexander Street, number 426, Apartment 106."

"This is great. Thanks, Sarge. You've really made our day! I'll see to it you get a letter of appreciation on this from our Chief."

"No need for that, Lute. I don't want to be involved in this if our boss doesn't approve the release. Just chalk it up to an anonymous informant if you have to use it before Monday."

"I understand," my voice said as my mind comprehended that cops were now afraid to even talk to other cops. As an afterthought I asked, "Sergeant, have you guys had any young kids killed out there recently?"

"Killed? No, Lieutenant. Nothing like that." There was a pause, a pause of about five or six seconds before Sergeant Alifano spoke again. "There was an abduction over in LeRoy, the next town over from here, but the kid managed to get away."

"When was that?"

"Let me see. We got it here somewhere in our roll call notes." Again there was silence as I listened to papers shuffle. Suddenly the Sergeant spoke. "It was back in November...November twenty-third."

"I thought so."

"Why, Lute? Do you think this Graham guy was involved?"

"Sergeant Alifano, I *know* he was involved!"

Ten minutes later I had Donovan on the phone, briefing him on the latest development from the town of Batavia, New York. Advising him that our Records Section was already working on getting a rundown on Kinkaid, I asked Frank to come back into the office with St. John while the others remained on the detail they had begun.

In sum and substance, Roger Kinkaid was a scumbag, a dirtball, an asshole, a mope. He had taken arrests for possession of cocaine, possession of methamphetamine, sale of meth, and two busts for contributing to the delinquency of a minor. Our Narcotics Squad knew the man as a low-level dealer who liked having kids front his dope for him on the streets. Consequently, it was that business habit of his that had led to the contributing to the delinquency charges.

Donovan, St. John and I kicked the issue around for a good half-hour. The smartest way to go was to have Kinkaid interviewed and see what he knew about Graham's whereabouts. The plan also had one major flaw. Kinkaid would sure as hell get in contact with Graham after our interview. All things considered, it was a risk we would have to take.

As it turned out, the interview with Roger Kinkaid amounted to a big, fat zero! He and Graham had met while they were doing time in the Monroe County Jail. After they both got released, they hung out together. When Graham vacated the Silver Street address, he bunked with Kinkaid, but usually stiffed him on the rent each month. Finally, after Wayne ended up with the traffic citations and getting Kinkaid's car towed, the two of them had a nasty argument and Graham went his own way. The bottom line was that Kinkaid had no idea where we could find Wayne Graham.

Although it concerned us at the time, it shouldn't have. The fact of the matter was, Wayne Graham was about to find us!

CHAPTER SEVENTEEN

DEATH AT A MERRY-GO-ROUND

By 10:00 p.m we were ready for Wayne Graham. A telephone trap had been set up at the Montgomery home. If he called there, the phone company would get an instant readout of the number and location from where he was calling. A detective from Lake Section would be with the family twenty-four hours a day to monitor the call—if and when it came—and he or she would then notify a telephone operator to retrieve the information from the trap. That information would be passed along to the police dispatcher and three cars would be sent to the location from where the call was being made.

The post office had been notified to set up a mail drop for the Montgomery home. All mail destined for the address would be held until an investigator could review it with the family before it was opened. That way, all the mail would be preserved in the condition in which the sender had mailed it...with as few extra fingerprints as possible. A surveillance had also been set up on the home. If Wayne Graham came anywhere on the block, he would be seized.

The consensus of the squad was that if Graham did kill Sandra Montgomery—and, God how I prayed I wouldn't have her life on my hands—he would place her body at or near the area of Charlotte Park, close to Lake Ontario. It was our best guess, somewhere between a hunch and an educated guess, but still a guess. In anticipation of that plausible possibility, Walz and Romano were put into the area in two separate cars. If they caught a glimpse of Graham they would stop him and search the vehicle he was using. Later, after the arrest, we would have—or invent—the probable cause needed to satisfy the courts. Nothing was going to be left to a judge's whim this time.

It was close to midnight when I got back to my apartment. The day had been long and arduous, but I couldn't sleep. It was 1:15 in the morning when I got out of bed and called Tommy Romano.

"How's it going, Tommy?" I asked.

"Boring and cold," he responded with a faked yawn. "It's colder than a nun's heart! Have you ever seen this place in the middle of January?"

"Yeah, I've seen it. Kind of depressing isn't it?"

Charlotte is an area at the extreme northern edge of Rochester. It's where Lake Avenue ends at Beach Avenue. Another hundred yards north is the southern shore of Lake Ontario, the smallest of the Great Lakes. In the summer, the place is alive with swimmers, sunbathers, families on outings, and lovers taking a stroll. In the winter, the entire place becomes a ghost town encased in ice and swirling snow.

Due to the absence of life in the area, placing a surveillance car in one of the Charlotte parking lots would be like trying to hide a submarine in the desert. Consequently, Walz and Romano had to constantly keep their cars moving so they wouldn't attract attention. As Gail moved her vehicle north, along the last mile or so of Lake Avenue, Tommy would drive south. Eight long blocks away from each other they would reverse their pattern, hoping to have Graham in sight...or at least between them.

"Give it another few hours," I suggested. "If you don't have anything by five or so in the morning, call it a day and we'll do it again tomorrow night."

"Why are you calling, Lute?" Tommy asked.

"I don't know," I was forced to answer in all honesty.

"Get some sleep, boss. Don't worry about it. We'll nail this bastard for you."

I returned to the bedroom and tried to sleep. At 1:35 a.m., while I lay in the warm bed, stroking Max's silky back, Wayne Graham called the Montgomery residence. Once he was assured he had the mother and father with their ears pressed to the phone, he had them listen as he choked their daughter Sandra to death.

I got the call from Gail Walz at 1:40 a.m. Her voice was between hysteria and brutal anger as she told me about the call.

"Where did he call from?" I asked without sympathy for her emotions.

"Lake Avenue and Stone Road. It's about a mile from Lake and Beach. Tommy's up there now. It's a phone booth. No one's around."

"Where are you?"

"I was down by the lake but I'm moving south now."

"Get back to the beach area, Gail! Stay at the beach!" I almost shouted.

"There's not a damn thing down there, Lieutenant. The fucking place is deserted. I'm going up to help Tommy."

"Gail, stay at the beach," I repeated evenly, emphatically. "You can't help Tommy with an empty phone booth. Stay at the beach! I'm on the way."

I was dressed and flying down the stairs in three minutes. On the way past Ann Salber's and Josephine Maira's apartment, I slipped my card under her door. It was going to be a long day, and Max was going to need the company of the two elderly women.

In the seven minutes it took to get from my place to the intersection of Lake and Stone, my anger swelled. I hated Wayne Graham and wanted the chance to kill him, to stick a gun in his face and let him watch me slowly pull the trigger. My thoughts were interrupted by Gail's strained voice as she called Investigator Romano and had him switch over to a secure frequency.

"Tommy...Tommy, I've got the body! Oh my God! The body's here."

"Where, Gail? Where are you? What's your location?" Romano asked as I gunned my motor.

"The Lake. The merry-go-round. The merry-go-round near the pier. Oh my God, Tommy. He did it. He dumped her right here."

"Is there a car?" Romano asked. "Do you have a car? A description of a car?"

"No, nothing. He's gone. I never saw him."

233

At that very instant I was just approaching the phone booth where Tommy was standing. I slowed enough to shout out the window, "You stay here and get the scene protected. I'll go to her."

In less than a minute my car sat next to Walz's unit. The tracks in the snow gave silent testimony to what had happened. The killer had pulled into the park through an opening in the fence that ran parallel with Beach Avenue. He then made a big, sweeping turn, rolled the young girl's body out of the car, completed his circle, and drove back onto Beach Avenue. Gail was kneeling over the body giving CPR. It took me a minute or so to get her to give up on the futile attempt to breathe new life into what was now a lifeless body.

Ten minutes later I was on the cell phone, giving Major Skip Winston the rundown. It was one of those briefings done in short, clipped sentences.

"After the phone company gave them the location from where the call was made, Romano headed for the phone. Walz hung back, but moved up a couple of blocks south, around Stutson Street. Evidently, while she did that, the killer was driving north. They must have passed each other somewhere along the way. She remembers one car going north as she was going south toward the phone booth Graham used. At the same time, as she saw the car, she was on the phone with me. When she tried to get turned around, her car got hung up on a snow bank for a minute or so until she could get some traction and get back on the street. By time she got up to Lake and Beach Avenues, all she saw was a set of tail lights going west on Beach Avenue, about two, three hundred yards away. She turned east on Beach to see if there was a car down here. That's when she saw the tire tracks leading into the park. She followed them and found the body."

"Does she know she screwed up, Mike?" my boss asked tersely.

"She knows it. We don't have to remind her. She's a basket case."

"What's being done now?"

"Tommy has shoe prints in the snow around the phone booth, but there are several sets of prints. The technicians will make castings of all of them. They don't see any fingerprints on the phone, but they're going to remove it and bring it in the Public Safety Building and let it warm up. We have some good tire prints down here at the merry-go-round, so the technicians are going to cast those also. They're—the evidence technicians—they're going to bring in their boss and a couple of more guys to help out."

"What about the car that Walz saw? Any description?"

"She says it was dark—dark colored and small. That's it."

The entire squad was in the office by 6:30 Sunday morning. Most of us had been up for over 40 hours and it was beginning to show in our faces and the ways in which we carried and conducted ourselves. Tempers were short and the gaps of silence were long. Eyes didn't make any effort to establish contact. Computers, desk drawers, and phones were cussed for not operating according to the user's expectations. For minutes at a time it was too quiet, and when the silence was broken it was done in a burst of profane anger.

The media had been calling ever since we entered the office. They had caught the bits and pieces of communication that sent the Medical Examiner, Crime Scene Technicians, and bosses north to the desolate beach area...and they wanted to know what the hell was going on. The order—like shit—had come rolling downhill from Chief Matthew Murphy. It was a simple order—I was to personally hold a press conference in the morning. The media briefing was to be short and concise. I was to be cooperative with the press and answer all their questions; and, at the same time, I was to tell them nothing.

By 8:00 a.m. Walz and Romano had already been sent home to get some sleep—sleep that would not come easily—if it came at all. Donovan and I entered my office with fresh coffee and *Sambuca* in our cups.

"You look like shit on a stick, Mike. You need to go home and get some sleep."

"Yeah. Right after this damn press conference." We sat silent for a minute before I took a deep breath and confessed, "Frank, the squad is falling apart. I can't hold it together any more. I've lost their faith, their trust. I'm thinking of stepping down."

"Don't be foolish, Mike. It's rough now, sure. But it's been rough before. We just need to get past this case. Once we nail this guy, things will change back to the way they were."

"I don't think so, Frank."

"Are you thinking about pulling the pin, about retiring?" Donovan asked.

The question went unanswered. As my nostrils drew in a clean stream of air, Bobby St. John walked into the cubicle without waiting for an invitation.

"Dispatch just called. They're forwarding a call to your line from a guy who says you want to talk to him about the killing in Charlotte. I told them to give it 30 seconds so I can start the trace."

"Is it Graham?" Donovan and I both asked.

"I don't know. He just said something like, he knew Amato wanted to talk to him about the kid we found in Charlotte."

Donovan grabbed a pen and pad. I stood up, lit a cigarette and filled my coffee cup. My mind wasn't ready for the conversation I was about to have. I had only ten seconds to get my thoughts and a rough plan together. The dialogue was going to be crucial. How much or how little I told the killer would impact the outcome of the case. Should I tell him we knew it was him who killed the Montgomery kid? Do I push him or pull him? What range of emotion should I show him? Anger? Humility? Should I come across superior or inferior?

Those questions and a thousand more like them ran through my mind as the phone on my desk rang and I looked down at the blinking white light. With another deep breath, I picked up the phone as my left hand was still attaching the tape recorder to it.

"Lieutenant Amato," my calm voice said into the mouthpiece.

"Can I still call you 'Mike'?" the caller asked.

"I guess so," I responded casually. "Everyone else does. But, by the way, who is this?"

"You know damn good and well who it is! It's Wayne, Wayne Graham."

"Did you do it?" I asked casually without even inquiring about why he was calling.

"Don't you want to give me my Miranda warnings before you ask me something like that, Mike?" Graham's voice was even, unemotional, as he asked the question. The way I heard him, he wasn't trying to be sarcastic. It was as if we were two old buddies trying to decide what to do this evening.

"I don't feel I have to, Wayne. Why? Do I need to?"

The fact of the matter was that I didn't need to give him any warnings at all. He was talking to me over the phone, from some unknown location. He wasn't in police custody or what the courts call a "police-dominated environment," so he wasn't entitled to hear his rights. It was another little convoluted thinking of our courts.

"Hey now, Mike, I want you to know something. I never wanted my attorney to fight the confession I made. I mean it! I didn't even know he was going to try to get the confession thrown out. I told your detective, what's his name, Bobby St. James or something? I told him to tell you I wanted everyone to hear that confession, and you know I did."

"I can buy that, Wayne. But like I asked you, do you think you need to hear your rights?" When he didn't respond to my last question, I pushed my voice up a notch. "Do you want to hear your rights, Wayne?"

"I just don't want to see you lose this case again, Mike. That's all."

The comment stabbed deep and the hairs on the back of my neck bristled as I snapped the pencil in my left hand in half. "I appreciate that, Wayne, but that's stuff for lawyers to work out. I'm just a cop, and all I'm trying to do is get down to some truth."

There was a pause in the friendly, easy conversation and I thought I lost him. I was about to give the customary, "Hello? Hello?" into the mouthpiece when Graham spoke.

"I'm really upset with you, Mike. This thing would have been over with if you would've kept your word. That's why I had to do this thing now, why I had to do it again. You didn't keep your word." There was just a slight twinge of anxiety in his voice now.

"What promise, Wayne? What promise did I break?" I asked honestly and with serious concern.

"You were supposed to tell the press, the papers, the TV people, why I did it. Remember? You were supposed to let them know all this stuff happened because of my father, because I was getting even with my father. You were supposed to say that, Mike. You were supposed to, but you didn't."

"Wayne, I'm sorry about that, but the truth of the matter is that's our policy. The Rochester Police Department's policies do not allow me to comment on any statements made by a suspect."

"You should have told me that, Mike. You should have told me that."

"I figured it would come out in court, Wayne. Don't go blaming me because *your* lawyer fought so hard to get your confession tossed out."

St. John came in and gave me a "thumbs down" gesture as he held a piece of paper for me to see. The note read, "Cell phone. No trace!!!!"

My low moan went over the phone, but before the tormenting bastard could speak, I jumped into the conversation. "Okay, Wayne, I have an idea. If you want your story told, if you really want it out there for the public to see, here's what you do. You write down what you did and why you did it. Okay? You write it all down. Then, you mail it to the newspapers, to the TV news people, to whomever you want to mail it...and then you come in and give yourself up? Okay? Is that fair enough?"

"I don't know, Mike. I don't know. What if they don't print it? What if the police department keeps them from printing it?"

"We can't do that, Wayne! We can't keep the newspapers from printing anything. Freedom of the press! Remember that? We can't stop them." My voice was rushing a little and I had to force myself to slow down.

"Yeah...maybe," he answered cautiously. "But maybe if I did it live, then you couldn't control it. Then the courts and the police department wouldn't be able to stop it."

"That could be the right way to go, Wayne. Okay, you may have a point," I conceded. "In fact, if you want, I'll even set it up for you. I'm meeting with a bunch of the press in about an hour. I know some of the better ones so, if you like, I'll set it up for you to do it live." I was dead serious! There was going to be no way on God's green earth his lawyer would be able to turn that type of confession into a violation of his sacred rights! Sure, a confession like that, live and on camera, would result in a change of venue for the trial, but so what? I sure as hell didn't care if the trial was going to be in Buffalo or

Albany or the moon for that matter…just as long as there was a trial…just as long as I got a second shot at him in a courtroom.

"I think you're right, Mike. Doing it live would be best."

"Sure, sure it is, Wayne. I'll set it up for you and you can call me back in an hour or so and I'll give you the particulars."

"No, Mike. No, I don't think so."

"What do you mean?" I asked in true bewilderment. He agreed he wanted to do it, and now he was saying no. What the hell was going on in this guy's mind?

"I mean *I'll* set it up. *I'll* take care of it. *You* won't have to do a thing."

With that, the phone went dead.

I had just spent almost five minutes on the phone with a demented killer of children, with a man who enjoyed twisting and torturing the lives of others, and the discourse had sounded as if two sane buddies were discussing a routine day on the golf course. On top of that, the conversation had netted nothing. There was no clear admission on his part, at least nothing that a baby lawyer couldn't rip apart in a courtroom, in front of the blindfolded broad, Lady Justice.

The press conference was the usual feeding frenzy of shouting news people trying to ask coy questions with the finesse of a fart in church. The questions were given thoughtful consideration and then given stock responses that we were working on "several leads" in which we expected a "break in the case within days."

"Isn't this Montgomery homicide very much like the series of three child murders your unit handled last year?" a baby-faced newspaper reporter in the group asked.

"There are similarities," I conceded.

"What if it turns out the same man who did those killings is also responsible for the killing of Sandra Montgomery?"

"Then, he will be charged," I answered the dumb question as if it was somehow akin to intelligence.

"I mean," the reporter persisted, "won't it reflect poorly on the police department that the man you let go free came back and killed again, that another life was lost after you let him go."

I could feel my jaws torque down and my eyes narrow in response to the question. Turning my instant dislike for the neophyte scribe into a soft smile, I flicked my eyebrows and said, "If you're referring to Wayne Graham, I may need to remind you that no one in this department let him go. His release from jail was the result of a judge's ruling. It was not a police decision. The decision came out of our courts."

"But you do understand what I'm asking here, Lieutenant, don't you? What I'm asking is how would you feel if you were to learn it was the same man?"

My eyes blinked a couple of times, and maybe because of my fatigue—maybe because the very same thought had been my thought for the past few days—and for one small second I let the assortment of print and electronic news gatherers see and get a quick peek inside Mike Amato.

"It would...would hurt me...hurt me greatly, if that were to be true," I answered as I looked down at the table and for some unknown reason began to pull on my right earlobe.

Monica Sheldon stepped in at that point and told the gathering I had been on my feet for almost two days, and that it was necessary to call an end to the press briefing. She volunteered to stay for a few minutes and answer any other questions the group or individuals might have. I got up from the table without the traditional crap about thanking them for coming and promising to get back to them as soon as we had a break in the case.

Noon was nearing when I finally hit the bed. I had retrieved Max from the Maira-Salber sisters' apartment, and they made it a point to tell me I really needed some sleep. Now, in my underwear, with my best buddy lying at the foot of the bed in his usual upside-down position with all four legs in the air, sleep came quickly and evenly for both of us. The mental list of things that still needed to be done was only partially completed as I drifted off.

By noon the faceless demons had come once again to follow me, to chase me down the blind alley, to lean over me as they pressed closer, to pull off their smooth-skinned faceless masks and ask over and over, one by one, "What about me, Amato? What about me? Why haven't you caught my killer?"

The only thing different about the dream was that Sandra Montgomery was now the closest face in the crowd. And her voice, though the softest, was the one to wake me and drive me into a hacking, gasping cough.

A shot of very good scotch and a cigarette finally got my hands to stop shaking. Once I crawled back into bed, sleep overtook my body.

It was exactly six o'clock in the evening when I woke up. I was sort of amused and slightly bewildered at how well rested I felt after the relatively few hours of sleep. In the shower I sang with my lousy voice, but still thought I sounded pretty damn good. Out of the shower, I dressed in casual slacks, loafers, a fresh shirt, and light sweater. I then summoned Max with a two-tone whistle. Patting the couch with my right hand summoned my little pal, and on his third attempt, he got up enough steam to get his growing butt up on the couch and set it down close to me. I scratched behind his ear the way Fast Eddy had done. When the contented pet laid down, he gave a sigh to announce his intentions for a fifth or sixth nap of the day.

As we sat side by side, I took my duty weapon off the coffee table, checked to make sure it was loaded, placed it behind my companion's right ear, and pulled the trigger. Without looking down to see the mess I had surely created, I sat back, opened my mouth, placed the gun inside it, angled the weapon up toward the roof of my mouth, and began to squeeze the trigger slowly, determinedly.

My cry, deep, guttural, and thunderous, filled the room as I sat upright and swung my legs off the bed in one, sweeping motion. Seeing Max at the foot of the bed, I surrounded him with my arms and gave him a visual check for any signs of wounds I may have inflicted during my tortured sleep. A warm kiss, planted with the full length of his very long tongue assured me he bore me no ill feelings for my nightmare.

It was actually almost ten at night when I awoke for real. This time it took four shots of Scotch and a couple of cigarettes to get my hands to stop shaking. And, when my hands were calmed, the rest of me continued to pace, to run my hands through my hair, to scratch at the back of my neck, sniff quickly two or three times in rapid succession…and do those things common to a man searching to get a grip on himself and his life. Max paced with me and every so often I would crouch down and stroke his back, telling him I would never really hurt him, my one real friend, my one contact with a normal world.

CHAPTER EIGHTEEN

ONE OF OURS

On Monday morning I elected—as I sometimes do—to avoid the expressway route into the city. Taking city streets that led south to the center of the city, was a change of habit I allowed myself periodically when I was early for work, or when, such as today, I wanted to delay the start of the day.

As the car passed the area of Aquinas Institute, the scene of Danny Martin's death, I made the Sign of the Cross and wished him the rewards of heaven. A couple of minutes later, a marked patrol car went speeding north, followed in a quarter of a minute by a second and third cop car with flashing red lights and screaming sirens. It looked like the cop business was starting the week off with an upswing in activity.

Realizing only then that I had not yet turned on the police radio, I reached down, switched it on and inquired about the nature of the call that was attracting three cop cars running with flashers and sirens. I was advised to call the dispatcher, "...by phone A-SAP."

"The cars are going to Dewey and Winchester. A girl was taken off the school bus by a man with a gun," the dispatcher said through my cell phone in the manner in which she had been trained...without emotion or anxiety.

"Sounds like a child custody thing, but if you want, I'll head that way."

"Does Detective Walz have a daughter, Lieutenant, a young daughter?" the voice on the phone asked with a tinge of hesitation.

"Yes, yes she does," I answered, not making the connection. "Is there something wrong with her daughter?"

"The child, the one the guy took off the bus, her name is Wendy Walz. It might be just a coincidence, but…"

I clicked the cell phone shut and threw it down on the passenger seat as my car made a wide arch in the middle of Dewey Avenue, causing other motorists to wish bad things for me and accuse me of sexual acts I had not even contemplated.

Winchester Street is a long street that runs east and west, connecting two of the major north-south routes, Lake Avenue and Dewey Avenue. It's a street of large, older, two and three story homes built back in the 1920's. It is also a street that shuttles many Kodak workers to their daily grind. Consequently, I encountered some confused and angry motorists as I approached the Dewey Avenue and Winchester Street intersection that was now blocked off by two patrol units.

Getting out of the car and walking the last fifty feet to the first police uniform I could see, I asked the standard cop-to-cop question, "What the hell's going on?"

"From what I pieced together, some jerk-off flagged a school bus down over around Dewey and McCall. I guess he stood right in front of it. When the bus stopped, the guy told the bus driver he was a cop and that he had been sent to get Wendy Walz. The bus driver asked for some ID and he told her he was undercover and was sent by Detective Walz to get her daughter. The lady driving the bus refused to open the door so the guy pulled a gun and told the driver he would shoot the kid in the first seat, and then the second one, and the third, unless she opened the door. When she opened the door, he grabbed the Walz kid and dragged her off the bus to his car."

"What kind of vehicle was he driving?"

"Over there," Officer Schaffer, a 20-some-odd-year veteran cop, said as he pointed to a car that was wedged between the school bus and a parked car. Waiting a second to see if I was going to again interrupt the briefing I had requested, Schaffer then continued. "The bus driver followed the car, got the plate, and then when he made the turn from Dewey onto Winchester the car slid out of control and

244

slammed into a parked car. When the school bus driver got there, she used the bus to block the asshole's car against the parked car."

Completing the last sentence, Schaffer motioned for me to follow him as he walked east. When we got to where he wanted to be, he pointed to a brown-shingle house on the north side of the street, about four houses away from where we stood.

"One of our cars was on a mail run to headquarters when he came up on the scene. He assumed it was an accident until the bus driver told him what had happened. By that time the guy had dragged the kid out of the car and was running up the street, going in and out of yards. Our copper gave chase and he has the bastard cornered in a garage in the back yard of that house."

"Description of the suspect?" The description wasn't needed. I already knew it was Wayne Graham. The bastard was evidently using the abduction of Wendy Walz to set up his press conference.

My assumption was confirmed when Randy Schaffer gave the description. "The bus driver says the guy is about six feet, thin built, longish hair, with weird eyes, and long nose.".

"I know this doesn't make much sense now," I cautioned Schaffer. "However, I want you to get a hold of two plainclothes cops, I don't care who, and get them down here with a video camera and a microphone. Get them here now! As quickly as you can. When they arrive, get them back to that garage to meet with me." I started to jog toward the house, stopped, turned, and asked, "Bosses notified? Perimeter established?"

"Bosses are on the way. The perimeter is the length of the street and from the backyards on the south side of the street to the cemetery on the north side."

"Notify Major Winston and my squad. Also get SWAT."

"SWAT's on the way. I'll get the rest post haste."

"If Gail Walz shows up, do not let her anywhere near that house."

When the cop mentioned the cemetery, it clicked that the homes on the north side of Winchester Street provided the south boundary for Holy Sepulcher Cemetery...an appropriate place to end Wayne Graham's life.

The garage at the rear of the house was just like the hundreds of other garages in this area of the city. It was a one-car, wooden structure, detached from the house. Two uniform cops stood at opposite corners of the worn, weathered building. The taller and younger of the two officers signaled me over to her.

"He's in the garage," she said. "He's got the girl with him and he's threatening to kill her...and he *is* armed. I saw the gun when I was chasing him."

"Can we see him or her?" I asked as I edged along the east side of the garage, toward a side door.

"There's a window and a door on that side of the building. The door is ajar about an inch. The window is dirty, but you can see the two of them if you expose your head to him. I peeked quickly, but I wasn't about to let him get in a head shot at me."

"Get over to the open door and stand there. If you hear a shot from the inside of the garage, kick that frigging door open and take your best shot at the bastard." I then asked, "Clear?"

"Clear, Lieutenant," she confirmed.

Moving toward the window, with my back to the wall, I reminded myself that I was just going to have to get in the habit - someday - of wearing my bullet-proof vest.

"Wayne!" I shouted loud enough for my voice to penetrate the wall. "It's me, Amato."

"Stay out of here, Amato. You try to come in and I'll kill her."

"You kill her, Wayne, and I'll drop you like a bad habit."

"It don't make any difference if you kill me, Mike. I don't care about dying."

"Yes, you do," was the best response I could manage under the conditions.

"No, I don't."

"Yes, you do," I answered before realizing we were beginning to sound like two schoolyard children in a "Yeah-Oh Yeah" verbal joust. "You have a press conference to attend." There was a pause before adding, "In fact, that's what all this is about, right? You want the media to hear your side. Right? If you want to do it now—and now seems like the time—I'll get the reporters here."

As he mulled that over, I peeked into the window. My target was crouched down on the flats of his feet and rump, in the far, back corner of the garage. Wendy was held closely in front of him, a handgun pressed to right side of her head.

"Let's do it right now, Mike," Graham said loud enough for me to hear.

My lips formed a tight smile at his response, but to stall I asked, "What? What did you say?"

He repeated his statement and again I told him I couldn't understand him. Before he could repeat himself again, I inserted, "Look, Wayne, this is bullshit. I can't hear you out here. I'm coming in."

"Don't do it, Mike. I don't want to kill you, but I will. If you come thorough that door, I'll kill you and then it'll be a really big press conference!"

"Okay. Okay, so I won't come in. Can I talk to you through the window? Huh? Do you mind that? I can hardly hear you out here." I moved closer to the window as I continued to crowd his mind with questions. "Do you mind that? Do you mind if I talk through the window? That's okay, isn't it? Huh? Do you mind that?"

By time I finished the last question I was at the window, peering in with my hands cupped around my face.

Graham caught sight of my mug at the window and appeared to be a little startled, but then smiled a crooked smile at me and said casually, "Hey now, Mike. How you doing?"

"Let the girl go, Wayne. She's got nothing to do with this thing. Let her go."

"Can't do that, Mike. She's my insurance policy."

"What?" I asked, reverting back to the hard-of-hearing rouse.

"Are you going deaf, Mike?" Graham asked with a broader grin.

Without answering him, I announced, "Wayne, I'm going to bust out this window so I can hear you and we can stop this mumbling crap." When I took my shot I didn't want there to be any chance of the dirty glass distorting my sight.

"Don't do it, Mike. You do that and I'll have to kill her."

"You're not going to kill her, Wayne. Like you said, she's your insurance policy. Without her, you don't have a bargaining chip to get your press conference. You kill her and before she hits the ground I'll put three shots in you—one in your ugly face and two in your chest. You'll be dead as dog shit, and I'll be the only one giving a press release."

"That's okay. You can tell them what I had to say about my stupid, faggot father," Graham countered.

"I won't tell them diddly-shit. All I'll say is that you were a perverted son-of-a-bitch with two wonderful parents who tried very hard to raise you the right way. I'll make saints out of both of them and I'll cry when I apologize to them for having killed their son who I know they loved dearly."

"You can be a real bastard at times, Mike," the suspect said seriously as if he had suddenly discovered what almost everyone else already knew about me.

"Yeah, well that's what they tell me. So now shut up and get a grip on yourself because the window is going to get smashed." With that, I pulled down the sleeve of my overcoat, gripped it between the tips of my fingers and the heel of the palm of my hand, and slammed my elbow into the center of the window frame. The four panes shattered with a noise that wasn't as loud as I expected.

When I re-focused on the inside of the garage, Wayne Graham was laughing. "They're going to make you pay for that, Mike. I should place you under citizen's arrest for damaging property."

"Hey, that sounds fair to me," I responded with an equal laugh. "Come on out here and I'll get the forms ready for your signature."

"I don't think so, Mike." Wayne smiled to show he was enjoying our verbal shadow boxing.

"Well, what the hell. It was worth a try," I said with a shrug and a wide grin of my own. Then instantly dropping the grin and having my face go stone sober, I instructed, "So let's cut the crap, Wayne. Send the girl out and I'll arrange your press conference. You have my word on it."

"Naw, Mike! I don't think so! But here's what I will do. You get a news team back here. I'll say my piece and then you can take me in. Okay? How's that?"

"Sounds like a plan to me," I said with a nod. "We can do that. Give me a few minutes to set it up."

I stepped back from the window, drew a deep breath and wiped my hands over my face. Only then did I sense how cold the morning air had become. The female cop's footsteps startled me as they crunched in the snow.

"SWAT's being deployed now. They already left the PSB" she said. "And, better than that," she added with a smile, "coffee is here. Schaffer arranged it somehow. He also said your camera crew is on the way."

I took the coffee and let it warm my hands before taking a long swallow and wished it was half full of *Sambuca*. "How long for SWAT and the guys with the camera?"

"Another fifteen minutes for SWAT—the guys with the camera are supposed to be only a minute or so away."

"Good," I said. "It'll be over with before SWAT gets here. But, if they do get here before the camera team, you make sure your bosses understand not to have SWAT come in without my okay. The suspect says he'll kill the girl the second he sees any SWAT team members."

"What's going on out there, Amato?" Graham shouted from inside the garage. "Don't you even think about rushing in here. I'll kill her the second someone even gets up to the door. Don't even think about it!"

"No one's going to rush you, Wayne," I assured him. "I'm out here waiting for the camera crew to get back here."

Taking advantage of the break, I lit a cigarette and blew out the smoke in a long exhale. By the time I was flicking the butt into a small mound of snow, the Johnson Brothers came walking up the driveway leading to the garage. Earl and Richard Johnson, weren't really brothers—in fact, Richard was white and Earl was black—but they had worked together for so long, the "brother" tag had been hung on them long ago. They were typical of a lot of other investigators in the city. The pair did good work day in and day out, but without any fanfare. They worked diligently, closing cases and making arrests, without the recognition they earned and deserved.

"What are we doing?" Earl Johnson asked.

I briefed the two on what had transpired to this point. "All you have to do is let him talk and ask a stupid question now and then, just like a real reporter. If he makes a move to harm the kid, get out of the way and give me a clear line of fire."

"Sounds like fun," Richard Johnson said. Holding his hand up for a high five from his partner-brother, he said, "Let's do it bro!"

Back at the broken window I explained to Graham he'd be given five minutes to tell his story to the news crew; then he would have to turn Wendy loose and surrender himself. He nodded in agreement before asking, "What station are they from?"

"What?" I asked, totally unprepared for the question.

"We're independents," Earl Johnson said as he stepped up to the window with the bulky video camera on his right shoulder.

"Independents?" Graham questioned suspiciously.

"Yes, independents," Richard Johnson said with a note of indignation as he stepped up to the window. His handgun was in his right hand, below the bottom line of the window frame. "We roam the city during the off-hours and try to get news stories. Then we feed the stories—for a fee—to all the stations." Turning to Earl, Richard licked the palms of his hands, glided them along the sides of his head in an effort to smooth his wind-blown hair, and asked—just as he had seen many egocentric veteran reporters do—"Am I looking good?"

"I never heard of any independents," Graham protested half-heartedly.

"That's right, kid. You probably never heard of us, but you see our stuff every night on every television station in the city," Richard Johnson said without missing a beat. His years on the streets had taught him to lie and bullshit his way through anything.

"I would rather have Channel 8 or maybe Channel 13 here," Graham said as he shifted his weight and I slipped my right index finger inside the trigger guard of the gun I was holding.

"Look...uh...what's his name, Lieutenant?" Richard asked with a look of annoyance on his face.

"Graham," I responded. "Wayne Graham."

"Look here, Wayne," Richard Johnson said. "You can have one of those guys and you can be on *one* station tonight. You go with us, and you hit all three networks, plus maybe CNN, FOX, and a couple of more. In other words, you go with us and you increase your exposure. It's your call, but personally, I could use the money, if you know what I mean."

Wayne seemed to be thinking the deal over.

"Give us a break here, will you, Wayne?" the cameraman, Earl Johnson, chimed in. "We cover seventy-five percent of the news you see on TV at night, and still everybody treats us like crap. We're the best damn news team on the streets and we're going to get you a hell of a lot of exposure. You can take that to the bank, my friend. Besides, like my partner says, we can use the dough this footage is going to bring in."

Graham thought about the option for a few seconds and then gave the Johnson Brothers a smile as he said, "Okay. I'll help you guys out. Let's do it."

"Then here we go," the white Johnson brother said with a smile and thumbs-up gesture as the black Johnson brother hefted the video equipment on to his right shoulder and said, "Lights, camera, action!"

Suddenly, a thought struck me. Maybe I should give Graham his Miranda warnings right on the tape…if there really was tape in the camera. Up to now I was going to tell any inquiring legal mind that I had advised the suspect before the camera got there. However, I wasn't about to take any chances. Graham was eager to give his little press conference, so I was confident he wouldn't balk when I gave him his rights.

"Before you start saying what you have to say, Wayne," I interjected as I stepped in front of Richard Johnson, "I need to let you know something." Then, to Earl Johnson I said, "Get the tape rolling and keep it going."

"It's going, Lute. Sound and video. Everything is rolling," Earl Johnson said without looking away from the camera's view finder.

"Wayne," I said and then cleared my throat. "I want you to know that you have a right to remain silent; that anything you say may be used against you in court. Also, you have a right to have an attorney present before you say anything, and if you can't afford an attorney, then one will be appointed to you, without charge, before any questions are asked or statements are made." I stopped and realized I had forgotten the fifth right!

Earl Warren's Supreme Court had given us four rights to tell every criminal before we talk to them. Over the years, somehow, somewhere along the line, a fifth right had gotten tagged on…but now I had forgotten it. Panic struck me as I pictured the case going down the tubes because I had forgotten a right I was supposed to give a man who was more than happy to talk to us. It was lunacy at it's best!

"Can stop at anytime," Earl Johnson whispered to me from behind the camera.

I nodded my thanks to the investigator and continued. "And, Wayne, if you do agree to give the statement you said you wanted to make to these gentlemen, you can stop at any time. Do you understand these rights, Wayne?"

"Come on, Mike," Graham said to me with a half-laugh. "Cut the cop-show crap. Sure I understand the rights. I'm no idiot, you know."

"Okay. I know you're a pretty savvy guy, but still I have to tell you your rights and make sure you understand them," I said with a smile and a friendly nod. Then I asked, "Do you want to waive your rights and make this statement?"

"Mike, you're pissing me off with all this legal shit," Graham said in an annoyed tone and without a smile. "I told you I wanted these guys here, and now you're asking me if I want to talk to them. Are you stalling for something? You told me that I had five minutes to talk to them, and now you're doing all the talking and taking up *my* time." Then, almost as an afterthought, he added. "This rights crap isn't counting against my five minutes, is it?"

"Wayne, I'm not stalling for anything. But still, I have to ask you these things. Do you want to waive your rights and talk to me and these men?"

"Yes, yes I do," he said louder.

I smiled at him, looked at my watch, made a mental note of the time of his right's waiver, and said. "Thanks, Wayne. Your five minutes will now begin."

For the next five, maybe six minutes, Wayne Graham spoke to the camera, telling it about the times his father had sexually abused him orally and anally. He described the incident with the football helmet and then listed three more examples about how his father had humiliated him. Next he went into a tirade about his mother failing to protect him. Looking directly into the camera, it seemed as if he was about to cry as he admonished the woman for failing to do her duty as a mother.

I listened intently to what he said, and while listening, my eyes scanned the man and selected a target for the bullets I was going to send spinning into his body the second Wendy Walz was out of harm's way. The cold, brutal pervert might feel comfortable laying all the blame on the doorstep of his parents, but I wasn't buying it...nor was I comfortable with the thought of allowing him to go free to kill again.

Investigator Richard Johnson played his newsman role well, but he still knew his job there was to get a confession, a good, complete, iron-clad confession. Consequently, every so often he threw in a question about one of the killings, and let Graham dig his grave deeper with a key admission or the addition of significant fact.

As the interview drew to a close, my conscience raised a question. Was I intent on killing Wayne Graham because he was a killer who preyed on children and I truly feared he would live and be free to do it again? Or, was I about to kill him because of the way he had humiliated the squad and perverted the system that was supposed to bring justice and order to society? I reasoned that I was going to kill him for the former reason, but the latter reason would make it more enjoyable.

"Okay folks, that's enough," I heard my voice saying. "Wayne, your time is up. I said five minutes and it's been almost ten minutes."

"Let me just make one more point, Mike. Just one more minute, okay?" he asked.

"One minute," I answered with finality.

During the one-minute extension, I told the female cop, "The second Wendy clears the garage door, you gather the kid up and run her out of the backyard." Then, out of Graham's line of vision I whispered so only Earl Johnson could hear me, "When the kid is out of there, shut the camera off and step out of the way."

"Are you...?" Johnson asked with the camera blocking his lips from the sight of Graham.

My left hand covered the microphone that stuck out over the camera lens. "You don't need to know and you sure as hell don't want to be a witness! When the kid is up, just shut it off and get out!"

"That's it, Wayne," I announced loudly as I re-entered the frame of the window. "It's time to let the girl loose. You promised. Now it's time to live up to the promise."

"You're right. Mike," he admitted as he pushed the palm of his left hand down to the concrete pavement of the garage and began to lift himself off the cold floor.

Once he was standing, his hostage's short stature gave me a clear shot at my enemy's complete upper torso and face. Smiling as if he was the tormenting devil himself, Graham looked me in the eye and ran his hand over Wendy Walz' flat chest.

"Wendy" I called out not too loudly, "I want you to walk over to this door over here, right next to the window. Walk to the door and there's a lady police officer there who's a friend of your mom's and she'll bring you to her."

Graham, with his left hand still pressing the chest of the quivering little girl as he rotated his hips forward against the back of her head, asked, "Is it okay if I just give her a little kiss before she goes, Mike? You know, just to show her I'm not really a bad guy."

My eyes narrowed ever so slightly and hate flared from them. My jaw locked as my teeth gritted together and my chin came up just a bit. My head swiveled only an inch, maybe two, right and left. There were no words. None were needed. Graham read the silent statement clearly.

The killer's hand released the child, and as she ran to the door with a terrified cry—her first sound of the morning—he lowered his gun. I felt the Johnson Brothers move away from me, and now I brought my gun up in my fully extended right arm as my left hand cupped against the fingers of my right hand which were wrapped tightly around the gun's grip. Only then did the killer drop his gun and raise his hands. I locked my arms in place and as my finger felt the rough surface of the trigger, Wayne Graham's affable smile disappeared and went through a slow-motion transformation that spoke of his terror as his mind told his face he was about to become a dead man. His eyes seemed to make a silent plea for mercy, but there was no mercy, no forgiveness in my heart or my mind. This man had taken four innocent lives. He had gone out of his way to torment the parents who gave life to the children from whom he had stolen life.

He had decimated the squad; had driven Jimmy over the edge; had invaded the private life of Gail Walz; had the balls to abduct one of our own children...and then molest her in front of me! Mercy was for God to bestow; but for me, mercy was not an option. My finger squeezed the trigger as my face went through its own transformation...from hate to a simple peaceful pleasure.

"Don't do it, Mike!" Donovan's voice said softly from my left side.

"Get the fuck out of here, Frank," I snapped back at him.

The large man gripped the barrel of my gun in his ham-sized hand and gently pushed it down. "It's over, Mike. We got him now. It's over."

I stepped back and reluctantly turned my prisoner over to Frank Donovan and two uniformed officers who had appeared out of nowhere. They ordered Graham onto the floor of the garage in a spread eagle, prone position. One of the cops handcuffed the killer, searched him, and then assisted him to a standing position. From somewhere outside of my body I watched the action as it moved in slow motion and I found myself hating the fact I had not taken the shot.

"Thank you, thank you for coming out," Graham shouted to the cameras and the sidewalk gawkers who had been attracted by the flurry of police activity. "Thank you, my fans. Thank you! Look for me tonight on the news."

Some of the younger members of the crowd cheered the rantings of the immoral bastard and applauded his brazen shouts. One woman yelled to the cops not to be so rough with the poor young fellow, and several of the citizens voiced loud concerns about the cops beating up the man once they had him in private.

Randy Schaffer turned to face the woman who seemed to be greatly concerned about our treatment of Graham. Going nose-to-nose with her, he shouted in her face, "He killed a kid, a child, you stupid broad! Now shut up and go get a life."

The word went through the crowd, sometimes loudly; sometimes it was said in whispers. "He killed a kid...killed the Montgomery child…killed that little girl…he's the one that's been murdering the little children…killed all those kids."

The taxpayers who demanded kindly treatment for the prisoner now turned on Graham and shouted for the cops to beat the crap out of the prisoner. One of the young ones who hooted and laughed when Graham had hollered his greetings to the crowd, now became boisterous and demanded the cops to turn the killer over to the crowd. "You pussy cops will just let him go again. Let us take care of the bastard."

I turned away from the maddening scene and longed to be home, in the quiet of my apartment with the songs of Joni James in the background, with Max on my lap, and a scotch and water in my hand. However, that was not an option. This thing had to be seen through to the end. There was work to do, and even though I knew I was not going to be the one to do the work, I had to be there to see that it was done.

Skip Winston and Deputy Chief Ernie Cooper approached me at the corner. The Major asked for—and received—a briefing as to what had transpired since my arrival at the scene. Cooper was quick to point out that I had broken a half-dozen General Orders by not waiting for the SWAT guys, unauthorized use of investigators who were not under my command, not notifying the dispatcher of my location, and some other gibberish.

"Yeah, Deputy. Whatever you say," I responded with a wave of my hand as I reached for the door of my car.

Arrangements were made to leave Tommy Romano and Bobby St. John at the scene to handle the evidence. They would have to track down the owner of the car that Graham used, make sure the garage scene was processed for any evidence, and coordinate the hundred other things that needed to be done. Gail was sent home to be with Wendy. I received official permission from Deputy Chief Edgy Ernie Cooper to make use of the Johnson Brothers after they booked the videotape into evidence. There would be enough work to carry the five of us into the late night hours.

Once in the PSB, I instructed Donovan to take over the investigation. There was no way yours truly was going to be a part of it at this juncture. My mind was too numb…and besides, my temper was never going to hold up if I had to sit face-to-face with Graham. Now that I had been denied the opportunity to kill the man, there was no way I was going to let myself stand in the way of the case going to court. Hopefully, I would live long enough to piss on Wayne Graham just before some warden turned on the juice to short circuit his ass and send his immortal soul to hell.

The DA insisted on the interrogation being videotaped, and that was just fine with the suspect. Donovan was beautiful in the way he wove his body language together with his words and led our killer through each one of the four killings.

The interview and subsequent stenographic statement lasted almost nine hours, from about ten in the morning until just after seven o'clock in the evening. At appropriate times Frank Donovan would ask Graham if he wanted something to drink or something to eat; if he wanted to rest; if he needed to use the latrine. Each time he granted the needs of the prisoner and treated Wayne Graham just as if he were a real human being. Twice he let the prisoner take a break for almost an hour so he could nap. After all, the courts and liberals are very sensitive about insuring that a busy killer receives his proper rest.

Through it all, Frank Donovan masterfully allowed the killer to go through the details of each of the four killings, how the abductions and the murders were committed, what vehicle he used, and how he had learned of Wendy Walz's school bus schedule.

There was one moment, right after six in the evening, when I froze in fear. Watching the conversation from the other side of the mirror, I was just about take a drag on my thirtieth or fortieth cigarette of the day, when Graham stood up and demanded, "Stop! I want to stop! Wait a minute here. I want to stop!"

My dread was that he wanted to invoke his rights and stop the questioning. However, as it turned out, his command was more narcissistic than that. What Graham wanted was to take a time out so he could see himself on the six o'clock news.

"Geez," Donovan said. "I would love to help you out, Wayne, but I can't."

"Why not?" the madman asked sternly. "I have a right to watch television, don't I?"

"I don't know about that, Wayne," Frank answered with a sympathetic smile. "I think maybe the Founding Fathers left that one out of the Constitution." When he didn't get a smile back, Donovan turned serious. "What I mean is that we don't have a television up here in the Detective Bureau. I don't know where to get one right now."

"You mean to tell me there isn't one damn television set in the entire Rochester Police Department?"

"Hey, Wayne, what can I tell you? The city doesn't even like buying us cars, much less TV sets."

"Don't bullshit me, Frank," Wayne said sternly, as if he was holding the deck of cards.

"Don't accuse me of that, Wayne," Donovan said with a hint of hurt in his voice. "I'm doing everything I can for you already. Don't you appreciate anything I do?" He let the plea for sympathy settle in Graham's sick mind, knowing that the son-of-a-bitch liked to be in the position of being able to give or withhold sympathy.

"I'm not saying you're lying," Graham backed off. "It just seems to me that there would be at least one television set around here."

"And I'm swearing to God there isn't one. But, I'll tell you what. I'll go out here and ask one of the guys to run over to my place and get my portable TV. Then, when the late news come on at eleven, me and you can watch it together. Okay? Is that alright with you?"

"Well, I guess so," Graham pouted.

"Can we go on now?" Donovan asked in a friendly manner.

"I guess so," the suspected said as he sat in his chair looking somewhat dejected.

Graham accepted Frank's offer and the interrogation continued without a hitch. On one of his trips out of the interview room, Donovan told Romano, "Go scrape up a TV so this sick motherfucker can see himself tonight. We don't need anymore shit in this game. I don't want some warped legal mind coming up with a 'Right to Television' argument." It was said sarcastically and was met with some laughter from the other cops, however, we didn't know how close to the truth Frank Donovan had come!

At one time, as the DA's stenographer was taking down the confession, Graham described how he had driven his thumbs into the neck of little Sandra Montgomery as he held her up to the telephone so her parents could hear her die, the steno began to cough. It was one of those coughs that stay in the throat and come in quick, repeated heaves of the chest.

Wayne Graham turned to the 40-some-odd year-old woman, touched her arm gently, and said, "I'm sorry if this is bothering you, honey. I know it sounds bad, but my father made me do all this." She pulled her arm away from him as he advised, "We'll get to that part in a minute, and you'll see."

By 10:15 p.m., Wayne Graham was ready to be booked into the Monroe County Jail. Donovan held off on it until after eleven o'clock so the defendant could watch his television debut. When the news program didn't show any footage of Graham's confession in the garage, he became very upset. Donovan got him to calm down by telling him it was probably too long, and the TV people would probably show it when they did a special program about the killer.

Skip Winston, John Niemeyer, and I went over every single development of the day. The consensus was we had built an airtight, solid, tamper-proof case against Wayne Graham. We toasted each other with cups of coffee and commended each other for a job well done.

Returning to the squad room without the bosses in tow, the scene was repeated, with the squad and the Johnson Brothers…and whiskey was added to the coffee cups.

When the place quieted down and I was alone, my attention was diverted to the message slips that had accumulated on my desk. Three were from Jimmy Paskell. He wanted to thank us for making the arrest. Two were from Gail. In the first one she let us know that Wendy was fine. In the second message she let us know Wendy was sleeping and she was grateful we had finally gotten Graham. She then added how guilty she felt about leaving her post at Charlotte Beach the night that Wayne Graham murdered little Sandra Montgomery.

This time there was no loud, boisterous party following the booking of Graham. When the work was done, members of the squad shook hands, patted each other's backs with comments of "Good job…Nice going…Thanks for the help"…and then drifted quietly out of the office.

I turned off the lights in the squad room and left the building. On the one hand it felt good to know the killer was now locked away; on the other, there was a nagging feeling that we had not yet won this thing…that there was more to come.

PART THREE:

JUSTICE TRIED

LOU CAMPANOZZI

CHAPTER NINETEEN

THE CIRCUS COMES TO TOWN

By the time May rolled around, the *new* Wayne Graham case had gone to court three times. The first event was the Preliminary Hearing. It was a simple process that lasted about two hours. Frank Donovan was the only witness the state presented. All we had to do at that stage of the game was to establish probable cause that a crime had been committed and that Graham was the one who committed it. It was a cakewalk and bail for the defendant was set at one million dollars.

The second court matter was that of the Grand Jury. Two days after Valentine's Day the body of jurors handed down its findings: indictments on four counts of murder, five counts of kidnapping (including Wendy's abduction), two counts of robbery, and one count each of assault with a deadly weapon, possession of deadly weapon, and possession of a stolen motor vehicle. The two robbery charges came from Wayne removing the guardian angel pin from Traci Taylor and the compass from Timmy Bidwell. The singular indictments related to the assault with a deadly weapon, possession of a deadly weapon, and possession of the stolen car, all stemming from Wayne Graham's abduction of Wendy Walz. Those charges were simply frosting on the cake.

On May fourth, the Huntley Hearing began. This was the third pre-trial hearing leading up to hopefully getting Wayne Graham convicted and executed. Jefferson Longler again appeared in behalf of Wayne Graham; and, John Niemeyer once again represented that nebulous body referred to as, "The People." Both men were set for the fight of their professional lives. Getting Graham's three, long, rambling confessions—one in the garage, the second one to Frank Donovan in the interview room, and the third one with Frank in front of the stenographer—thrown out was going to be the only way in which Longler was going to get his client off...and enhance his career. Getting any one of those confessions admitted to trial was going to be a key factor in nailing Graham with a death penalty or at least several life sentences. Getting all three of the confessions admitted to the trial stage would definitely enhance Lethal John's career.

The judge assigned to the case, Judge Anita Kaseman, is a no-nonsense woman who rules her courtroom with a great deal of courtesy and respect for all parties—courtesy and respect that are sometimes mistakenly taken as a personal weakness. Anita the Hun, as she is referenced by some, is not above verbally reducing a neurotic lawyer to a mass of quivering jelly when the acceptable limits of argument are pressed too far. She is not a bully, nor is she a pushover.

Fifteen years earlier the woman had established herself as a defense attorney who fought for her clients as if she personally were on trial. If the cause was just—and she believed the innocence of the person she was defending—Kaseman was not above taking on a controversial case. Within ten years of her being admitted to the Bar, she had built up a successful practice that spread itself over a broad range of criminal cases, business mergers, divorces. and small business law disputes with the same level of energy. Then, in a period of less than six months, the defense of two separate clients turned her sour to the role of being the sword and shield for the defense.

In one case, she successfully argued the innocence of a man accused of scamming a large number of elderly. So the story goes, within a month of being released, the same man ran a confidence game on Anita's aunt and relieved her of almost $20,000. It was shortly thereafter that Kaseman happened to be standing in the wrong courtroom at the right time. A young couple had been accused of physically abusing their five year-old daughter. Both were indigent, but the Public Defender's Office—due to issues of conflict interest—could only handle one of the parents as a defendant. The judge scanned the room, saw Anita Kaseman in the back of the room, waiting for a client to show up. In that instance her fate was sealed and she was assigned to defend the woman. True to her oath, the lawyer did her best to offer a proper defense for a woman she loathed. Kaseman's defense was good enough to have the brutal, child-beating woman go free...only to severely batter and kill the same child less than three months later.

Enough was enough for Anita Kaseman. She changed sides and went to work for the District Attorney. "The money sucks," she was quoted as saying. "But now I won't be forced to take on evil clients and become a partner with the devil. At least, in the DA's office you can throw in the towel if you know you are backing a loser."

In a little over two years as an Assistant DA, the woman built a reputation as a tenacious prosecutor. Two years ago she was tapped by the Democratic Party to fill a judge's vacancy that had suddenly come open with the death of Judge John Manning. Due to Manning's reputation for starting court late, having extended lunch periods, and never allowing a case to go beyond three-thirty in the afternoon, the rumor mill stated he had died years earlier but his passing had only recently been noted in an official declaration of death. Within a week, Anita the Hun let it be known she would not follow her predecessor's lax schedule.

It was the time of year when flowers were just beginning to come to life after a long, cold winter had dumped well over a hundred inches of snow on the town. The day was cool and the courtroom was comfortable...so I couldn't offer an explanation as to why I was sweating as I approached the witness chair to be sworn in. A year and a week had passed since the last time I took the stand against Wayne Graham in another courtroom regarding the legality of his confession. Mistakes made then would not be repeated now.

Jefferson Longler had already been hard at work in his representation of Wayne Graham. He had already filed a motion to suppress the evidence we located in his client's home. Claiming we did not have the owner's permission, Longler then filed a motion to suppress the evidence we found in the car Graham had stolen. Another motion alleged I did not have probable cause to arrest Graham in the garage on Winchester Street as he pointed a gun at Wendy Walz's head. I was very glad to hear the pear-shaped attorney with the fat, droopy lower lip lost each of those efforts.

Now it was time for Longler to go after the biggie - the confessions.

I walked into the large, marble-floor courtroom and heard my heels click off the walls and twenty-foot high ceiling. At the witness chair, I stood to take the oath. In doing so, my eyes shifted over to Graham, slouched in his chair next to his attorney. The murdering bastard wore a stupid little grin and fiddled absent-mindedly with a paper clip. When I sat in the witness chair, Graham looked up as if seeing me for the first time.

"Hi, Mike. How you doing, buddy?" he asked loudly.

I took the opportunity to look at the judge and raise my eyebrows. Then looking at the man I nodded and said, "I'm fine, Wayne. Thanks for asking." It was all an act, but it was one I hoped would let the judge know that Wayne considered me a friend and not a rogue cop who had beaten a confession out of him.

The defendant then stood and stated, "Your Honor, I move to dismiss this hearing. The confession I gave was a valid one after having been advised on my rights. We are only here so my fat, little lawyer can get extra money from the state for defending me!"

The outburst caused quite a stir for a minute or two. Anita the Hun ordered Longler to quiet his client. Longler then moved for a dismissal of the charges on the grounds that Graham's statement had unduly affected the judge's ability to render a fair and impartial decision. When that was denied, Jeff Longler moved to have Judge Kaseman removed as the hearing judge. That also failed. Finally, things returned to normal…at least in terms of what is *normal* for a courtroom.

Lethal John asked his questions in short, concise bursts that allowed me to get in only the information he wanted to be admitted at this point of the proceedings. My direct testimony took less than a half-hour. The cross-examination was to be even shorter…much shorter.

"Who were the men operating the camera and asking the questions for this alleged television interview?" Jeff Longler's question was benign in its delivery but devious in the way the disheveled man delivered it.

"Investigators Richard Johnson and Earl Johnson," I answered succinctly.

"Do either or both work as news reporters?"

"Not as far as I know, Sir."

"By whom are they employed?"

"The City of Rochester."

"In what capacity?"

"As investigators for the Rochester Police Department."

"I have no further questions, Your Honor."

I had looked over to Graham a couple of times during my testimony—once when he giggled for no apparent reason, and once when he began to whistle something that sounded like a Cavalry charge.

The Johnson Brothers were the next two witnesses; Earl was first and Richard followed. Each one faced questions from Longler, questions very similar to the ones asked of me. Both of the Johnson Brothers were off the stand in less than fifteen minutes after the cross-examination began.

Next came Frank Donovan's testimony. Due to the amount of time he had spent with Wayne Graham, the detective was on the stand for the remainder of the day. At ten after five in the afternoon he called me.

"I'm done. Let's grab a beer," he said in a voice that let it be known he was exhausted and mentally drained.

"How did it go?" I couldn't wait until we got to the Robe and Gavel to ask the question.

"Good. Damn good," he answered. "Don't sweat it. We've got this one nailed down tight."

"Longler pulled out all the stops," Frank summed up his testimony as he downed the fifth beer. "Finally Kaseman told him to move onto something new or put a cork in it. That was it!"

"Did they show the videotapes the Johnson brothers shot in the garage?" I asked although I knew the answer.

"Tomorrow. They're going to show the tape taken in the garage and the one taken later when Graham was interviewed at our office. The judge ordered both videos to be on hand and the attorneys ready to proceed by 8:30 a.m."

"Those two tapes are going to going to cinch it," I said after draining my beer.

"You bet your ass they will. Longler will be trying to cop a deal with Lethal John by early tomorrow afternoon."

"You got that straight," I said…and I wondered why I was doubting my optimism.

The first court argument of the day came the next morning at about 8:31 a.m. when Jefferson Longler stood up, smoothed his unsmoothable sport coat with his fat fingers and said, "Your Honor, I object to the showing of this videotape."

"Oh really, Mr. Longler," Judge Kaseman said with a smile. "And on what grounds is that objection offered?"

"The videotape is a travesty of justice, Your Honor. It is rooted in deception, trickery of the foulest nature, and deceit."

"Clarify the objection in a manner that is relevant to a point of law, Counselor."

"Your Honor, the purported evidence that is about to be displayed to the Court was obtained illegally. It was garnered through a ploy and should not be allowed to see the light of day in this hallowed place of law."

"Mr. Niemeyer, do you wish to respond to Mr. Longler's eloquence?"

"I do, Your Honor. I most certainly do," Niemeyer said as he stood and buttoned his suit coat. "First of all, the tape is being offered for Your Honor's scrutiny. That is why we are here, having this hearing. How can we offer it for that scrutiny if you are not allowed to view it?" Not waiting for a response, he continued. "Secondly, the tape will allow us to see and hear that the defendant was properly advised of his rights by a person he knew to be a law enforcement officer; that he was advised the tape recording may be used in a court against him; and, that he waived his rights regarding self-incrimination." Pausing to smile an impatient smile, the prosecutor then added, "Third, Your Honor, who shot the video and who the defendant believed was shooting the video are irrelevant. The defendant made the statement in the presence of a person he knew to be a police officer after that officer had Mirand-ized Mr. Graham and he waived those rights. Last of all, whether or not the defendant believed the camera operator and interviewer to be police officers, the King of England, or Harpo and Groucho Marx is irrelevant to the matter being heard. If there was trickery or deceit, it was not rooted in duress or coercion. Now then, Your Honor, The People beg the Court to allow us to proceed."

Longler was not giving up. "But my client was tricked into believing the video was being shot by a news team. Your Honor, how may this Court condone trickery and subterfuge to be a means to bring so-called evidence into a place of law?"

"Did your client really believe that a news crew was shooting the video and that they were going to put it on the evening news?" Kaseman asked suspiciously.

"He most certainly did, Your Honor. He had no way of knowing those two men with the camera and microphone were cops. In fact, they even told him they would make sure the video was given to all three television news stations."

"Then I believe you have overruled your own objection, Mr. Longler."

"Your Honor?" was the only thing Longler could come up with.

"You stated your client expected the videotape to be aired all over the city. Right? Therefore, I believe you would have to agree it was done voluntarily and that he had no expectation of privacy regarding the statement."

"But...but it was trickery, Your Honor. It wasn't done fairly."

"Life's not fair, Mr. Longler. Get used to it."

"But..."

"Enough, Counselor. Your motion is overruled. Now let's move on."

"But..."

"Your exception is noted. Now then, one more 'but' by you is going to be met by 'Contempt of Court' by me. Are we clear, sir?"

"Yes, Your Honor," Longler conceded as he plopped himself back down in his chair.

After the tape was shown, Jeff Longler made another passionate plea for the Court not to allow evidence that had been obtained under false pretenses.

"What next, Your Honor?" he asked. "Will we allow the police to sit in a confessional booth, dressed as a priest, and solicit a confession from an unsuspecting, down-trodden soul."

"As long as that priest has a cop in there with him, and the cop gives the down-trodden soul his Miranda Warnings, and the poor soul waives those rights, then yes, Mr. Longler, we will allow it."

Lethal John couldn't help rubbing salt into the wounds heaped on him by Judge Kaseman. "Very well put, Your Honor. I think you have made that matter of law blatantly clear to my opponent."

"Don't suck up, Mr. Niemeyer," Anita the Hun said. "It doesn't become you." She then called for the second tape—the one shot in the interview room—to be shown.

The second legal argument came at about 10:45 a.m. when Jefferson Longler jumped to his feet and shouted, "Stop the tape! Stop the tape right there!"

"I beg your pardon, Mr. Longler," Judge Kaseman said flatly as she looked at the dumpster-diving appearance of the defense attorney over her half-glasses. "Would you like to put that outburst into the form of proper decorum that is acceptable in my courtroom?" Anita the Hun asked with a notable tone of annoyance.

"Your Honor," Jeff Longler said as he stepped in front of the TV set. "The defense requests the opportunity to once more review that last minute or so of the recording. I believe it goes to the heart of the matter regarding the voluntariness of the statement."

"Go back about a minute in the tape, Bailiff, and re-play that portion again." Kaseman then turned her attention to Longler. "When we get to where you want to be, Mr. Longler, you may *respectfully* ask the Court to stop the tape."

The tape began again at a point where Graham was describing the abduction of Sandra Montgomery. Then, without any warning it was about to happen, the TV monitor showed Wayne Graham jump to his feet and say, "Stop! I want to stop! Wait a minute here. I want to stop!"

It was the point of the interrogation when Graham demanded to see himself on the six o'clock news. The tape went on to show Donovan dealing with the TV issue and then asking if they could continue.

When the defendant answered, "I guess so," Longler took a step toward the judge's bench and stated, "We respectfully request the Court to stop the tape at this point."

Kaseman instructed the Bailiff to stop the tape. Turning to Longler, she asked, "And your objection is...?"

"Your Honor, my client clearly asked for the interrogation to stop. That is his right, Your Honor. It is a request that should have been honored. Detective Donovan and Lt. Amato both advised my client he may stop the interrogation at any time. At that point when he said he wanted to stop, Mr. Graham should have been afforded an opportunity to either cease all interrogation, or at least be allowed to counsel with an attorney before proceeding."

Lethal John was on his feet and responding without waiting for the judge to ask for his input. "The defendant requested only to stop so he could see himself on the news. I did not hear him asking to stop the interrogation, nor did I hear him ask for an attorney. He simply requested a pause to exercise his vanity."

"Whatever the reason, he asked to stop," Longler said loudly as he looked at the prosecutor with disdain.

"He did no more than say he wanted to stop to watch TV. He could have asked to stop long enough to go to the bathroom. It's nothing more!" Lethal John Niemeyer said with a will-you-get-serious look on his face.

"It's a lot more!" the defense attorney shot back.

"Gentlemen! Gentlemen!" Kaseman said above the voices of the two men. "You will address the Court! We will not have shouting matches in my courtroom." Having gotten their attention, she turned to Longler, and asked, "Is that your motion, or do you have more?"

"Your Honor, the New York State Court of Appeals and the Supreme Court of this country are very clear on this matter," Longler said as he moved toward the elevated workspace of the judge. "Once a suspect has asked for an interrogation to stop, that request must be honored until such time as an attorney has had an opportunity to review the matter with his client."

"Mr. Niemeyer?" the judge asked over her glasses.

"The Court of Appeals has never said that an interview has to stop just because some suspect wanted to watch the news," the Assistant DA stated with just the hint of a smile on his face. "What we have here, on this tape, is the defendant saying, 'Hey, I want to stop so I can see if I made the evening news.' The detective tells him that there are no TV's available, and then even goes so far to ask the defendant if it is okay to continue. And, as Your Honor and the rest of us saw, the defendant agrees to continue."

"Your Honor," Longler said and then stopped to make sure it was allowable for him to continue without being asked by the judge to do so. Kaseman gave the man a nod, and he went on. "My client does not agree to go on. He merely says, 'I guess so.' He is confused and bewildered. He has had a very long day, Your Honor. He is now undergoing a grueling interrogation and he asks to stop. The detective merely dances around my client's passionate plea to stop and asks if they can go on. My client, in his exhausted, beleaguered state, gives in to the detective's badgering and says simply, 'I guess so.' There was a clear request to stop, Your Honor, and there was no clear permission to go forward."

"Do People wish to respond?" Kaseman asked Niemeyer.

"Your Honor, the People do not wish to become involved in wasting more of the Court's valuable time. The issue is clear. There was no request to stop the interrogation, only to interrupt it. The defendant was given an explanation as to why his request could not be filled. He obviously understood the reason and agreed to go on."

"Defense?" the judge asked.

"I believe I have made myself clear on the matter, Your Honor," Longler said and I mistakenly thought he was going to shut up. He then continued, "Our state courts have ruled a person undergoing a police interrogation may ask to stop the interrogation for any reason. It might be because he is tired, or maybe he is frightened over the tactics being used. He may ask to stop because he wants to watch television, or maybe he might want to stop because he just wants to stop. The courts have never said there has to be a *good* reason; nor have they said there has to be *any reason.* The right is one that belongs to the suspect. The police are not allowed to interpret it."

The courtroom fell silent for perhaps a quarter of a minute before Judge Anita Kaseman said, "I'll take it under advisement." Niemeyer and I looked at each other in shock as the judge ordered, "Now let's see the rest of the tape."

Longler continued to challenge every minor thing he saw on the TV monitor. Once he argued the detective could not be heard; later he objected because Donovan was speaking too loudly. Finally, when he wanted Kaseman to take note of the fact that Donovan had supplied Graham with four soft drinks in an attempt to keep his nerves on edge with caffeine and sugar, Anita the Hun had had enough. With nine well-spaced words and a stiff, pointed forefinger as she leaned over the bench, the five-foot, three-inch woman told Longler she had had enough of his crap. "Make it legitimate, or don't make it at all," she cautioned the defense attorney as he popped up from his chair for the twentieth time in less than a half hour.

The day concluded with Kaseman asking if there were any other motions before she set a trial date. Longler responded like a school kid bringing forth his error-free homework. He submitted two new motions to the Court. First came a motion to dismiss the indictments against Graham on the first three murders, citing Double Jeopardy as the basis. He then submitted a motion for Change of Venue, arguing that—due to the publicity the case had been given—his client could not get a fair and impartial trial in the Rochester area.

Anita the Hun tapped her gavel on the round, oak piece of wood that sat on the left side of large, ornate judge's bench, advised one and all she would have decisions within two weeks, and adjourned.

"How do you think she'll go on all of this?" I asked Lethal John as we exited the courtroom.

"She's no one's fool. Kaseman knows when she's being snowed, and what we had in there was a blizzard!"

"What about the double jeopardy motion?"

"It won't fly. We never prosecuted the case. Remember, I told you I would move for dismissal of the first case...without prejudice? Well, Mike, I did. LaVacca granted the dismissal without prejudice and that gave us the leeway to re-open the matter now. Remember?

Way back then after the first Huntley Hearing, I told you to hang loose on it and wait for something to shake loose."

"Yeah, and it did. The bastard killed another kid."

Two weeks later, Judge Anita Kaseman handed down her findings. First and foremost, she ruled all three confessions would be admitted as evidence in the trial. Secondly, she found that double jeopardy was not a factor. And, third, there would be no change of venue.

"True, Mr. Longler, this case has gotten its fair share of publicity. However, I believe the police and the prosecutor have done an admirable job of keeping their case under wraps. There has not been any publicity splash by them, and there has been no exposure given to your client's confessions and the other evidence the DA's Office will be presenting at trial. Now then, in order to keep the lid on things, I am placing a burden of silence on both sides of this case. In essence, there is a gag order in place. Neither side will discuss the case, the evidence, or their opinions. There will be no press conferences, no on-the-street interviews and no news leaks. For now the Court is adjourned. Trial is set for July ninth. Good day gentlemen."

The Huntley Hearing had gone so well, but still a cloud of pessimism hung over me like a black cloud. Consequently, I was angry but not surprised when I learned Jefferson Longler had gone to the Monroe County Hall of Justice the very next day after Judge Kaseman's findings. Appearing before the Administrative County Court Judge, Longler filed two new motions. Both were potentially lethal to our case.

In the first new motion, Longler asked Judge Anita Kaseman to recluse herself from the case. The basis for the motion was an alleged conflict of interest. It seems that six years earlier she had represented Florence Graham—the mother of Wayne—in a minor auto accident case. It was a bullshit deal in which Kaseman, as a private attorney at the time, wrote some letters and made a phone call for Mrs. Graham in order to achieve a quick settlement for the woman. Nonetheless, Longler made his usual verbose argument asserting Kaseman's affinity for the family. Now, in light of Wayne's accusations against his parents, there existed, Longler proposed, a potential for the judge to be prejudiced against his client.

The second motion was also a bombshell. Wayne Graham, he submitted, was suffering from symptoms of mental illness. Based on what he allegedly observed during the Huntley Hearing two weeks earlier, Longler advised the Court his client was incompetent to stand trial, and that even if he did so, he was criminally insane. In doing so, he changed Graham's plea of "Not Guilty" to "Not Guilty By Reason of Insanity." So as not to miss an opportunity, Longler suggested Graham was bi-polar and was suffering from paranoia, schizophrenia, manic-depressive manifestations, social anxiety, socio- and psychopathic behavior, post-traumatic shock as a result of physical and mental abuse suffered as a child, multiple personalities and, to round it all out, low self-esteem. Surprisingly, the son-of-a-bitch left out psoriasis and halitosis in his laundry list of modern day psycho-babble.

The case was now going to be pushed back at least two months...two more months of waiting for the other shoe to drop...two more months of waiting for justice.

The news hit me like a ton of shit—I didn't know it was coming, and I sure as hell didn't like it!

It was on a Tuesday morning, and I was just about to drop Max off at the apartment of my two senior citizen neighbors. With my finger on the power button of the TV's remote control, I froze as I heard the female part of the morning talk show make the announcement to her male co-host. "A new judge has been named to the Wayne Graham trial. Our news team has learned that later today, Judge John LaVacca will be named as the judge who will hear the murder trial of Wayne Graham, the alleged killer of..."

The string of Italian-English profanity drove Max off the couch and under the kitchen table. How could they do this to me? Didn't anyone in the courts have any brains, any common sense? If Anita Kaseman had been taken off the case because of some supposed prejudice against Graham, didn't it also follow that John LaVacca had some prejudice *in favor* of Graham? Vodka LaVacca had let the

275

killer off! He was not going to admit that error by now finding him guilty! Had the entire, frigging world gone nuts?

This wasn't going to be a trial! It was going to be a goddamned three-ring circus!

CHAPTER TWENTY

DÉJÀ VU ALL OVER AGAIN

I pulled into my assigned parking space at the PSB and headed directly for the District Attorney's Office. Once at his office door it dawned on me he wasn't going to be in at 7:25 in the morning, so I taped a note to the door leading to the entrance of his secretary's outer office, asking that D.A. call me A-SAP.

Back at the office, the question asked by each arriving investigator was, "Did you hear about…?" The answer came in a rich stream of profanity that was usually introduced with, "Fucking courts…"

When everyone was in, we began our morning briefing. The topic was the murder of a mid-level drug dealer from New York City who had the audacity to come into *my* city to be murdered. That was *supposed* to be the topic of discussion, but instead we turned our conversation to facing the arrogant and blissfully ignorant Judge John LaVacca.

"Does he have to review everything that Anita the Hun ruled on?" Romano asked with a raised eyebrow.

"Review it? Yes," St. John said. "He won't have to hear the evidence all over again, but he will review the transcripts."

"Aw shit! Here we go again!" Romano cried.

Just then, my phone line rang. It was John Niemeyer. He was in his office, waiting to see me.

"Nothing personal, John," I told him. "I don't want to see you. I want to see the man, your boss."

"Rudy will meet with us. He asked me to call you. He has a tight schedule this morning, but he's holding open a 15-minute window for us."

"I'll meet you at his office in three minutes," I responded and hung up the phone.

Rudolph Jameson Cantor was Monroe County's District Attorney. Known simply as "Rudy" to one and all, the D.A. is not a man to stand on a lot of formality. Although it seemed he had held his present elected position since dirt was invented, Rudy is not the type of guy to be overly impressed with himself. I guess it was fifteen, maybe seventeen years ago when Rudy won the election and took over the DA's role. At the time, people said he was too young. Now they were saying he was getting too old. Rudy Cantor, like me, didn't get too worked up over what people said.

John Niemeyer was just arriving at the outer door of the District Attorney's Office when I got there. Without waiting to exchange niceties, he knocked on the door, waited a comfortable three seconds, and then entered.

"Don't start any shit over this, Mike," were the first words out of the District Attorney's mouth.

"Then you know why I'm here?" I asked.

"Sure! This thing with LaVacca."

"You know he's going to set Graham free, don't you, Rudy?"

"I know no such thing, Mike. In fact, when I got word of this thing last night, I called John right away and we discussed it at length. John will roll it out for you as soon as we break up. I don't want to waste time doing that now. All I do want to do is make sure you keep your cool about this LaVacca thing. You let us do our job and Graham will fry...or at least he'll spend four life times in jail."

"Is there anything you can do in order to get LaVacca removed from the case?" I asked, sounding very much like Jimmy Paskell when he implored me a year earlier to do something about the media's coverage of Graham's confession being tossed out of court.

"That's out of our hands, Mike. The Administrative Judge decides who he's going to be assigned to a case." Rudy Cantor put up his hands and added, "End of the story on that! There's nothing I can do about it." The District Attorney looked up at me as he finished stuffing two folders into his briefcase. "Any questions?"

"For one," I began, "does LaVacca have the power to overrule what Judge Kaseman ruled on regarding the confessions?"

"*Can* he change her ruling? Yes, he can! *Will* he change it? I'll bet you your retirement pay he won't."

"Why not?" I asked.

"If he tosses out the confessions now, after Judge Kaseman admitted those statements and other evidence, LaVacca will look like he's second guessing. No judge wants to overrule a peer judge, especially on a case like this. Sure, the higher courts will overturn a judge from a lower court, but it's not a good thing for a judge at the same level to do that to another judge from the same court." With a grin, he added, "It's considered to be kind of tacky. Also, my friend, because he tossed out the first Graham case, LaVacca isn't going to now toss out the confessions after a judge like Anita Kaseman has ruled they're admissible."

"But you do realize he'll have to save face with this case," I stated flatly. "I mean he set Graham loose the first time. It's going to be hard for him to eat crow and find him guilty now. Am I right?"

"You're right…but!" Cantor teased with a wide grin.

"But what?" I asked.

"LaVacca is a pompous bastard. He wouldn't know the law if it hit him in the face or bit him in the ass. He's obnoxious, overbearing, and conceited; however, the man is no fool. Once this trial gets going and the press latches on to it full-force with coverage every night, LaVacca is going to have to let things slide our way. Besides, he has an honorable out."

"And that is?"

"I'll talk to him before the trial and let him know I appreciate the fact that he kicked your ass in the first trial. I'll tell him he has forced the police to do their job better…and suggest he can see how much better they're doing their job by the way you have prepared such an airtight case matter. As I said, the man is no fool. He'll get the hint, and he'll use it from the bench. LaVacca will take credit for setting the police straight and insisting they do a better job of preparing cases. It not only gets him off the hook, but it makes him the champion of justice he fancies himself to be. I'll have to sacrifice you, but what the hell," the D.A. said with a big smile and a wink, "you're only a civil servant."

Giving the man a crooked grin I asked, "You're sure he'll bite?"

"Mike, I'm sure of nothing but constipation and taxes. However, on this matter, let's just say I'm confident it'll work out...as long as you don't go making problems and shooting your mouth off to the press the way you sometimes like to do." He gave me the election poster Rudy Cantor smile, and said, "I've got to run now. Just stay cool and let John do his job."

On Friday afternoon Lethal John called the office. He had just gotten the word from LaVacca. The judge had some heavy-duty vacation plans for August, so he was giving both lawyers less than a month to have Graham's sanity - or lack thereof - evaluated. The competency issue would be heard by him on June twenty-eighth. July ninth was still set as the target date to begin the trial.

According to Lethal John and Dr. Zack McGill, there were several ways in which Jeff Longler could go about proving his client was legally insane or incompetent to stand trial. For one, he could show that Wayne Graham was so far out of whack he wasn't able to take part in his own defense. In that scenario, Longler would try to make the argument that his client was mentally unable to sense what was being said about him and therefore he couldn't provide his lawyer with the information and assistance needed to defend himself. In order to make that case Longler would need to prove Graham was totally out of touch with reality.

Another tactic would be to propose Graham had suffered a severe enough head trauma—or repeated head trauma—to render him mentally unfit to stand trial. That approach would require medical testimony to be bolstered with CAT scans and MRI's.

Or, Longler could try to prove to the Court and Jury that Wayne Graham was mentally unable to decipher—in a moral sense—wrong from right, and that would support the innocent by reason of insanity defense.

Zack was betting that Longler would pursue all three courses of action.

"Take a look at it, Mike," McGill said as he sipped water from a plastic bottle. "When you grabbed Graham the first time, he went on and on to tell you about how his father beat his head into the wall. Right? If I recall what you told me, didn't the guy tell you that was his father's favorite form of punishment—to bang his head against the wall and tell him he was trying to beat some sense into the kid?"

"Yeah," I agreed. "He sure did."

"Now, maybe he can't get a neurologist to come up with the CAT scan to prove it, but he could raise the issue for the jury to hear. Even if he can't win on the concept, he'll still get some jury sympathy." Then, as if I had to be reminded, he added, "Remember, it only takes one juror to hold out!"

"So, if he has that going for him, what makes you think he'll go after the I-can't-tell-right-from-wrong angle?"

"It's the easiest issue to raise and the hardest one to disprove." Zack paused to toss me an apple from the fruit bowl he kept on the left side of his desk. Then, selecting one for himself, he bit into it, chewed it a few times, and continued. "Look at it this way. Let's say you're Joe-the-Juror or Jane-the-Juror. You come from a nice family, live in a comfortable home in the suburbs, and love your kids. Being a good person, you constantly worry about Johnny's buckteeth, the friends he and Suzie hang around with, and their chances of getting into a good school. Okay? Got it? Now I come along and I tell you that there's a guy who enjoys strangling kids...in fact, he likes it so much, he's done it four times. You reel back in shock," Zack said as he held his hand to his chest and stumbled back toward the mahogany credenza at the far wall of his office. "You say, 'Oh my God! The poor guy must be...'"

"...crazy," I said to finish his sentence and to make his point.

"Exactly, my man! Exactly right. It's the one approach that's the easiest one for jurors to grasp as a concept. Unfortunately, those detailed and chilling confessions you have from Graham's lips will help his attorney establish the ever-popular nuttier-than-a-fruitcake defense. And once again, it only takes one juror to create a hung jury or a lead to a finding of not guilty."

"Yes," I conceded before advancing my argument. "However, being criminally insane and being walking-around-crazy are two different things. I mean, a guy can be crazy, nuts, whacko, insane, bonkers, whatever else you want to call it, but still he may not be *legally* insane."

"Good point!" the shrink admitted. "You know that, I know that, Longler knows that, Lethal John Niemeyer knows that, Graham probably even knows that, and maybe even that dumb shit LaVacca might know that...but can a jury make the distinction?"

"Well then, what about Son of Sam?" I asked rhetorically.

"What about him?" Zack asked in a challenge.

"The guy says he went out and shot, what was it, five, six nice young kids, and then he comes up with the bullshit that his neighbor's dog told him to do it! That's pretty far-fetched!"

Zack shrugged his shoulders as if to say, "So what?"

"So," I continued in response to his silent challenge. "Evidently there are ways of convincing the jury they're being snowed."

"Yes, there are ways of doing it. The question that still remains is—will the jury get it? Will they understand they're being buried in horse crap? "Now get the hell out of here and let me get some work done. Quit worrying about it. You're going in with just about the sharpest Assistant DA we have. Every time he gets in front of the jury box, John plays those juries like a fine violin."

I felt better when I left the psychologist's office. I assured myself I went there to get his professional input, but I had to admit it was also good for my mental health. Walking out to my car, I caught myself whistling. The whistling would soon fade when Jeff Longler announced his next two surprises.

Surprise number one, and not a big one, was that the defense was going to go after the insanity plea on all three arguments. The big one, surprise number two—Longler was making a request for a trial *without* a jury...a trial to be heard and decided by one man...Judge John Joseph LaVacca.

The nice thing about going on a date with your ex-wife, especially one with whom you get along, is that you don't have worry abut impressing her. Diane knows all my bad traits and she has either mitigated or learned to tolerate each one.

We started the evening with nice meal at Red Fedele's place on West Ridge Road, on the outskirts of Rochester. Red's restaurant had been a favorite haunt of ours ever since we first married. His new place was larger and brighter than the former location, a two-story white farmhouse with bright red shutters, farther out on West Ridge Road, or what the locals refer to as, "The Ridge." The good smells of tripe, *calimari,* shrimp scampi, sausage and peppers, veal, and herb-rich sauces hit our noses as we entered the restaurant. Diane, always impressed by people who enjoyed a certain amount of fame, took time to study the pictures of Red and assorted celebrities that hung from the twenty-foot walls in the main lobby of the place. The 50 or 60, maybe 75 pictures, showed the portly red head posing with athletes, entertainers, politicians, and assorted local and national celebrities. While she absorbed the pictures, I had our name added to the waiting list, and was told to expect the customary half-hour delay before being seated.

"You're getting the *calimari,* right?" Diane asked with a smile.

I responded with a shrug.

"You're so predictable, Michael," she said with a laugh.

"I'm predictable? Me? I'm the only one here who is predictable? Like you're not going to have a glass of white wine, and then order the Veal *Franciase*?" I mockingly questioned. The observation made us both laugh.

The meal was good and the conversation was light. During dinner I discovered, for the first time, that Diane was aging. It was something I had not seen—or at least had not been aware of—before that night. The thin lines in the corners of her mouth and eyes did nothing to distract from her attractiveness.

Following the meal and an after-dinner drink—predictably a *Sambuco* for me and Irish Cream for her—we drove over to my place, picked up Max, and then drove to Ontario Beach Park for a walk.

"You're getting nicer to be with, Michael," she commented casually.

"Well, others have noted I do clean up rather well. I'm also bright, witty, charming, charismatic, and bordering on handsome."

"Don't push it, buster," Diane laughed as she nudged me in the ribs with her elbow.

We had parked the car by the pier and walked toward the beach area. Along the way we passed the merry-go-round. Although it was summer now, with the air warm and humid, I could still see the tire prints in the snow and the discarded body of Sandra Montgomery lying, there just west of the carousel.

"Is something wrong, Michael?" my date asked.

"This is where we found the Montgomery girl," I answered.

"Who?" she inquired with a wrinkled brow. Although she had been a cop's wife for ten years, Diane was not unlike the general public in that respect. Six months was a long time for them to remember the name of a homicide victim.

"The last kid Graham killed. He dumped her body near here."

My former spouse let the distraction go without admonishing me for allowing the job to interfere with our summer night's walk. Just as I had learned to clean up my language and cut way back in my drinking in order to please her, she had learned not to be so critical of my ties to police work. We walked a few minutes before she spoke.

"How's that case going? I think I read it's coming up for trial pretty soon."

"It will probably be delayed a few weeks. The defense is asking for a competency hearing and they just announced they're going for an insanity plea."

"What's all that mean, Michael?"

"You don't want to hear all that."

"No, Michael, I do. I want to try to understand more about what you do and why it all seems to bother you." There was a pause before she added, "You've changed for me, and I need to change for you."

I couldn't decide if she was just being polite or if she really wanted to understand. As we walked along behind Max who seemed to be inhaling most of the beach with his nose, I lit a cigarette, blew the smoke out, and decided to go for it.

"The competency hearing is for the judge to decide whether or not Graham is competent to stand trial. In other words, to determine if he's able to understand what's going on, and whether or not he's able to take part in his defense. If the judge rules he's competent, then we go to trial."

"And, if he decides he is incompetent, then what?"

"Then Wayne gets shipped off to the State's Psychiatric Ward until such time as he is competent. That may be six months, a year, five years, maybe never. However, if he's later declared by the shrinks to be competent, then we go to trial."

"What's the other thing you mentioned?" Diane asked. "The insanity plea...what's that all about?"

"If we do get to have the trial, we then get to present all our evidence. After that, his lawyer has the opportunity to prove that although the crimes were committed, Graham is really innocent because he's insane. His lawyer has to be able to prove that Graham did not understand right from wrong; that he didn't know what he did was wrong. If they can establish that, then Graham's found not guilty by reason of insanity."

"And he goes free?" she asked with notable disbelief.

"Yes, no, and maybe," I answered. "He'll be sent to a state hospital for the criminally insane for what they call 'an indeterminate sentence'. Once he's there, he gets evaluated periodically. If, at some time, any time in the future, he's found to be stable enough to join the rest of us in society, he gets turned loose. End of matter!"

"Do you think he is truly insane?"

"Insane? Yes! However, the question is this—is he *criminally* insane? There's a difference. You can be crazy like the Son of Sam, Charlie Manson, any one of those guys, and still not be *criminally* insane."

We stopped walking long enough to look out at the lake. The sun was going down now and the water took on a pinkish hue. It was a nice moment...a quiet moment. Max moved ahead of us but turned around to see if we were following. When he saw that we weren't, he returned to us and gave a couple of barking orders to continue walking. We did.

"I don't believe for a minute the man is criminally insane," I said as we strolled in the direction of the pier. "He knew what he was doing was wrong. He covered his tracks, hid evidence, tired to keep his identity concealed, used a false name when he took one of the kids to a motel. You don't do those things if you don't know, don't understand what you're doing is wrong."

We had reached the old bathhouse, but before turning around, Diane embraced me…and we kissed. It was a kiss that was long enough to make Max bark at us, telling us he didn't like being ignored.

"Is he always this jealous?" Diane asked.

"Only when I love the woman," I answered with a big smile. When she didn't respond I asked, "Do you want to walk out on the pier?"

"Sure," she said. "I guess so. Do you have time?"

"I don't have to be anywhere until eight tomorrow morning," I answered as I attached the leash to Max. Letting him roam the beach was one thing. I was not about to risk allowing him to go free out here, on the concrete pier with river water splashing one side of it, and the lake water on the other side.

"You two sure take good care of each other," Diane noted as she petted Max's head.

"He's a good guy."

"Do you think you could ever pay this much attention to us, to our relationship?" she asked.

"I don't know. Do you fetch?"

When she slapped my back with an open hand, Max took a step toward her and gave three sharp barks to let her know that was not acceptable behavior. We began walking again in a nice, comforting silence. Every so often we would wave at the people on the sailboats who were now returning from the lake to docks along the Genesee River.

"You've changed considerably, Michael. You stop to see the sunsets now. You listen. You've slowed down. You've learned to give something of yourself to others…even if it is a dog."

Looking due north across the lake, I lowered my head down toward Diane's shoulder and whispered, "Not so loud…Max doesn't know he's a dog."

Diane just smiled and gave a soft chuckle and gripped my arm closer to her.

CHAPTER TWENTY-ONE

A MATTER OF COMPETENCY

Less than a week before the competency hearing was scheduled to begin Tommy Romano stood in front of my desk with a big, stupid grin on his face. I looked up, stared at him for a few seconds, and finally was forced to ask, "Do you have gas or are you in love with me?"

"Lute, although you love me already—and I believe you really and truly do love me—you're going to love me twice as much when I tell you what I have to tell to you."

"Is this going to lead to sex between us, Tommy?" I asked.

"That will be your choice, Lute! But please be gentle with me...I *am* a virgin!"

"I'll keep that in mind," I said as I tossed the pen on the desk. "Now cut the crap and tell the nice Lieutenant why you're here standing in front of him with that asinine smirk on your face."

"I have an aunt," Romano said as he nodded his head up and down as if to affirm the statement.

"I'm glad for you, Tommy. Now, go do some work."

Undaunted, he continued. "This aunt of mine, Aunt Carmel, has a sister-in-law, Filomena Romagnola. Aunt Fanny is what everyone calls her. The sister-in-law, Aunt Fanny, has a neighbor. The neighbor has a grown daughter." He paused and then asked, "Are you following me on this, Boss?"

"I am if you're going somewhere with this genealogy...otherwise I'm totally ignoring you."

287

"Just hang on a second because here comes the point. My aunt's sister-in-law's neighbor's daughter works at the library, the main branch of the library!"

"That's nice, Tommy. I'm very happy your family's relatives are gainfully employed. Still, I need to ask, so what?"

"So, this girl takes note of certain people who come in and out of the place. In particular she takes note of one Wayne Graham—*who* she recognizes from the nightly news! She recalls he comes to the library every so often and asks for certain books. 'What types of books does he like to read?' you might ask," Tommy asked rhetorically. "He likes books that are about mental illness, criminal insanity, mental incompetence!"

"No shit!" was my astute observation.

"Now then, if you would like to offer me the weekend off, I will be more than happy to share the name of that girl with you."

I offered the man a cold look, tucked my chin down into my neck, and peered up at him from under my raised eyebrows.

"I'll take that as a 'No'!" Romano observed correctly. He then promptly volunteered the information. "The girl's name is Cassandra Mosehauer."

"Where is she? Get her address and get out there with Bobby and get her interviewed. See if she'll go for a signed statement and get her to agree to testify."

"Done," Tommy said with a proud smirk. "I talked to her last night, right after I got the information. Here's her statement."

As I glanced over the statement the investigator had obtained from the Mosehauer woman, Tommy filled in the blanks. This new and very important witness had taken note of Wayne Graham when he began to come to the library following his release from jail last year. She kept an eye on him because she was concerned he might try to approach some of the children in the place. Because Mosehauer worked in the area where medical and psychiatric books were kept, Graham would often come to her to ask where he might find books concerned with mental illness and legal issues related to mental illness. The librarian also observed that Graham carried one of those reddish-brown, cardboard, accordion files with him that held together with a couple of wide rubber bands. After finding the books he had asked for, he would sit for two, sometimes three hours, reading and taking notes. This went on right up until the time of his last arrest.

"This is absolutely dynamite, Tommy!" I exclaimed, unable to contain my delight. "Get it over to Lethal John right away. Under the rules of discovery, he's going to have to make it available to the defense attorney. Longler will raise holy hell that he didn't get it sooner, but Niemeyer will have to deal with that."

"On my way, Boss!"

Two minutes later I briefed Skip Winston regarding the librarian. He was so excited he called Deputy Chief Cooper, and I'm confident that Cooper then called Chief Matt Murphy. What Romano—through his network of relatives—had uncovered would be a strong piece of evidence to prove Graham had contrived his mental incompetence and alleged insanity.

The competency hearing is commonly referred to as a "7-30 Proceeding." The reference, I have always assumed, is made to the section of the New York State Criminal Procedure Law that allows for such matters. And it was at 10:35 a.m. on June twenty-eighth that Judge John LaVacca pounded his gavel and announced the rules of engagement.

"In *my* courtroom, gentlemen, a 7-30 Proceeding will not become a circus in which you tramp through a small army of psychiatrists, psychologists, psychotherapists, and other such people. I will allow you each to present two witnesses, and that's it! If you go over your limit of two witnesses, that third guy better have some very new and special testimony for this court to hear. Have I again made myself clear?"

Both attorneys affirmed it was clear.

"You may also want to advise your witnesses that I am no fool, and I am well versed in matters of psychiatry, so they better shy away from redundant testimony where they make the same point over and over again with different professional jargon. I will catch them and they *will* be embarrassed. Now let's begin."

I didn't stay for the long-winded testimony of the four shrinks. Prior experience had shown me they take the first twenty or thirty minutes going over their education, membership in assorted associations, certifications they've been awarded, papers they published and presented at various conferences, and their affiliations with different institutions. They would then go into the tests they performed on the defendant and their observations and conclusions regarding those tests. The end result would be the two shrinks for the defense would have come to a totally opposite conclusion than the one reached by the two shrinks for the prosecution. In short, it would end up being a draw and the judge would have to reach his conclusion by—in a figurative sense for most judges, but not necessarily for Vodka LaVacca—tossing a coin.

I was later told that Wayne Graham staged a couple of outbursts as the psychiatrists testified. A couple of times he chanted to them, "Liar, liar, pants on fire!" On one occasion he threw pencils at one of the defense witnesses; another time he tried to moon the witness, but Longler pulled him down to his chair and asked the judge for a brief recess.

The difference in this 7-30 hearing would be the testimony of Cassandra Mosehauer. As instructed, the bailiff at the hearing gave me a call when the librarian was about to take the stand. I arrived at the courtroom moments before she was sworn in.

Lethal John ran her through the preliminary stuff regarding her name, place of employment, how long she had been so employed, and the duties of her position. Then the main course began.

"What first drew your attention to the defendant in this case?" the ADA asked.

Cassandra—she preferred to be called Cassie—was a young woman, probably in her late 20's, with an unmistakable beauty that is not usually associated with librarians. She had a serious look about her and seemed to be absorbing the entire room, the various people, and the nuances of the proceeding, with her calm, warm eyes.

"Well, at first he just struck me as being odd. I say that because he would come into the library and wander around without apparently looking for books or anything in particular. When he would finally come over to me and ask for certain books, he would leer at me, smirking, as if there was something funny and I was missing whatever was amusing him. Then, one evening, I saw his picture on the evening news."

Niemeyer asked Mosehauer if the same man she saw on the news was present in the courtroom, and she confirmed he was, pointing to Wayne Graham and commenting, "The man over there."

When pointed to, Graham stood up and took a graceful bow.

The prosecutor ignored the stunt and asked if Cassandra recalled any of the titles of the books the Wayne Graham had requested.

"Oh, yes, of course. I began to keep a list of the books."

When the ADA asked for it, Cassie Mosehauer read the list of books that Graham had used as his research material. Lethal John made special mention that two of the books were written by one of the defense's psychiatric witnesses.

Suddenly Graham came to life, standing up and yelling at the witness, "Tell them how you gawked at my crotch every time I came in. Why don't you tell them how you lusted after me? That's why you remember me! You wanted me!"

The witness blushed her annoyance at the defendant as LaVacca threatened to remove him from the court.

When things calmed down, Lethal John used his questions to summarize and repeat the relevant points he wanted to get into the proceeding. The young woman was then turned over to Jefferson Longler for cross-examination. His questioning was short...but effective.

"Miss Mosehauer, do you have any people who come in and ask you for medical books on such subjects as, let us say, on illnesses such as cancer, muscular dystrophy, heart ailments, or diabetes?"

"Yes, yes, I do," the witness responded in her serious manner.

"Do you know, of your own personal knowledge, if any of those people actually have some of those illnesses...illnesses related to the book they are requesting?"

"Some do."

"Do you know of any person, or perhaps a few people, who suffer from some particular disease and ask for reference material related to that particular illness or disease?"

I hung my head. It was obvious where he was going with the line of questioning. Unfortunately, Cassie Mosehauer was not familiar with the traps that lawyers set.

"Well, yes, I do. There are several."

"Would you tell us about one or two of those people."

"Objection, Your Honor," Niemeyer said as he rose to his feet. "I dispute the relevancy of this line of questioning; also, it's beyond the scope of my direct examination of the witness." He made the statement, but he knew the relevancy better than I.

"Mr. Longler, do you care to respond?"

"May I approach the bench, Your Honor?" Longler asked. It was obvious he didn't want to discuss the relevancy of his question within earshot of the unsuspecting witness. It is also a serious no-no to get too close to a judge's bench without his permission.

Both attorneys huddled with Judge LaVacca on his sacred ground for less than a minute. When they broke the huddle, LaVacca stated, "I'll allow the question. Objection overruled."

"Tell us about one or two of those people, briefly, if you would, so as not to take up too much valuable court time."

"Well," the attractive, serious girl with the bright eyes said, "there is one lady who has breast cancer. She told me she's trying to use diet as a way to treat the cancer. Another person, a young man with diabetes, does a lot of reading on that illness. He has told me he's made some startling discoveries on ways he can control the disease and reduce his insulin intake."

"Interesting," Longler said as he stroked his chin. "So then, following what these most unfortunate people have told you, would you say that these people are reading up on cancer and diabetes because they are trying to fake the disease, or are they doing so because they want to understand it?"

"I object, Your Honor," the prosecutor said as he jumped to his feet once more. "The question is leading and it asks the witness to draw a conclusion."

"Your Honor," Longler said in a whine as he flapped his short, stubby arms up in the air and back down to his rounded hips. "The witness has testified she talks to these people, engages them in conversation. She has necessary information to draw the conclusion. In fact, she's not even drawing a conclusion; she is merely stating what she knows, through her conversations, to be true."

"I disagree, Your Honor," Niemeyer said as he took a bold step toward the bench and drew a warning glance from LaVacca. "These people have merely *told* the witness they have the diseases they claim to have. She has not testified to having any medical knowledge or medical documentation that they actually do have the diseases they purport to have. They *also* could very well be faking their alleged illness, and seeking information on how to continue the fraud. And, for that matter, for her to repeat what they have said, would be nothing more than hearsay."

"Your Honor," Longler said a little to loudly and too sharply for LaVacca's ego to accept.

"You keep a civil tone in your voice when you talk to *me*, young man," Vodka LaVacca commanded.

"I'm sorry, Your Honor. It won't happen again," Longler back-peddled.

"It better not," the judge stated flatly. "Now if you have something to say, say it and keep it short and respectful."

"Yes, Your Honor. I will, sir. Thank you, Your Honor," Jeff Longler said in rapid succession. It was hard for me to decipher if he was overreacting, sucking up, or actually trying to vex LaVacca. "My point is the prosecution has no foundation on which to lay that allegation. He doesn't know if these poor, sick people who go to the library for knowledge and understanding are pretending."

"And that, Your Honor," Niemeyer interjected, "is exactly my point! I do not know, he does not know, and surely the witness does not know. He is therefore asking her to draw a conclusion she is not qualified to make."

Vodka LaVacca looked as if he could have used a good, stiff drink as he hesitated and tried to put some understanding to the exchange between the two attorneys. Finally, without making a ruling, he instructed the defense attorney, "Re-phrase the question."

"Do you, Miss Mosehauer, have any direct knowledge that either of these two people you mentioned have the disease they claim to have?"

"Well, the woman told me she had a breast removed about…"

"Objection, Your Honor," Niemeyer said, not bothering to stand. "More hearsay."

"Objection, my ass, you fool!" Graham shouted as he stood.

"Sit down, Mr. Graham or I shall have you gagged!" LaVacca said with exhausted patience. "Objection sustained," he then ruled as he turned his attention and ire to the witness. "Young lady, I don't care what they told you. I don't care what you think, feel, or suspect. All that is being asked of you is what you *know* as a fact to be true. Do you *know* anything in that pretty, but dense little head of yours?"

Cassandra Mosehauer could not understand why the judge and the prosecutor were suddenly mad at her. Was she not doing the right thing? Was she not being a good citizen in coming here? What had she done to earn their anger? Not being able to sort it all out, she drew herself erect in the chair, looked squarely at Longler, and said, "I do not have any such knowledge as to the accuracy of the claims that those people have made to me."

"Thank you for your testimony today," Longler said with sincerity. Then, turning his attention to the judge, he stated, "I have no further questions, Your Honor."

"Anything from you, Mr. Prosecutor?" asked of Niemeyer.

"Nothing more, Your Honor."

The testimony of Cassie Mosehauer had resulted in little for the prosecution. Niemeyer had drawn—for the court's benefit—the inference that Graham was studying ways to create the appearance of criminal insanity; Longler had created the insinuation that poor old Wayne was simply trying to understand his mental affliction.

"The witness is excused," LaVacca proclaimed. "You may leave, deary."

Cassandra Mosehauer stood up, smoothed her skirt as if she was brushing off a stench. She then turned to John Judge LaVacca after stepping down from the witness platform, and said, "I may not know if those people are really sick, but I do *know* this; you are a rude, obnoxious person, and you should be ashamed of the way you treat people who come here!"

LaVacca's jaw fell as John Niemeyer covered his mouth to stifle the laugh.

"One more remark like that, young woman, and I will hold you in contempt!" LaVacca barked as he pointed the handle of his gavel at the proud, bold witness.

Cassie replied with an audible, "Humph!" and walked to the massive doors sealing off the hallowed chamber from the rational world. Having pushed the door open, she turned once more and said, "You couldn't begin to measure the contempt I have for you!" And, with that, she was gone.

LaVacca began to sputter and stammer as he ordered the bailiff to seize the woman and bring her back in the courtroom so he could, "...deal with her!" However, to everyone's pleasure, Cassandra Mosehauer had disappeared and was nowhere to be found. The bailiff returned to the court huffing and puffing, to advise the judge, "I can't find her...she must have taken the stairs." The bailiff did not volunteer the information that he had been the one who scooted the brazenly brave Miss Mosehauer away from the elevators and to a staircase. There were some things the judge didn't need to know!

The clock was teasing four o'clock in the afternoon when John Niemeyer called the office to announce that LaVacca had already ruled on the competency matter.

"I'll come over and you can buy me a cup of coffee as you give me the bad news," I said with surrender in my voice.

"No, I don't think so, Mike," he responded. "However, you can come over in about a half-hour, pick me up, and take me out to dinner...because my dear, old detective buddy, we won! LaVacca held that Graham is competent to stand trial!"

"No shit?" I yelled into the phone. "Really?"

"No shit!" Lethal John responded proudly. "Really!"

Forty-five minutes later the two of us were standing at a small bar of a restaurant hidden away in the back of a large, old house over on Park Avenue. Even though the bar is small, the restaurant portion of the joint does nice things with *portabello* mushrooms.

"Give me the details, John," I insisted as we clinked our glasses together in a salute. "How did it go down?"

The prosecutor explained all of the shrinks had basically cancelled out each other. Cassie Mosehauer helped us slightly...up to the point when she—verbally, at least—flipped off Vodka LaVacca.

"So if it was all a draw, and Mosehauer didn't really help us, how did you pull it off?" I asked with an eager grin on my mug.

"Well, it just so happens that *I am* a brilliant lawyer," John said as he huffed a breath on the tips of the fingers of his right hand and then brushed the fingertips on his chest. "Besides, I live right, am nice to children and small animals, and I pay my taxes."

"Cut the crap! How did you do it? Really, how did you pull it off?"

"When LaVacca gave us each five minutes to make closing statements, Longler took the time to try to re-cap what the doctors had said, and then went into the malarkey about poor old Wayne going to the library so he could understand the mental illness that was plaguing him."

"And?" I asked.

"And LaVacca, although he was still pissed at the librarian, wasn't buying it." The tousled-hair guy took a long, draining swig of his beer, set it down and signaled for two more before he continued. "However, when it was my turn, I told the judge he had a difficult decision to make, but I wanted him to know that I had seen our buddy Wayne—on at least four occasions—pass notes to his attorney during the day-and-a-half of the proceedings. I then added that I had seen him whisper to his lawyer at least a half-dozen times during the same time period. Just to give it some umph, I volunteered to take the stand and give him the same testimony under oath. To my shock and great pleasure, LaVacca said, 'There won't be any need for that Mr. Niemeyer because I have made the same observations!' Naturally, he had to outdo my observations and say he had seen him do the same thing; however, *he* had seen Wayne pass *five notes* and whisper to Longler *eight times*. With that, he raps the gavel a couple of times and says it's his finding that Graham is competent to take part in his own defense, and had evidently been doing so in spite of his outbursts. So, Graham is going to trial. End of story. Period!"

We high-fived each other and then sat down to a great dinner. During the meal I pressed him for more of the details about who said what, but the details weren't relished as much as the bottom line...I was going to get *my* day in court with Mister Wayne Graham!

After dinner, as we walked to our cars, I asked, "Why do you think LaVacca sided with us on this deal? I mean, what the hell, he could have just as easily gone the other way."

"I think he really did see it loud and clear that Graham was faking, and it pissed him off. I may be wrong, Mike, but that's the way I took it. Besides, Rudy did have a talk with LaVacca. I truly don't know what was said, but I guess it made an impact on our dear judge."

"Well, don't misunderstand me, John. I mean, I'm so happy I could shit, but still, we're going to have to face LaVacca in the trial. The long and short of it is I don't trust him. The guy is frigging weird! He doesn't just march to his own drummer; the son-of-a-bitch has his own orchestra! He's too much of a renegade! He likes being unpopular."

"Funny," John said as he unlocked his car door. "It seems to me people have said the same things about you!"

"Thanks for the low blow, asshole!" I said as I threw a feigned punch at him.

"Don't sweat the trial, Mike," Niemeyer advised. "Graham screwed up the competency hearing and he'll probably do the same thing at his trial."

It was a good thought on which to part. However, what neither John nor I suspected that night was that Graham was more legally astute than we gave him credit for being. What we didn't know at that time was that Wayne had intentionally blown the competency hearing. He wanted to go to trial!

CHAPTER TWENTY-TWO

THEY CALL IT JUSTICE

Playhouse 90 was a popular television show back in the mid-1950's. The show presented viewers with a live, hour-and-a-half presentation of a stage play. "Playhouse 90" is also a phrase used by cops— Rochester cops, at least—to describe a confusing crime scene that included a large number of people playing the real-life roles of victims, suspects, and witnesses. For many obvious reasons that phrase, "Playhouse 90" kept creeping into my mind as I watched the murder trial of Wayne Graham unfold.

As scheduled, the trial began on July ninth with Assistant District Attorney John Niemeyer presenting the state's case with a parade of witnesses. Included in the procession were the parents of the murdered children, crime scene technicians, the uniformed cops who were first to arrive at the homicide scenes, and various investigators who played a role in finding witnesses and evidence. Finally, one by one, virtually every member of the Violent Crimes Unit followed them.

Romano, St. John, and even Jimmy Paskell testified to our hunt for the murderer of Becky Chilsom, Traci Taylor, Timothy Bidwell, and Sandra Montgomery. I offered testimony about confronting Graham in the garage on Westminister Street and his subsequent confession. Donovan, the old pro, was magnificent as he recaptured the defendant's detailed confession after the arrest. Gail and Wendy Walz also appeared as witnesses. Gail testified about her role as one of the detectives who worked the case; Wendy gave flawless testimony as to the abusive cruelty of the defendant.

Finally, Niemeyer put on Doctor Zack McGill and two other psychiatrists who had evaluated Wayne Graham and found him able to decipher right from wrong. Each one of the professionals stated that a person who would conceal facts and take steps to elude the police—in the manner described by the squad—would know he was doing something wrong and would then try to conceal it, and therefore would not be criminally insane. After getting all three of the shrinks to admit it was very possible to fake criminal insanity, Niemeyer brought Cassie Mosehauer to the stand for one more appearance. LaVacca glared at the attractive, self-confident woman most of the time she was on the stand, and I'm not really sure he heard any of her testimony.

During the entire trial Lethal John did not spare the court one iota of detail in reconstructing the cold killings committed by Wayne Graham. His questions were direct and to the point. When it was necessary to be amiable, he was gentle in pulling out the information he needed to make his case "beyond a reasonable doubt." When there was a need to be aggressive, his words lunged and attacked reluctant witness, extracting the verbiage, the information, the very nuance he needed to make his case. Some witnesses cried as they testified; others presented the information they held in a cool, business-like manner.

Jefferson Longler cross-examined each witness with an almost blasé, ho-hum line of questions that were usually short. He didn't seem to care that each witness shoveled more shit into his client's grave, for it was not his tactic or his need to prove Graham did not commit the killings. In fact, Longler worked hard to pull out the gory details of what the man seated at the defense table had done to young human life. What Jeff Longler *did* need to prove was that Wayne Graham was insane, crazy, nuts, demented, deranged, psychotic, whacked out, sociopathic, or whatever the hell else one wanted to label the condition. No, Longler did not need to prove his client was incapable of such acts. It was quite the reverse. He needed to paint Mister Wayne Graham as a lunatic, and specifically, a *criminally insane* lunatic.

With nearly every witness, the disheveled defense lawyer closed his cross-examination with two questions. "Do you think this was a horrible thing that was done?" was the first of the closing queries. It was then followed with, "Wouldn't a person have to be insane to do such a thing?" Each time he asked the question of a witness, Niemeyer would state, with a bored, how-foolish-can-you-be tone of voice, "Objection, your Honor...the question seeks an opinion the witness is not qualified to offer." And, each time the objection was presented, Vodka LaVacca would sustain the objection and forbid the answer from being given. Only the three psychiatrists who testified on behalf of the prosecution were spared the last question, for Longler knew their response would only damage his case.

As the trial moved on doggedly day after day, Wayne Graham did his best to play the role of deranged defendant. He was not above shouting at witnesses, Niemeyer, and even Judge LaVacca. One time our boy went off on a tangent about the uselessness of Number 1 lead pencils, insisting the court supply him with Number 2 pencils.

"You tell me I'm competent enough to stand trial, and then you give me these useless Number 1 pencils that don't write worth a damn."

"Sit down!" LaVacca demanded.

"How the hell can I defend myself if I can't write because of these fucking shitty pencils?" Graham insisted on knowing.

On another day Graham came to court with the word "GUILTY" scratched across his cheeks and nose. When LaVacca inquired as to the meaning of such an act, Longler began to explain that his client had used a metal tab from a soft drink can to etch the word into his skin. Unlike his attorney, Wayne was more direct in his response.

"What the fuck do you think it means, you dumb shit? IT MEANS I'M GUILTY!"

"You can't wear that...that sign, that message in here, young man."

"Why can't I?" Graham challenged. "It's my damn skin. I can do whatever I want to with it. I have rights you know!"

Once again LaVacca got roped in. In a feat of stupidity above his normal range of ignorance, the judge blurted out, "It could prejudice the outcome of the case."

With that, Jeff Longler was on his feet asking for a mistrial. His argument was long-winded legal crap, summed up by noting, "In short, Your Honor has admitted he has been prejudiced against my client."

"I did not!" LaVacca bellowed.

"You did so!" Jeff Longler shot back.

"Perry Mason was never as good as this," Tommy Romano whispered to St. John as we sat in the back row of the courtroom. "We are witnessing the very intricate judicial debate known as the 'Did Not—Did Too Argument.' I'm impressed, very impressed! It surely can't get much better than this!"

Meanwhile, the legal argument between the two stalwartly representatives of jurisprudence continued.

"You stated my client's wounds would prejudice the outcome of this case," Longler insisted.

"I did not say that, Counselor," LaVacca shot back. "I merely stated a person, any person—a witness, one of the people observing this proceeding—*could* be prejudiced by seeing those marks on his head. I am certainly not prejudiced by it. That type of activity does not prejudice a judge of my caliber!"

"The people back there can't see his forehead, Your Honor," the defense attorney said as he pointed to those of us watching the farce. "Besides that, they and the witnesses do not determine the outcome of this trial. You do! *You* render the decision and you can see the word on this poor soul's face. *You* raised the matter of prejudice."

"That's enough, Counselor!" the judge almost shouted so as to keep himself from getting anymore entwined in his own gross ignorance. "Your request for a mistrial is denied."

"I take exception," the other clown said.

"Your exception is noted!"

Once more Tommy Romano leaned over to his partner and asked, "Who won that little exchange…Tweedle Dee or Tweetle Dum?"

"Now have that man removed from this courtroom," LaVacca was saying as he pointed to Graham. "Do not allow him to return until that word is either healed or covered."

"FUCK YOU, ASSHOLE!" Graham shouted. "I'm staying! How can I defend myself if I have to depend on this idiot lawyer and you?"

"You may watch the proceedings from a back room that has closed-circuit television. If you have comments for your lawyer, you will be allowed to send out notes! However, you may not stay in *my* courtroom with that word on your face. If you want to stay, it will have to be covered."

The defendant finally agreed to the judge's request and was led out of the courtroom while a brief recess was called. Later, when Graham re-entered the sacred chambers with six band aid strips criss-crossed over the middle of his skinny, drawn face, I busted out laughing and had to quickly seek refuge in the hallway.

Every day Wayne Graham worked diligently to prove his insanity. Three separate times he was removed from the courtroom because of the havoc he caused. Another time he politely asked to address the court, and then went off on a nearly lucid argument that if he were to be found guilty, he would lose his voting rights. His point was his right to vote was a federal guarantee and the state-level court could not abridge his constitutional rights.

LaVacca listened patiently to the ten-minute rambling and then calmly said, "Thank you for sharing that with court, but your argument has no legal bearing."

"I didn't think so either, Your Honor," Graham said with a devilish grin. "But, what the hell, I thought I would give it a try." He then turned and bowed to all those assembled.

A few days later, in another effort to further his cause, Graham fashioned a dunce cap out of a couple of sheets of paper and a few paper clips. LaVacca had excused himself from the courtroom so that he could attend to some "pressing paperwork" he had suddenly decided needed to be taken care of that very moment. When he returned, Graham had positioned himself in a chair, on top of the defense table…with the dunce cap balanced precariously on his head.

When Lethal John announced, "The People rest, Your Honor," Jeff Longler leaped into action. It was now his turn to prove that his client, although having committed all the crimes of which he had been accused, was—in the eyes of the law—not guilty by reason of insanity. He did not have to disprove or even attack the evidence and testimony that had been introduced; all he had to do was convince the judge that Wayne Graham was so mentally deficient he could not or did not comprehend the wrongfulness of his acts. The defense began their parade of so-called expert witnesses to state Wayne Graham could not possibly understand the acts he had committed were, in a legal and moral sense, wrong.

The trial that Judge LaVacca had scheduled for two weeks, spread over into a third week as Jeff Longler took time to re-show portions of the two video-taped confessions of his client to the psychologists and psychiatrists that he had summoned. Although the prosecution had introduced the tapes to prove the confession, the defense now used them to promote the argument of Graham's insanity. Frequently ordering the tape to be paused, the rumpled defense attorney would ask each shrink to evaluate a look, a word, a gesture, or a phase made by Graham.

"Does that appear to be normal?" Longler would ask. "Is that the way a criminally sane person would act or speak?" Again and again, the videos were paused so the defense attorney could further his cause. "Would a rational person say something like that? Isn't that the behavior of a person who does not know right from wrong?"

And, as we all knew the defense witness would do, each sided with Jefferson Longler's point of view on the matter.

Lethal John, being one to make a little hay himself, would, in cross-examination, ask only a few questions of the shrink-of-the-day. "Let's suppose," he would offer up to the witness as if he was asking the question for the first time in his entire life. "Doctor, let's just suppose you wanted to convince others you were criminally insane. Could you fake it? If you knew what the criminally insane act like, could you then pretend that you were criminally insane?"

Each of the defense's mental experts would try to dodge the question or dance their way around it, but sooner or later, Niemeyer would corner them and they would have to admit that most mental illnesses could be faked. Some of them would make the admission, but only with the caveat that the pretender would have to be fairly intelligent.

The ADA would pounce back with, "When you tested Mr. Graham, what did you find his IQ to be?"

"One hundred and thirty-seven," they would be forced to say.

"That's 'fairly intelligent', isn't it, Doctor?" the prosecutor would ask and the witness would have to admit the score was in the higher end of the general population's range of IQ scores.

On the other hand, Jefferson Longler also scored some major points when he asked one of the psychiatrists, "Did you ever find out what motivation my client had for committing the crimes for which he has been accused?"

"I did," Doctor Bertram Stiller stated flatly.

"What was that motivation?" Longler asked, and then stepped back to give his witness the stage.

"Mr. Graham suffers from a type of post-trauma disorder. It caused him to want to make his parents suffer for the way they treated him as a child. He wants to embarrass and humiliate them, to expose them to loathing by their friends and associates. In his own mind, Mr. Graham could not fathom a way to do that; a way to get everyone's attention to what he wanted to say. He therefore contrived this plan of doing something so bizarre, so extreme, it would attract the entire city's attention, perhaps even the attention of the country. In his attacks on those children, he was crying out, 'Hey, look at me…take note of me!' Mr. Graham was laboring under the belief that once he was found out, everyone would want to hear from him, to learn why he was doing such a dastardly thing." Doctor Bertram Sills took a few seconds to sip the water the bailiff had placed next to his right arm. He then continued. "He didn't plan on going to court. He wasn't capable of playing the matter out that far. In his mind, he only looked forward to the day when his story would be in the newspapers and everyone would know Graham has a father who verbally and physically abused him."

It went on like that until the third day of the third week of the trial. Finally, the defense rested. It was over. All that was left was for both sides to sum up…and for the Honorable John Joseph LaVacca to render his decision.

The next morning, every news operation in the city was in court to hear John Niemeyer sum up the prosecution's case.

"Wayne Graham is a cold-blooded, calculating, manipulative murderer," Niemeyer said as he looked squarely into the eyes of the judge. From that point Lethal John pointed out each one of the steps Graham had taken to cover up his crimes, to hide the victims while he abused and killed them, to conceal evidence, to secrete himself from the police. "These are the acts of a man who knows right from wrong, who knows good from bad, who knows he is evil," Niemeyer said as he pointed to the sky beyond the ceiling of the room. His words were well spaced and delivered with deliberation so they would be heard and absorbed by the judge who would make the ultimate decision.

"Wayne Graham is a crafty killer...and he practiced his craft skillfully," Niemeyer said as he stood in front of the defense table. As he spoke the words, he looked the killer squarely in the eyes. "He sought out books on the subject so he could study his craft. He read up on the insanity issue and then came to court to play out his drama in front of a good and honorable judge. And, in doing so, Wayne Graham made two mistakes." The prosecutor paused so he could look first at the judge, and then at the defendant. "Your Honor, his first mistake—contrary to the supposition made by his attorney—was Mr. Graham never used the knowledge he sought in those books to seek out a cure, to seek out treatment. And, the second mistake he made was being so transparent in the theatrics he used in this courtroom for your benefit. Wayne Graham took the information from those books in the library and then formed an act, a play...and opened his play in this court. Your Honor, he wasn't able to fool you during the Competency Hearing, and I trust he is not able to fool you now. The People place their faith and hope in you, Your Honor. We do trust and have confidence you are not duped into accepting this thinly disguised masquerade as a real defense...a defense that shames justice."

Personally, I thought it was a brilliant closing statement. In one swoop, Lethal John had pointed out all the inconsistencies in Graham's play acting, had paid homage to LaVacca's over zealous ego, and, he had challenged LaVacca not to make an ass out himself in front of the entire world.

Unfortunately, Jefferson Longler was not lacking in his own brand of brilliance and bullshit. He began his summation by shouting one word, "TEL-A-VI-SION!" Letting the four syllables play in everyone's mind for a quarter minute, he paced away from the defense table and began talking to the Assistant District Attorney.

"What sane man, when captured and cornered with a victim in his arms, asks to go on television? What sane man, when confronted with a policeman holding a gun, a policeman who may be just itching to kill him, smiles and asks to go on television? What sane man seeks out a television news crew in order to tell the world, 'Yes, you have me…I killed four children.' What sane man smiles and cries as he looks into the camera and tells all who are looking—or at least all he believes who will be looking—at him on the evening news, that he is a despicable man who abducts children, fondles them, and then kills them?"

Longler allowed his opening premise to sink in as he turned slowly to face the judge. "And what sane man, Your Honor, abuses and curses the man he wants to protect him, to find him innocent. Your Honor has suffered greatly during this trial, and I apologize to you for that. You have been mocked and ridiculed, cursed and damned by my client. I apologize to you that it happened, and I beg Your Honor's forgiveness that I had to allow it to continue. I am not a great attorney, Your Honor, but I am an honest one. I had to allow my client to go on in his abuse of you because it demonstrated the depth of my client's illness. The prosecutor would have you believe my client is a cunning, calculating person. However, I ask you this, Your Honor, what sane man who needs your support, would make you suffer the slings and arrows cast upon you by my client? I submit to you that if my client wanted to fake his insanity, he might very well have verbally abused the prosecutor; he may have sworn his filthy words at a witness; he may have even made me the brunt of his antagonism. However, my client attacked *you* just as he attacked some of us. Does this seem to be the act of a sane man?"

Longler went on at length to summarize the observations and professional opinions of his witnesses, and when he finally concluded almost an hour later, it was Judge LaVacca's turn to speak.

"I want both Counselors to know that I am well aware of their ploys to win my favor in their summations," Vodka LaVacca said with disdain on his face and arrogance in his voice. "Those efforts, I assure you gentlemen, were wasted. I have listened intently to the witnesses and observed carefully what has gone on here in my courtroom. Using those observations and all the legal guidance I have available to me, I will render my decision Monday morning at 10:00 a.m. Court is now recessed!"

July and August can be brutal months in upstate New York. On that particular morning when Judge LaVacca ruled on the case, as August was advent, the heat and humidity were battling to outdo each other. By 10:55 a.m., when LaVacca finally pounded his gavel and announced, "Court is now in session," the humidity, at 99 percent, was ahead of the temperature by a mere three units.

"The role of this court is to judge," LaVacca began in a stately voice. "I have sat here for almost a month and listened intently to witness after witness. I have also, in that time period, observed. And, at night, when I should have been sleeping, I have reviewed those words of testimony and sought meaning to my observations. My task is not an easy one. No matter which way I rule, there will be those who will second guess and deride my decision; they will scoff at my decisions and mock my finding. However, I cannot bend to that probability. I must do that which I know to be right, and allow my detractors to have their fun. This decision has weighed heavily on me, but it is mine to make, and I *will* make it." He then paused to move some papers around his desk, take two sips of water, and sigh deeply. The pause also allowed the reporters to capture his words for posterity's sake.

Having allowed the news people time to catch up on their notetaking, LaVacca began anew. "The Defense has raised an affirmative defense, that of criminal insanity. And, as is the case with all such affirmative defenses, they have the burden of proof—proof beyond a reasonable doubt—that there is such insanity." Again there was a pause as the judge sipped water and looked out at the reporters to see if they were getting all of this down on their pads. "Although there is no doubt in my mind that the defendant did willingly and intentionally take the lives of four children…"

The word '*Although*' made my heart stop. I knew right then what was coming but thought that if I kept calm and trusted in God, the judge would not say the words I believed he was going to say.

"…and held another child against her will. Now, the question I am forced to grapple with is did he do so with a clear and sane mind." LaVacca again paused to sigh. "In analyzing this entire case, there are a few significant matters that stick in my mind, and try as I may, I cannot ignore them. I have to wonder about a man who is on trial for murder, but is so taken with the type of pencil he has been provided that he interrupts the proceeding. I have to wonder about a man who stands here accused of the most shocking sorts of crimes, and yet beseeches the court to consider the fact that he will lose his right to vote if he is convicted. These acts, are to me are at least, not the musings of a sane man; they are not the rationale of one who is facing a lifetime behind bars…or death. Based on that and the astute observations of some the greatest mental health minds in this area, it is therefore my finding that there is a level of proof beyond reasonable doubt that Wayne Graham is insane in the legal sense of the word. I, therefore, find that he is innocent of these crimes by reason of insanity."

Over the quiet and not so quiet words being shared among those of us who were but spectators to the farce, LaVacca pounded his gavel and commanded, "Order! Order! There will be order in my court!" When the room was somewhat quieted, he finished his sentencing quickly, "And he will be remanded to the State of New York for placement in a suitable institution for the criminally insane. He will remain in such custody for an indeterminate amount of time or until he is deemed sane enough that he does not present a danger to himself or others. At such time, should it occur, he may be returned to society. The matter before the court is closed!"

And that's how it ended. It had been 22 months since we found Becky Chilsom's body on Scrantom Street. All the work, all the hours, Jimmy Paskell's peace of mind,. the tears that had been shed, the families that had been torn apart, the hundreds of thousands of dollars that had been spent investigating and prosecuting the case, the fear that had seeped into every home in the city…had been for nothing. The squad was in shambles because of the case. Gail Walz and Tommy Romano barely spoke, and when they did, it wasn't even close to being civil. Frank Donovan talked about retiring to Florida to avoid another Rochester winter. Bobby St. John had reconciled with his wife but was now quieter than ever. The Almost Monthly Poker Game had faded and became only a memory of better days. And as for me, well, I simply existed. Only hatred kept me going—hatred for Wayne Graham and for the system that had failed to obtain that elusive animal we call justice.

Wayne Graham would now go to the State Hospital where—for a year or two, maybe three—he would be able to see the sky, eat his meals, speak and mingle with others, watch television, touch the grass, walk about with the living, receive medication for his ailments, and enjoy this thing we call "life." Then, when he chose to set aside his counterfeit insanity, when he acted remorseful, when he woke up from his feigned lunacy, when he cited examples of right and wrong for his doctors, he would then be declared to be sane, or at least *sane enough* to mingle with society and its children.

There was no doubt in the minds of many that Wayne Graham would then, once he was set free, see another child, lust for his control over the child, seize her, torment her, and finally kill her. Each detective in the squad knew one of us would once again knock on a door, stand there to announce the news of death as wails and agonized moans would fill yet another home. And I knew that *if* I hung around long enough there would be another smooth-skinned face in the crowd to chase me into an alley, loom over me, and ask, "What about me, Amato? What about me?"

Not only had we failed, justice had failed. Truth had sneaked past Lady Justice, standing there tall and blindfolded, with her sword unused.

Walking out of the building into the heavy, hot, oppressive wet heat, I pulled a cigarette out of the pack, cupped my hands around the lighter, lit the butt, and then looked up to see the words on the building. Standing there, looking at the words, my face remained unchanged. I neither frowned nor snickered; I simply looked. Finally, I had to shake my head in disbelief, turn my back, and walk away from the *Hall of Justice*.

CHAPTER TWENTY-THREE

JUSTICE ABDUCTED

The taxi rolled to a stop in front of Wegman's Super Market in Pittsford Plaza, an upper-middle income suburb south and east of downtown Rochester. The cabby hated these calls in shopping plazas. More often than not, they came from stupid kids who were just fooling around. And, in those cases where it was a legit call, the passenger usually ended up being some old lady who not only expected a ride to her doorstep, but also expected the hack to carry her groceries up five flights of stairs and into her kitchen.

Not seeing anyone around who appeared to be trying to get his attention, the cab driver used the time to catch up his trip sheet. The pumpkins displayed in front of the grocery store reminded the cabby he had to pick up two of them before he got off work tonight so he could enjoy one of his family's traditions—carving scary faces into the orange gourds.

It was only ten in the morning, and he was already behind on the log he was supposed to complete after every call. However, before he could complete the paperwork, his peripheral vision caught sight of an elderly man walking his way. The old man waved his right arm and extended his cane in the direction of the cab, and the driver was comforted to see there were no bags of groceries in the old guy's arms.

"State Hospital. Elmwood Avenue," the old man said as he sat himself onto the back seat and then, with some effort, pulled his legs in behind him.

When the car was out of the busy parking lot, the driver asked the rearview mirror, "Going to see someone?"

"What?" the old man questioned in return as he smoothed his mustache with his right hand which still gripped the cane. His attention had been on the cars on the street, and he did not hear what the driver had said.

"Are you going up to visit someone up there in the State Hospital?"

"Yes," the passenger said, and with that the conversation ended.

When the cab pulled into the long driveway that led up to the non-descript, high-rise brick building the old man spoke up. "You wait for me? Yes?"

"I'll have to leave the meter running," the cabby explained. "How long will you be?"

"Twenty minutes. A half-hour maybe," came the reply as the passenger now labored to move his legs out of the cab and onto the pavement.

"That may run you fifteen, maybe eighteen bucks, or so. But before you leave, you'll have to pay what's on the meter already." Then with a smile he added, "I'm not saying *you* would—you look like a pretty nice guy—but we do get stiffed now and then when people go in these big buildings and then don't come out."

"I understand." Out of the cab, the old man handed the driver two twenty-dollar bills and suggested he keep it until they settled up after the trip was completed. "If I no come back when meter say forty-dollars, you wait. I pay more." He then shuffled off toward the high-rise building.

Inside the state hospital the man moved in the manner of old men. The soles of his feet slid forward, rising not more than an inch from the smooth, well-buffed floor. At the information desk he stopped to inquire where he might go to visit his friend. Moving to the elevator, the old man squinted through his eyeglasses circled in plastic frames that time had yellowed. Once in the elevator and alone, he used his left forefinger to depress the button for the floor he desired, and simultaneously pressed the fingertips of his right hand to his mustache for the third or fourth time in the past quarter hour.

Arriving at the ward, he approached the thick window that was meant to keep people from busting out instead of intruding in.

"I come to see my friend, Charlie VanVorhiss," he announced as he leaned forward to form his words into the circular metal mouthpiece in the center of the window.

"Your name?" the male attendant asked with a quick, insincere smile.

"Markel Sopovich."

"Relative?"

"Friend. Family friend."

"Wait here," the attendant in the white uniform said before disappearing for a full five minutes.

As the old man waited into the fourth minute, he began to wonder if it would not be prudent for him to leave. He was beginning to sweat—sweat caused more by his nervousness than the heavy, over-sized coat—and he wondered if the sweat was affecting his appearance.

Finally the attendant called to him. "Mr. Sap-o-vich?"

"So-po-vich," he clarified as he moved toward the man.

"Well maybe that's the problem why…"

"Problem? There is a problem?" the old man asked as he measured the distance to the elevator door.

"Well, it seems Charlie is being a little obstinate today. He says he doesn't know you and he won't see you. However, it may be that I mispronounced your name, and that is why he doesn't make the association."

"I am old friend. Family friend. I come to make visit. It is Christian duty to visit sick. Maybe he does not remember me. Please, not to make trouble, will you go to him again. Name is So-po-vich. You can say?"

"So-po-vich," the attendant repeated and nodded.

"Tell him I am long-time friend. If he does not remember me, I understand. You tell him I say to him, 'There is rain in the forest'. It is family joke. Maybe he will remember me if you say that. There is rain in the forest. Okay?"

"I'll tell him Mr. So-po-vich," the man said with a more earnest smile as he broke the name down into the syllables and proper pronunciation.   "We'll see if we can get Charlie to be more cooperative."

In the absence of the male nurse, the old man tried to catch a glimpse of himself in the window that looked down six floors to the driveway where the taxi waited. The reflection was not the best, but the man was fairly confident his semblance had remained intact.

Finally, another male in a white uniform came to the door that was one separation point between the patients and freedom. Calling the visitor in, the worker explained the visitor would be escorted to a day room where he and VanVorhiss could talk.   There would be an attendant present at all times and if there were the least bit of agitation on Charlie's part, the visitor would be promptly escorted out of the area.

In the day room, the old man stood near the center of the room. He could not be sure how VanVorhiss would handle the meeting and he began to worry that perhaps he was entering too far into dangerous waters.

Machine Gun Charlie VanVorhiss entered the day room cautiously. He had gotten a little heavier and maybe a little older. His round face screwed up to try to make sense out of the presence of this old man who he did not know, but then again, he reasoned, he did not know all the agents.

The two men moved together as the attendant went to a far corner of the room to look for a magazine.

"There is rain in forest," the old man whispered in a mixed Jewish-German-Slovak accent as he embraced the patient.

"There is snow on the lake," Charlie replied, still not too sure of the visitor and the situation.

"And the house is filled with smoke," the old man said without any hint of an accent.

Moving over to a window that was covered by a heavy-gauge metal screen, the two men began their conversation. Whenever the attendant looked their way, the old man would smile and make some comment in a language that sounded German or maybe Russian. The nurse noted that Charlie seemed to be slightly confused by whatever the old man was saying, but at least he was calm and he seemed to be enjoying himself.

Five minutes later the old man was on the main floor of the building and walking to the waiting taxi. While his visitor rode in silence back to Pittsford Plaza, Charlie VanVorhiss went over his instructions in his mind.

The assignment was rather simple and direct. Another patient in the same ward, was a foreign agent. He had been sent to the hospital to recruit spies for the Communists. Now it made sense to Charlie why he instinctively hated the man. The foreign agent was a loud and bossy pain in the ass who enjoyed taunting the other patients. VanVorhiss usually avoided the man, not wanting to become a target for his rowdy intimidation. But now, now he must get close to the man he disliked…close enough to kill him. Charlie's country needed him and the need would not be denied.

At 5:15 in the afternoon of the old man's visit, Charlie got up from the table that held his evening meal. The butter knife was slipped up the right sleeve of his flannel shirt and never came into view until he stood behind his espionage enemy. Then, in what could be referred to as the blink of an eye, the knife slid down the palm of Machine Gun Charlie's hand, was gripped tightly with the thumb over the hilt of the dinner tool, and plunged into the neck of Wayne Graham. The first thrust went past the jugular vein and entered the throat. The second thrust caught the major artery and pushed through it. The third and fourth thrusts simply did more damage.

At 5:18 p.m. Wayne Graham had bled to death.

EPILOGUE

I didn't set up Graham's death and I'll go to my grave denying I have any idea about who did do it. In fact, what little I do know about the case came to me by way of two New York State Police Sergeants, John McNall and Steve Bowman.

Because Graham's murder took place on state property, i.e., the State Hospital, it was the New York State Police who handled the investigation. It was early in their investigation that they learned about the old man who visited Machine Gun Charlie just hours before the killing occurred. Besides that tidbit of information, there was little on which to build a case. Charlie was of very little help to Sergeants McNall and Bowman. All VanVorhiss would contribute to the investigation was that he had plunged his knife into Graham as an act of patriotism to protect his country from foreign agents and that he could not disclose any additional information without the sergeants having the appropriate clearance.

"So where were you when it went down?" Sgt. McNall asked me as we met for beers late one afternoon.

"I took a few days off and drove down to Connecticut for some R and R.," I answered with a grin.

"Why the grin?" the investigator asked.

"It sounds like I'm a suspect," I answered through the smile.

"You are," was the unsmiling response.

"Then shouldn't I be advised of my rights?"

"You're not in custody, Lieutenant," Bowman stated flatly. "This is just a preliminary discussion that's taking place in a restaurant. You're free to leave anytime you want."

"So, you two really think I had something to do with the killing of Wayne Graham?" I asked with less than a grin.

"You or Tommy Romano, or maybe Jimmy Paskell, or, as far as that goes, maybe Gail Walz," McNall answered.

Without being asked, the State Trooper laid out his theory to me. Tommy, Gail, Jimmy and I all had a motive to kill Graham after he had beaten us in court on two separate occasions. The four of us also fit the basic height, weight, and build of the old man, Markel Sopovich. Donovan was excluded because he was too big; Bobby St. John was eliminated based on his skin color. Tommy and Gail were both working the day of the killing, and Jimmy had a good alibi with his wife and children. That left me.

"Check the records, John," I said casually. I believe I signed into the Ramada Inn in Meriden, Connecticut, at about three-thirty Saturday afternoon, two days before Graham was killed. I didn't come back to Rochester until late Tuesday afternoon…the day after the killing. I went down there to see a couple of friends, and while I was there I spent a lot of time doing some gambling at two of the casinos in the area. I believe an ample amount of ATM records will show I was at those two casinos on Saturday, Sunday, and Monday."

"If you wanted to, you could have driven back up here early Monday morning, talked to VanVorhiss, and then driven back to Connecticut right after," Sgt. Bowman commented.

"That's an interesting theory, but it's simply that, a bullshit theory!"

"And," McNall added, "there is the fact that when you were in the Tactical Unit, you were assigned to the Street Crimes Unit, and as such, you sometimes disguised yourself as an old man when you were working the mugging detail."

"That's ancient history!" I protested with a laugh. "And besides, so did everyone else who worked the detail." After that point settled in, I added, "I think you're groping in the dark, John."

"Okay, then, if not one of your squad, who would *you* suspect as having done this?"

"Take your pick," I answered before I took a sip of beer. "Anyone of the parents of the kids who the son-of-a-bitch killed; any citizen who saw it as a brand of justice; maybe one of Charlie's street buddies. Who knows? Then again, maybe no one. Maybe Charlie VanVorhiss did it all on his own. He does have an extensive rap sheet regarding violence and dealing with what he called 'foreign agents'."

"True," McNall said as he nodded. "But it's quite a coincidence that he went months without any violence, then, right after this old man—who has actually been dead for three-and-a-half years—visits and suddenly Charlie is off on a rampage."

"Stranger things have happened," I noted with a tight smile.

"So what did you do in Connecticut...besides gamble?" Bowman asked.

"I saw friends, Steve and Patty Walsh, and I did stuff. If the need arises I'll call on them for their testimony. Other than that, I'm not sitting here and taking shit any longer. If you want to talk to me again, bring a lawyer with you...because I'll be asking for one."

Justice is an elusive bird, and I won't sit here and try to convince you that two wrongs make a right. Whoever it was who set up Machine Gun Charlie to take out Graham does not have my best wishes, my appreciation, or my sympathy. The person does, however, have my understanding. I understand completely how a person could be driven to such a rage of anger that he—or she—would want to see Wayne Graham on a cold, metal slab of stainless steel at the Medical Examiner's Office.

No, I don't condone what happened, but I do understand it. I understand how one might sit home at night after a long day and wish Graham to be dead. I fully understand how someone could take weeks and months in planning the contrived killing of Wayne Graham. I truly understand the fear in the heart of person who envisioned Graham walking out of the State Hospital one day after he miraculously became sane once again...and how the killer would then pick out his next victim. I'm not making excuses...I'm just saying I understand.

Justice has such an evasive, gossamer meaning. I don't know what it is, and I don't know how to define it. Through the years I've looked to the courts for justice, and when it failed to deal out what I thought justice should be, I kind of shrugged my shoulders and blamed the ignorance of lawyers, judges, or juries. That's the way everyone should have seen the court trial of Wayne Graham. He went into the courtroom, took his best shot, and we sure as hell took our best shot. He won. We lost. It was best if it ended there.

I won't try to convince you to exonerate one who takes the law into his own hands, because I personally cannot exonerate the act. If we do not live according to our system of courts and jurisprudence, then we are doomed to live in lawless confusion, of roaming mobs casting their concept of justice on all they encounter. Murder does not justify another murder. Vengeance cannot be substituted for the concept of justice; nor can it become synonymous with the word, "Justice." I understand what could drive a person to want to assassinate a cold-hearted killer such as Wayne Graham...I understand it, but I can't and won't condone it!

But then again, I guess a man's got to do what a man's got to do!

#

"Justice is always in jeopardy."

Walt Whitman

"I don't want to know what the law is, I want to know who the judge is!"

Roy M. Cohn

"You go looking for justice and that's what you find...Just-Us."

Richard Pryor

"Swift justice demands just swiftness."

Supreme Court Justice Potter Stewart

"Without justice, courage is weak."

Benjamin Franklin

"Judges are the weakest link in our system of justice, and they are also the most protected."

Alan Dershowitz

"I know this—a man got to do what a man got to do."

John Steinbeck in "The Grapes of Wrath"

Comments and orders for JUSTICE and the author's other two novels, THE KILLING CARDS and GROUND LIONS are welcome at www.loucampanozzi.com

---

ABOUT THE AUTHOR

Louis Campanozzi was born and raised in Rochester, New York. After serving in the military he returned home and joined the Rochester Police Department. During his 22 years with the department, Lou worked undercover narcotics, commanded the homicide and robbery squad, and served as District Commander on the city's West Side. Campanozzi investigated some of the community's most notorious crimes and later wrote about the sometimes-mean streets of Rochester as an author of mystery novels.

Lou was one of the three founders of BowMac Educational Services, founded in 1980. BowMac is a police training-consulting firm. Lou designed the company around idea of teaching "young cops" how to interrogate suspects like some of the more successful investigators he knew. Lou taught the basic and advanced interrogation courses and also assisted in developing a "Police Involved Shooting" course that deals with police - involved shootings. Lou has taught hundreds of cops and now thousands use the techniques taught by Campanozzi to this day. In turn, tens of thousands of criminals are put behind bars because of his teachings.

After retiring as Captain from the Rochester Police Department Lou relocated to Albuquerque, New Mexico where he worked for the New Mexico State Police in addition, he continued to teach nationwide for BowMac. He later took on the position of Chief of Police of an Indian Reservation in Albuquerque, New Mexico.

Lou Campanozzi was married to wife Nancy for over 35 years. They have two grown children, Marc and Kim and three grandchildren, Zachary, Mackenzie and Cassandra.

Lou's two other novels in the Mike Amato Detective Series, "The Killing Cards" and 'Ground Lions" have been well received by both the police community and devoted murder mystery readers. "Justice" is Lou's final novel in the Mike Amato Detective Series.

Printed in the United States
1428300003B/44